I0763136

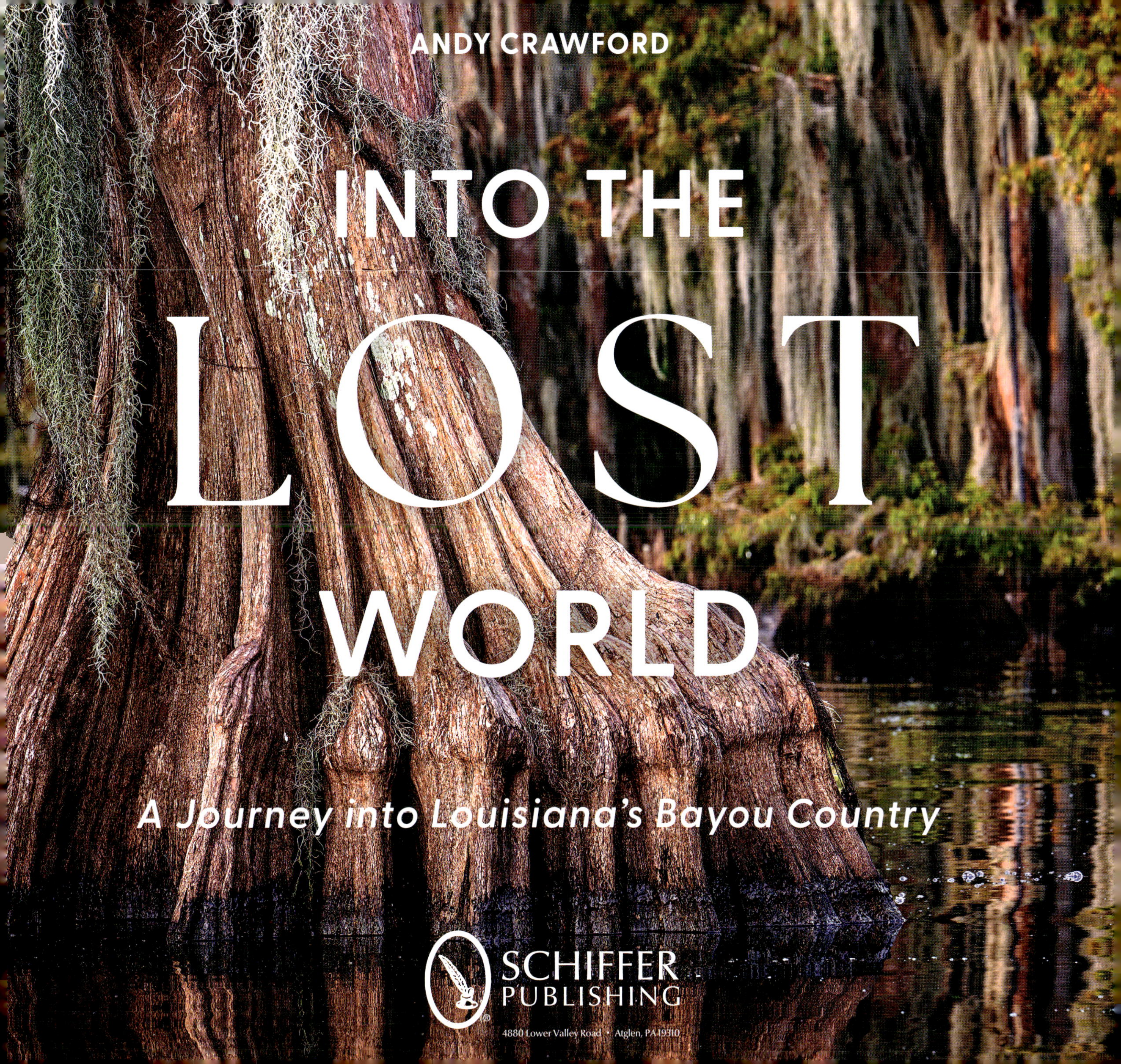

ANDY CRAWFORD

INTO THE LOST WORLD

A Journey into Louisiana's Bayou Country

SCHIFFER PUBLISHING

4880 Lower Valley Road • Atglen, PA 19310

Other Schiffer Books on Related Subjects:

New Orleans: Elegance and Decadence, Richard Sexton and Randolph Delehanty, 978-0-7643-6598-0
Jammin' Through the South: Kentucky, Virginia, Tennessee, Mississippi, Louisiana, Texas, Daniel Seddiqui, 978-0-7643-6748-9

Library of Congress Control Number: 2025942149

Book cover and book design by Molly Shields
Introduction photography by Rick Berk
About the Author photo by Kevin M. White
All other photography by Andy Crawford
Edited by Kaylee Schofield
Type set in The Seasons/Cambria

ISBN: 978-0-7643-7111-0
ePub: 978-1-5073-0670-3
Printed in India

10 9 8 7 6 5 4 3 2 1

Published by Schiffer Publishing, Ltd.
4880 Lower Valley Road
Atglen, PA 19310
Phone: (610) 593-1777; Fax: (610) 593-2002
Email: info@schifferbooks.com
Web: www.schifferbooks.com

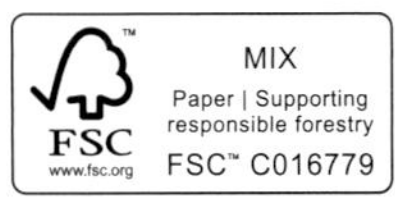

To Yvette, my greatest champion and most honest critic. I wouldn't want to make this journey with anyone else.

To my parents, Allen and Margaret, who instilled in me an appreciation for nature's beauty—along with a healthy dose of wanderlust.

ACKNOWLEDGMENTS

This book wouldn't be possible without a multitude of people who have encouraged me along my photographic journey. Too many people to name have cheered me along a path that has taken me from a newspaper reporter to an outdoor writer to a full-time sports and landscape photographer.

Even when my career decisions probably made no sense to them.

It's impossible to overstate the influence of folks like Matt Vincent, who gave me a jewel of advice that constantly floats through my head: "Stop making something for someone else and make something for yourself."

Bassmaster photographers James Overstreet and Seigo Saito took me under their wings and mentored me in action photography, greatly expanding my skill set. Tim Stanley, Dave Morefield, and James Eastham have dragged me along on landscape trips and given me confidence as I have grown photographically.

Award-winning landscape photographer Rick Berk has generously shared his skills and pushed me to constantly improve. My Into the Swamp Photo Workshops, through which I share the South Louisiana swamps with other photographers, came about largely because of his encouragement.

A huge "thank you" goes out to everyone who has pushed me along the path leading to this book. You don't know what your support means.

INTRODUCTION

Everyone takes their surroundings for granted. It's just human nature. Ask someone who grew up in the shadow of Wyoming's Grand Teton, and, sure, they'll admit it's beautiful. But they drive past it every day without a second glance.

That was the story of my life, growing up within an hour of some of the most remote, beautiful, and inaccessible wildernesses in the United States. For much of my first four decades of life, I didn't give the Louisiana swamps much thought. Sure, I knew those vast wetlands were gorgeous, and I spent a lot of time there—but they were just part of everyday life.

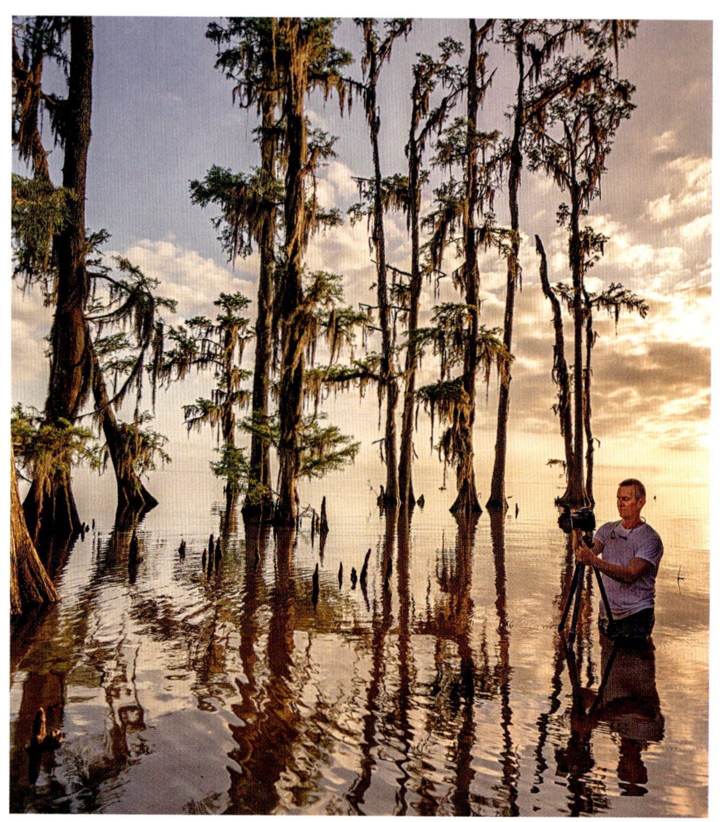

The author stands waist deep in the black waters of Lake Maurepas as he photographs the beautiful swamp during a brilliant sunrise.
Courtesy of Rick Berk Photography

It took a turn in career to reveal the full scope of my love affair with those swamps. In my late forties I turned from writing hunting and fishing stories to traveling the United States for upward of 20 weeks each year as a photographer for a bass-fishing organization. That opened my eyes to the true beauty found across this great country.

The old saw is true, however: Absence makes the heart grow fonder. It was only when I was removed from the beauty of the swamps for roughly half of each year that I came to fully appreciate the incredible beauty found in the wetlands near which I grew up.

Louisiana's swamps are wild. They are largely untouched by civilization. They are filled with amazing wildlife. Hordes of mosquitoes await fresh meals.

And I cannot get enough of them, retreating there as often as possible. It's where I go when I get bored with office work, whenever ennui creeps into my psyche. It's my refuge, far from the sounds of civilization, with no cars whizzing by and only the occasional sound of a boat reminding me a mechanized world still exists.

The simple act of launching my boat melts away stress, and I'm soon immersed in natural beauty that should be on the top of any nature lover's list. It soothes my soul and revitalizes my senses.

I truly believe Louisiana's swamps are a national treasure, and one of the best-kept secrets in the world. For those outside South Louisiana, swamps can be misconstrued as dark, foreboding places. That's the furthest from the truth, and I work to correct those assumptions through my photography

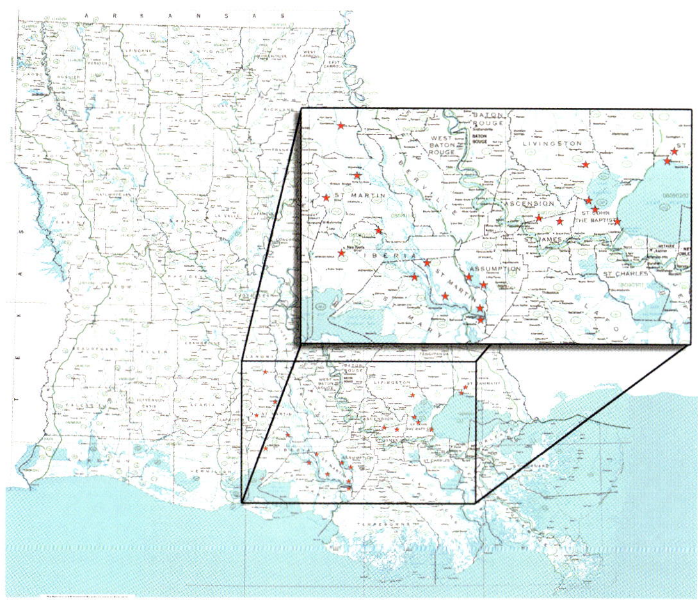

The author travels Southeast Louisiana in his pursuit to document the incredible beauty of the region's swamps.
Courtesy of Library of Congress, Geography and Map Division

The biggest challenge to Louisiana's swamps is accessibility: There are few roads through these wetlands, and those that do exist provide the barest impressions of the breathtaking beauty found a few hundred yards away.

That means most of the country has no clue that the natural wonder of our swamps exists. People in New York, Wyoming, Tennessee, and California have probably heard Louisiana has swamps, but they don't know the breadth of the wetlands and the sheer beauty found by pushing off from the boat launch and moving through the flooded cypress-tupelo swamps.

They can't just drive down and check it out, as they can in so many of this country's landscapes. There are no grand overlooks. They largely can't go hiking, unless they don hip boots. Thus, it's not your fault if you have never felt the glorious weight of these soggy environs.

So come with me on a journey into the wilds of South Louisiana and discover a world that has been largely forgotten. My hope is that by the time you turn this book's last page, you'll have fallen as deeply in love with our swamps as I did.

CHAPTER ONE

SUNRISES

Darkness envelops the swamps ahead, the shapes of cypress trees barely discernible. The silence is broken only by the soft splash of a paddle and the occasional fish, along with the hum of mosquitoes looking for the night's last meal.

Moments later, first light seeps over the eastern horizon, and the trees separate from the darkness to become more distinct. A thick veil of Spanish moss hangs limply from the old cypresses in the humid stillness of morning.

A mixture of yellow, gold, and magenta soon sweeps across the thin clouds above, creating a fantastical color palette reflected in the languid black waters below. The silhouetted trees contrast perfectly with the garish colors.

The colors flare and then fade, only to slowly reappear moments later as the sun finishes its approach to the horizon. And then the sun peaks over the trees, casting golden light into the cypress boughs. The normally gray moss seems to gather the light, glowing like living lanterns.

As alligators slink into the shadows from a night of hunting, other wildlife begin to wake up. Silent no longer, the swamp becomes a cacophony of sound. Great blue herons croak. Egrets shake off sleep and fly to prized feeding spots. Owls hoot deep in the cypress-tupelo swamp. Kingfishers twitter as they make swooping passes through the trees, ready for another day of plucking fish from the dark waters.

There's nothing like being in the Louisiana swamp to witness the beginning of day. That first touch of color along the eastern horizon never fails to make me smile at the promise of another day in God's great, wild creation.

Opposite page: Most people focus on the skies directly above the rising sun, but there is often a more subtle light show happening along the opposite horizon. That's what happened during this sunrise, when the western skies behind this Lake Maurepas cypress tree were painted in wonderful pastels.

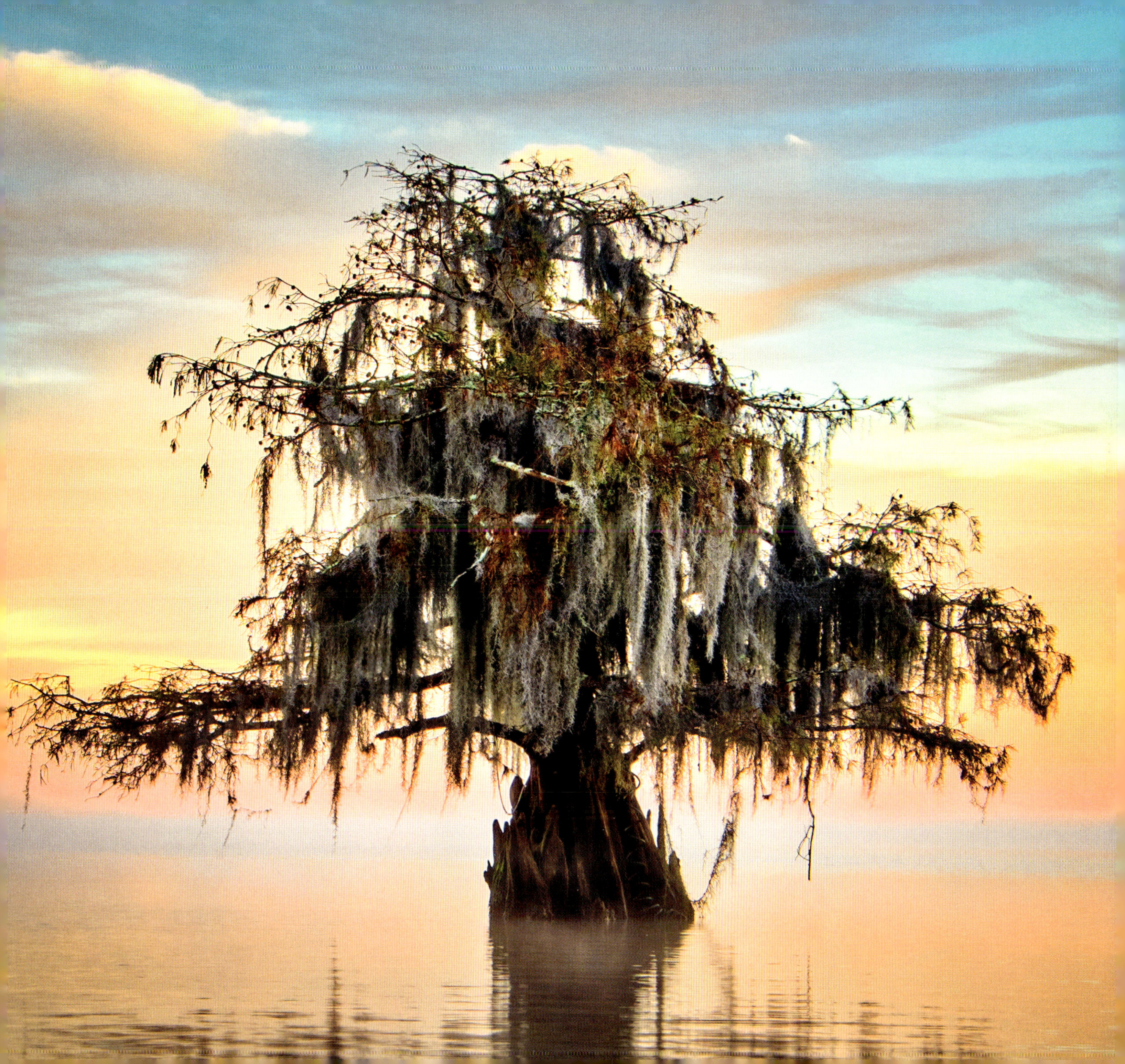

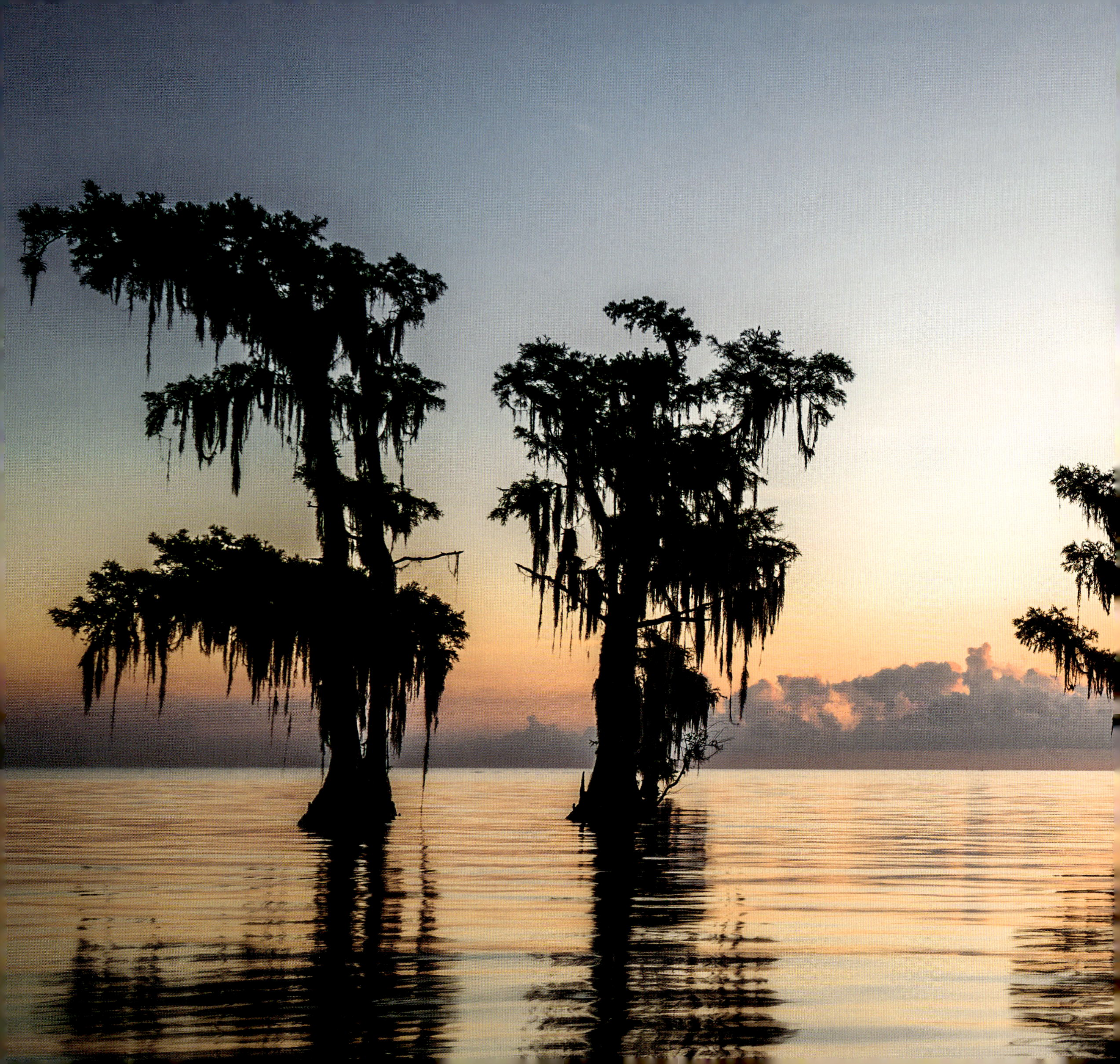

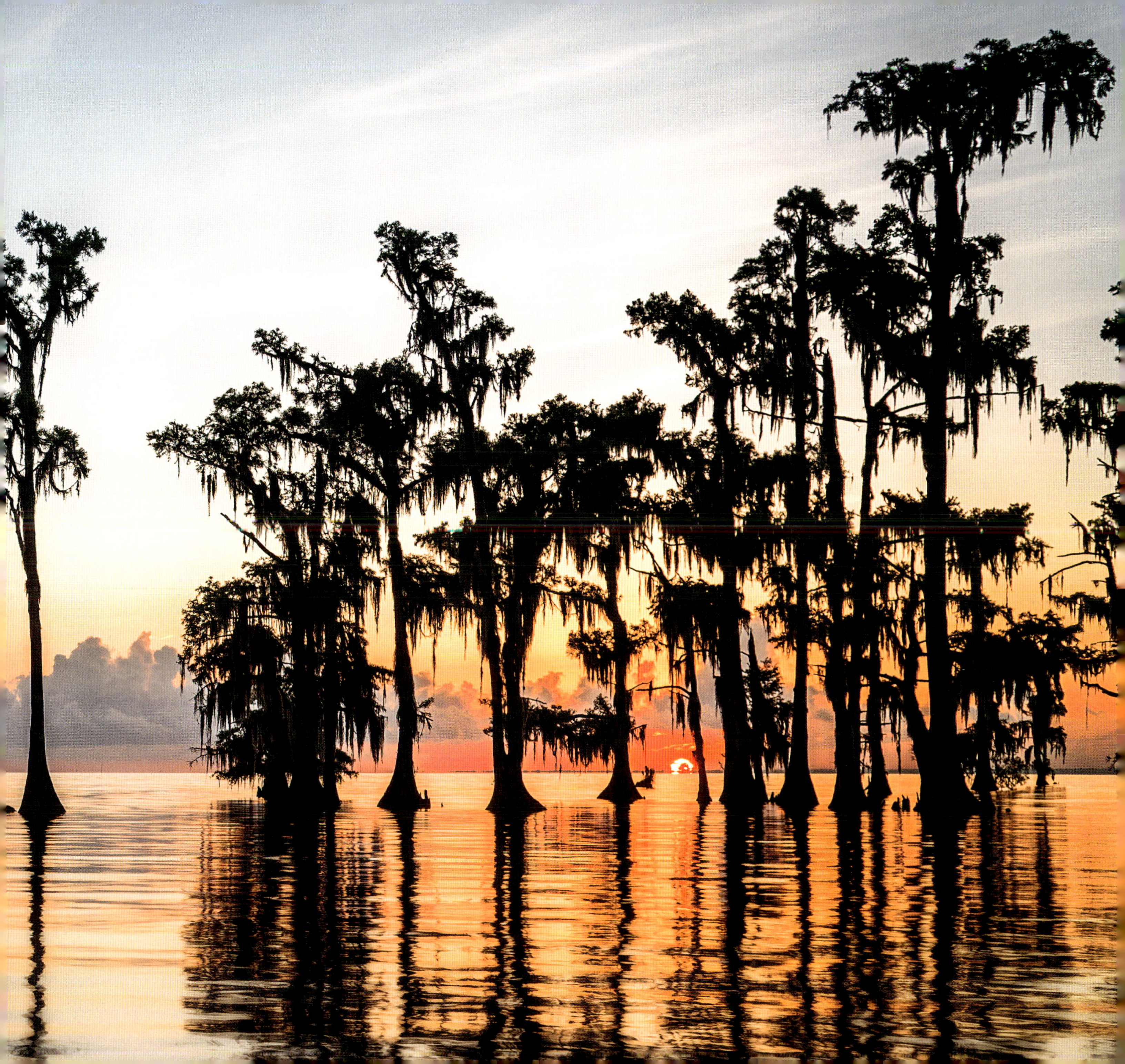

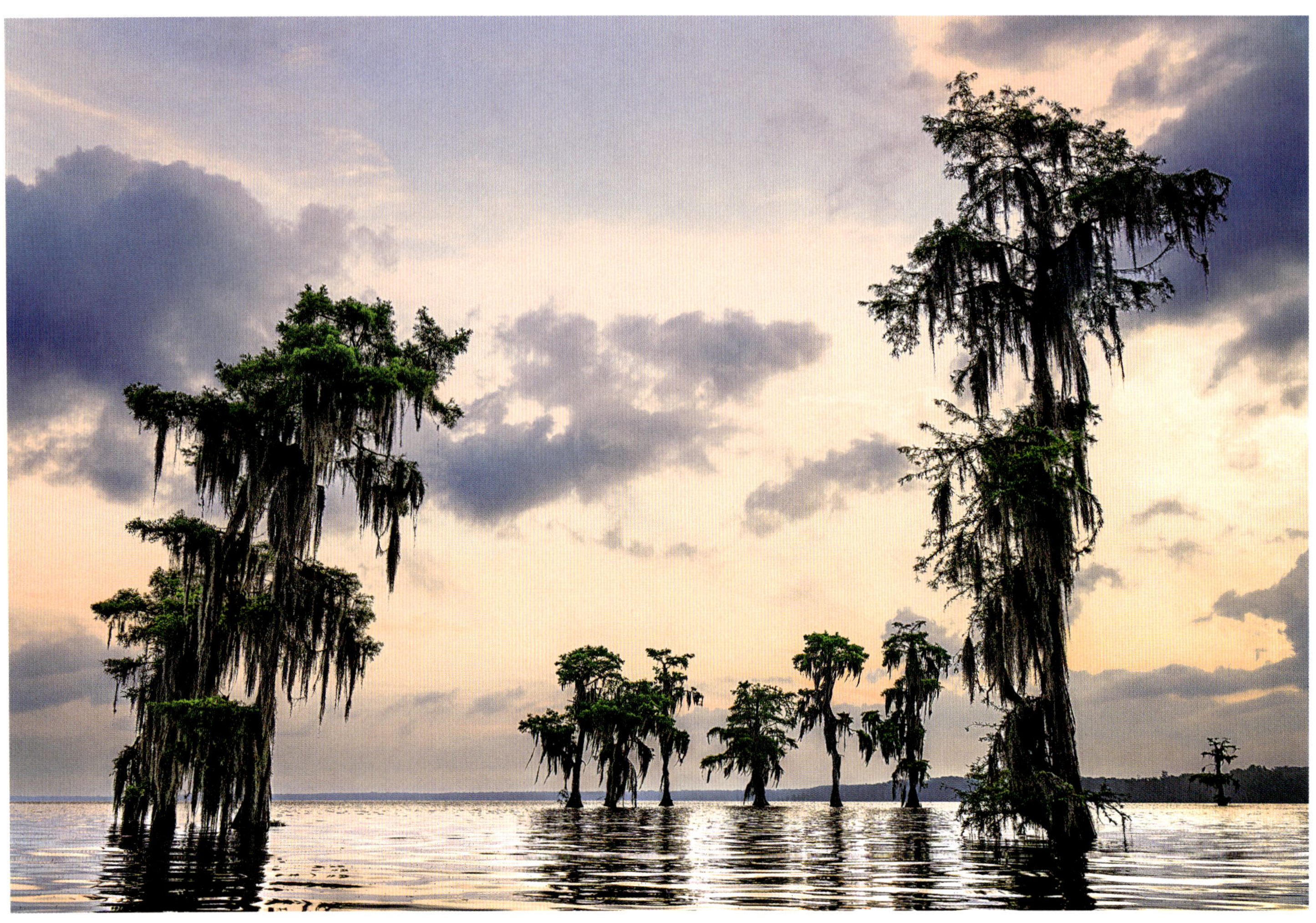

Thick clouds on the eastern horizon tamped down the predawn colors on this day of paddling Lake Palourde. A few minutes after sunrise, however, soft pastel colors blossomed across high, thin clouds 90 degrees from the actual sunrise. It was the perfect opportunity to show not only the colors of the sky but the lushness of the cypress trees standing on the edge of the lake.

Opposite page: I believe that the predictable rhythm of nature is proof a creative God exists. For instance, the sun rises and sets in different but scientifically known locations each day. That predictability allowed me to use an app to determine exactly where the sun would rise, so I could position this Lake Verret cypress to frame it through the far-off trees.

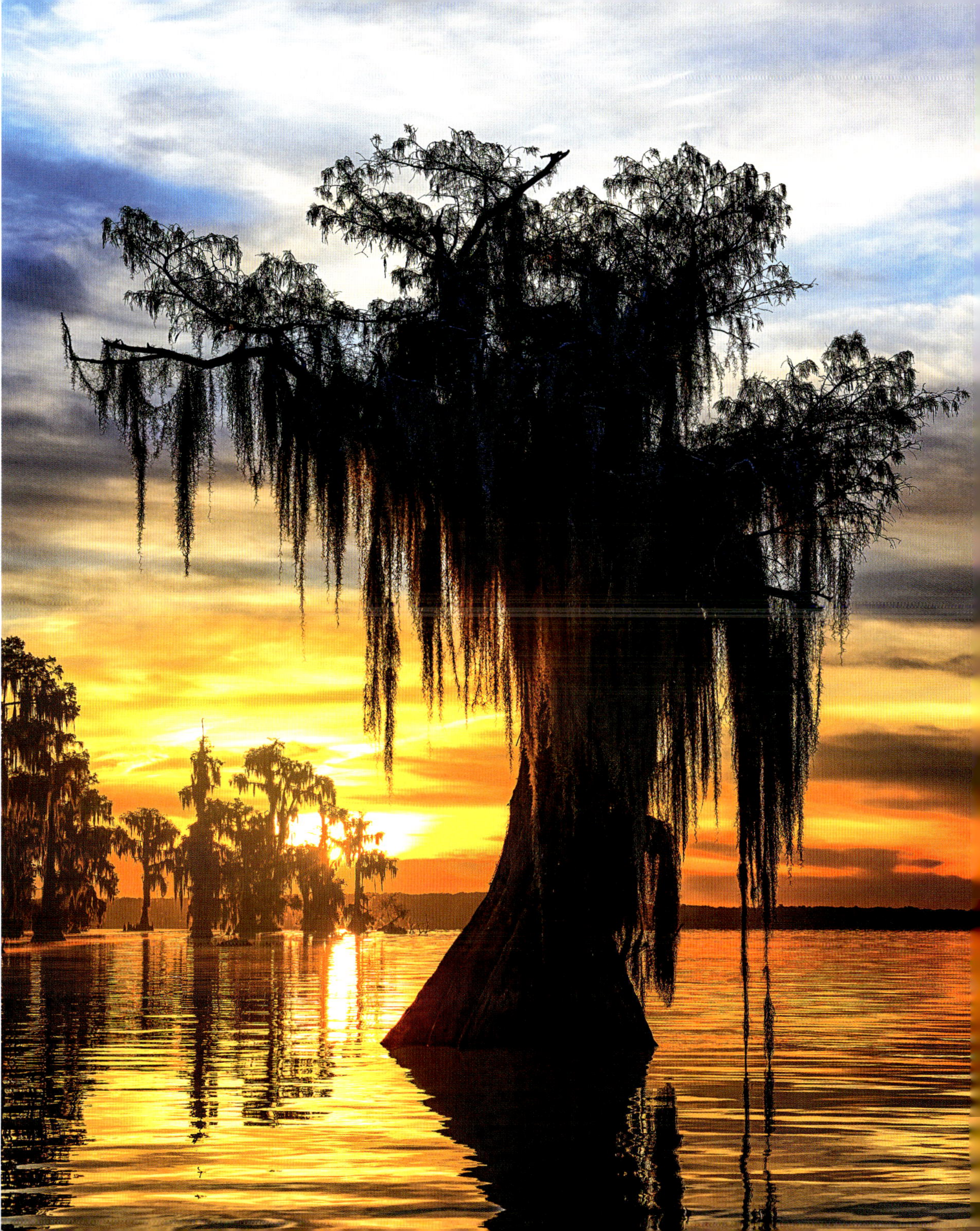

Cypress trees often form lines on the outer edges of the Louisiana swamps, like in this sunrise scene a short paddle away from Lake Verret's Attakapas Landing.

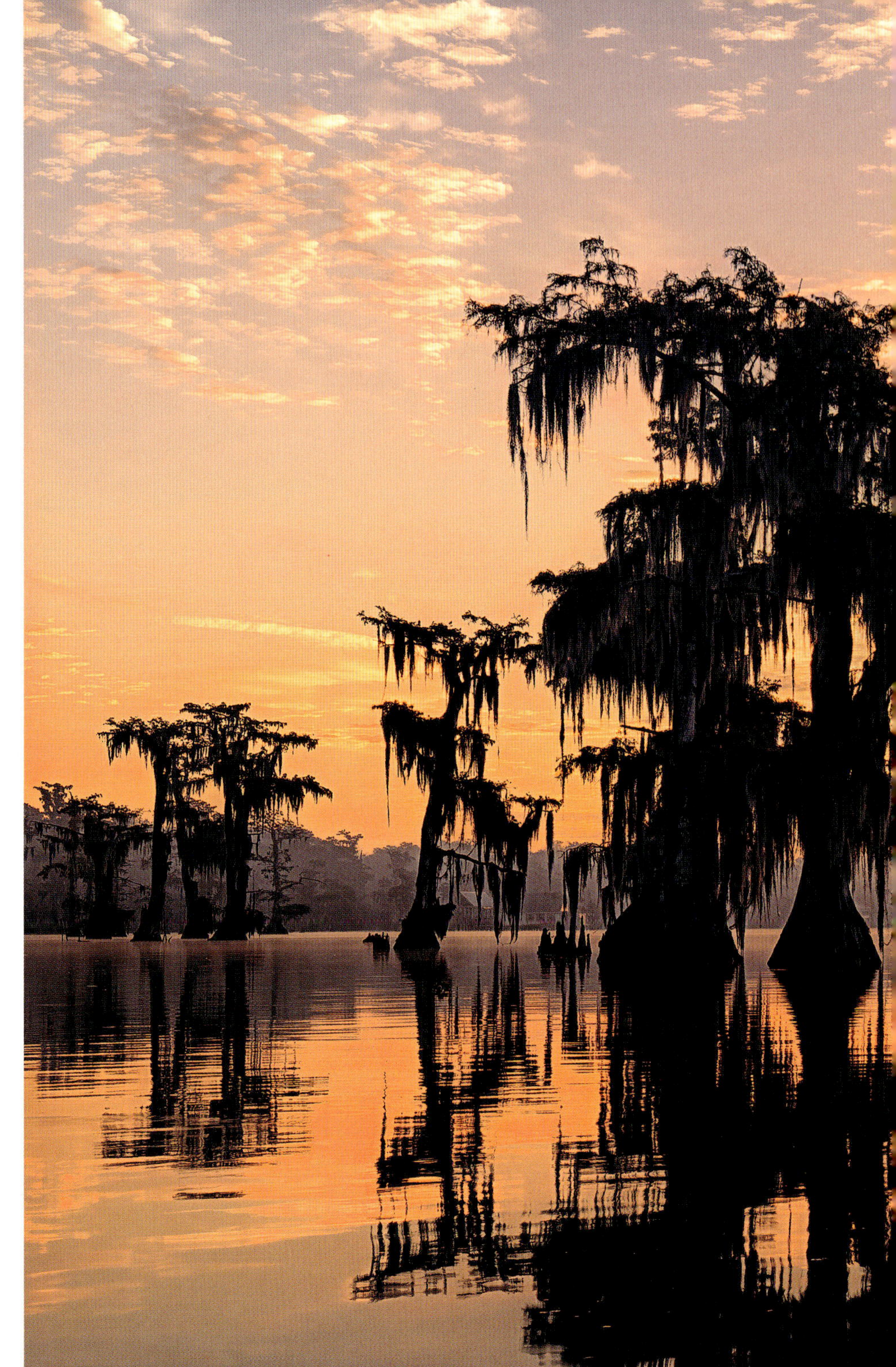

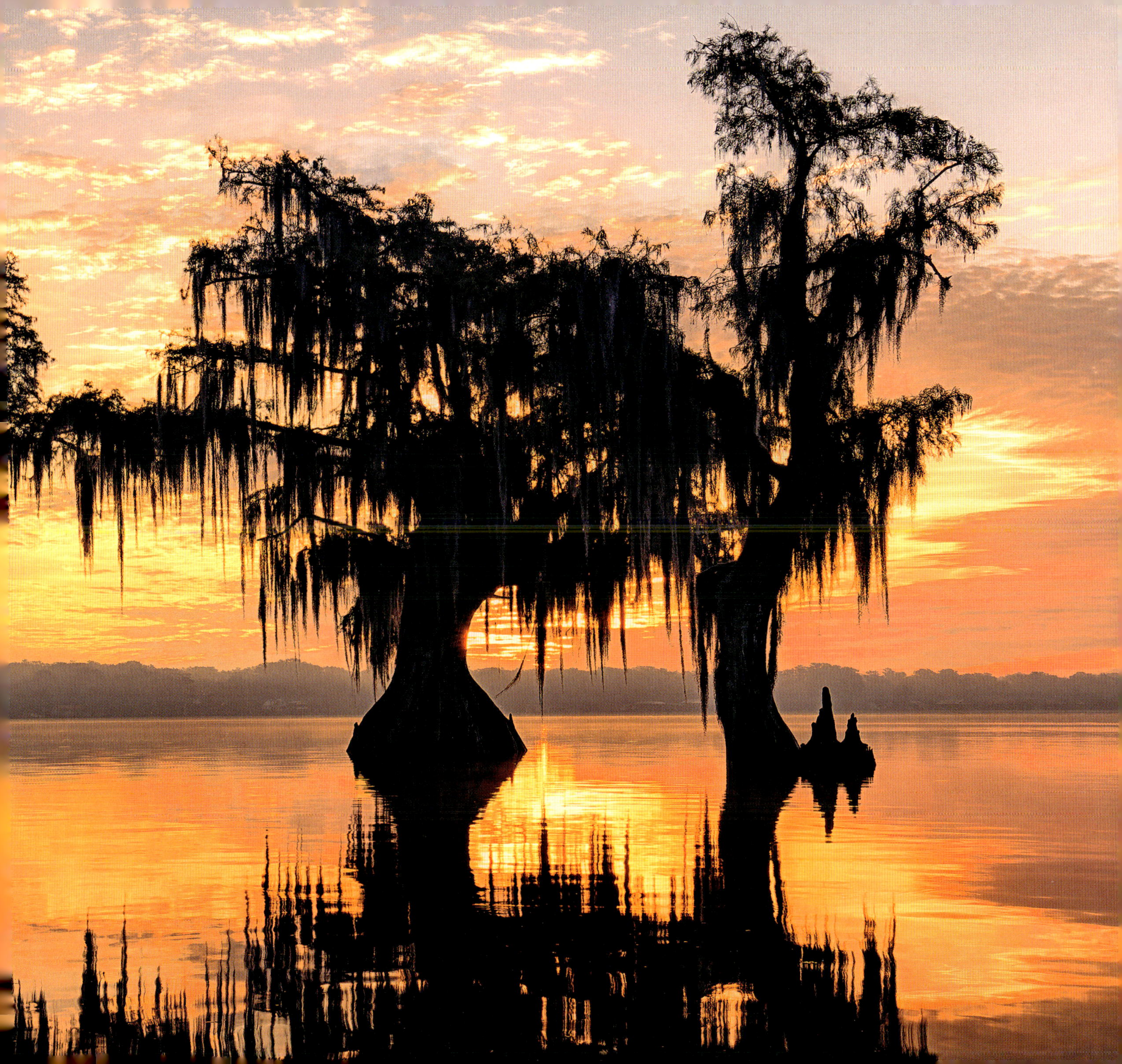

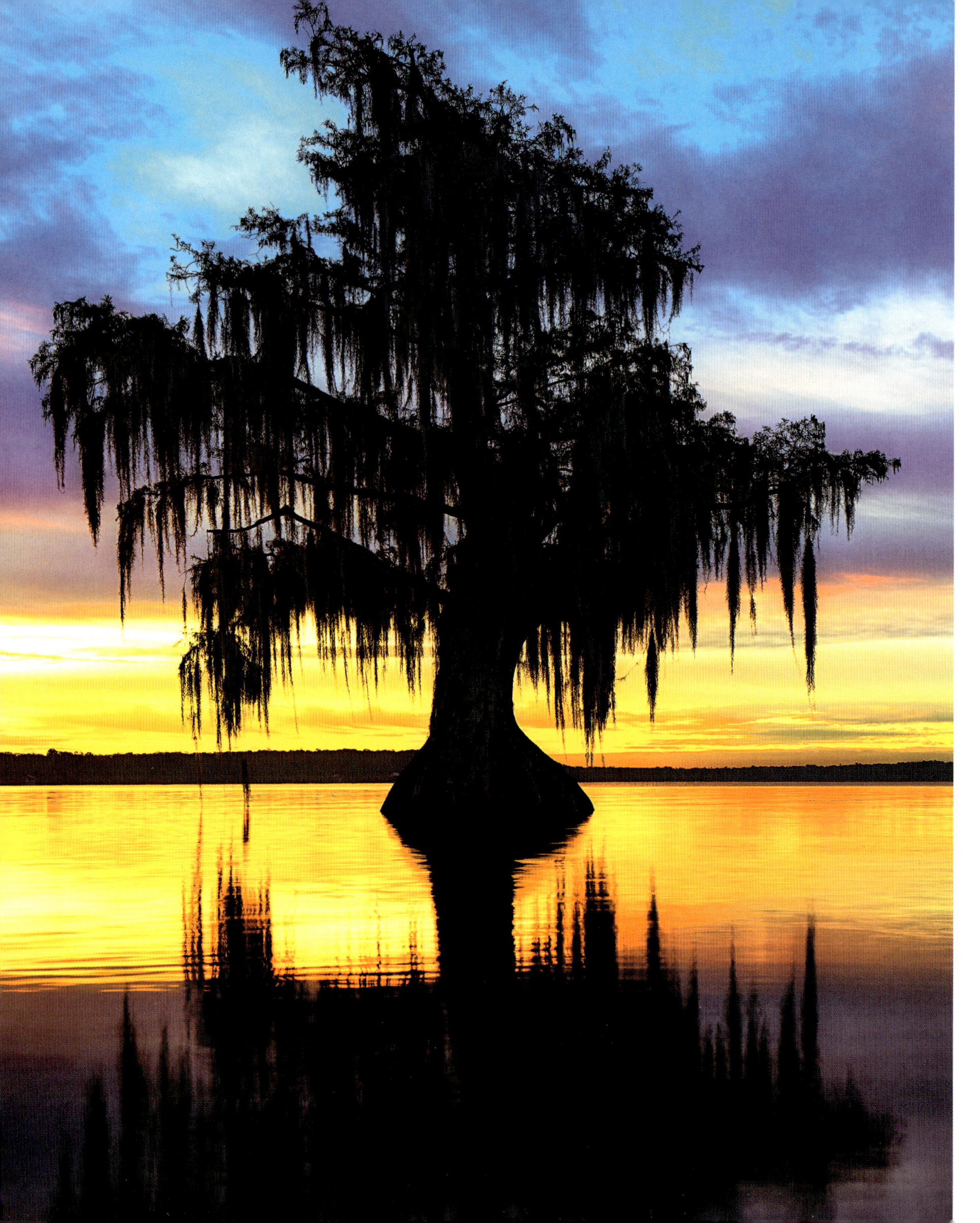

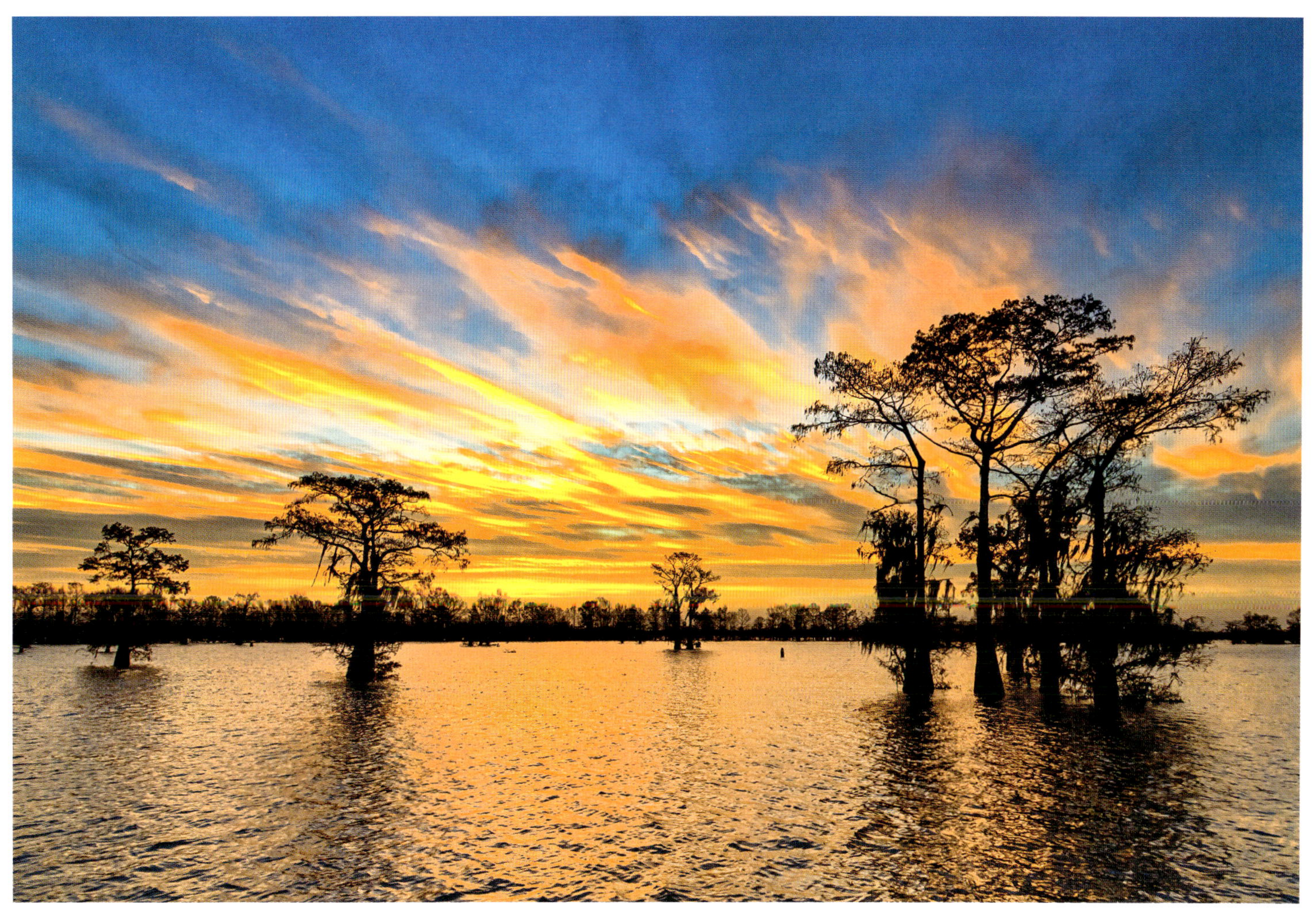

A colorful sunrise is all about clouds, which reflect light and add interest to the sky. And streaking clouds created by upper-elevation winds can turn a scene from nice to amazing.

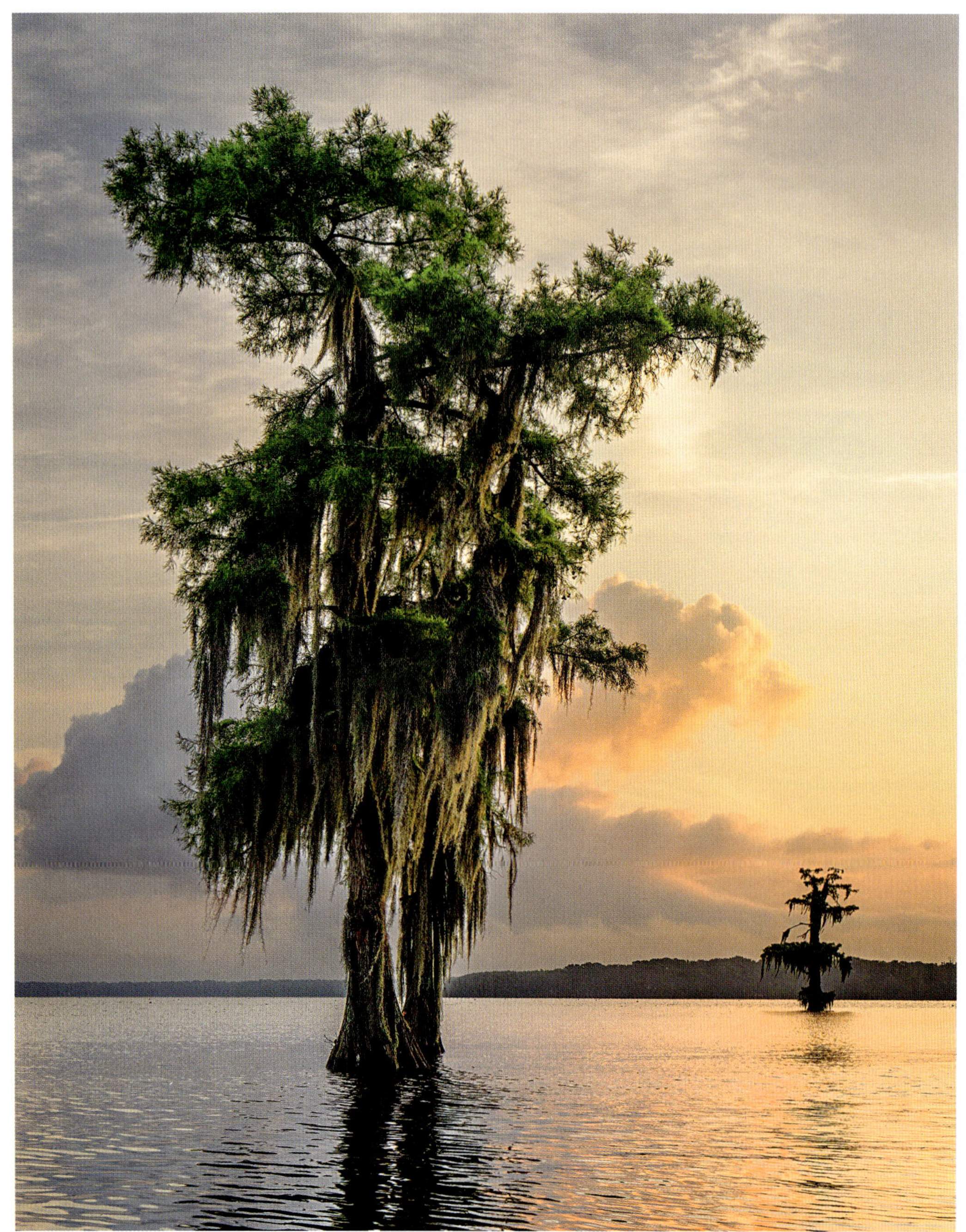

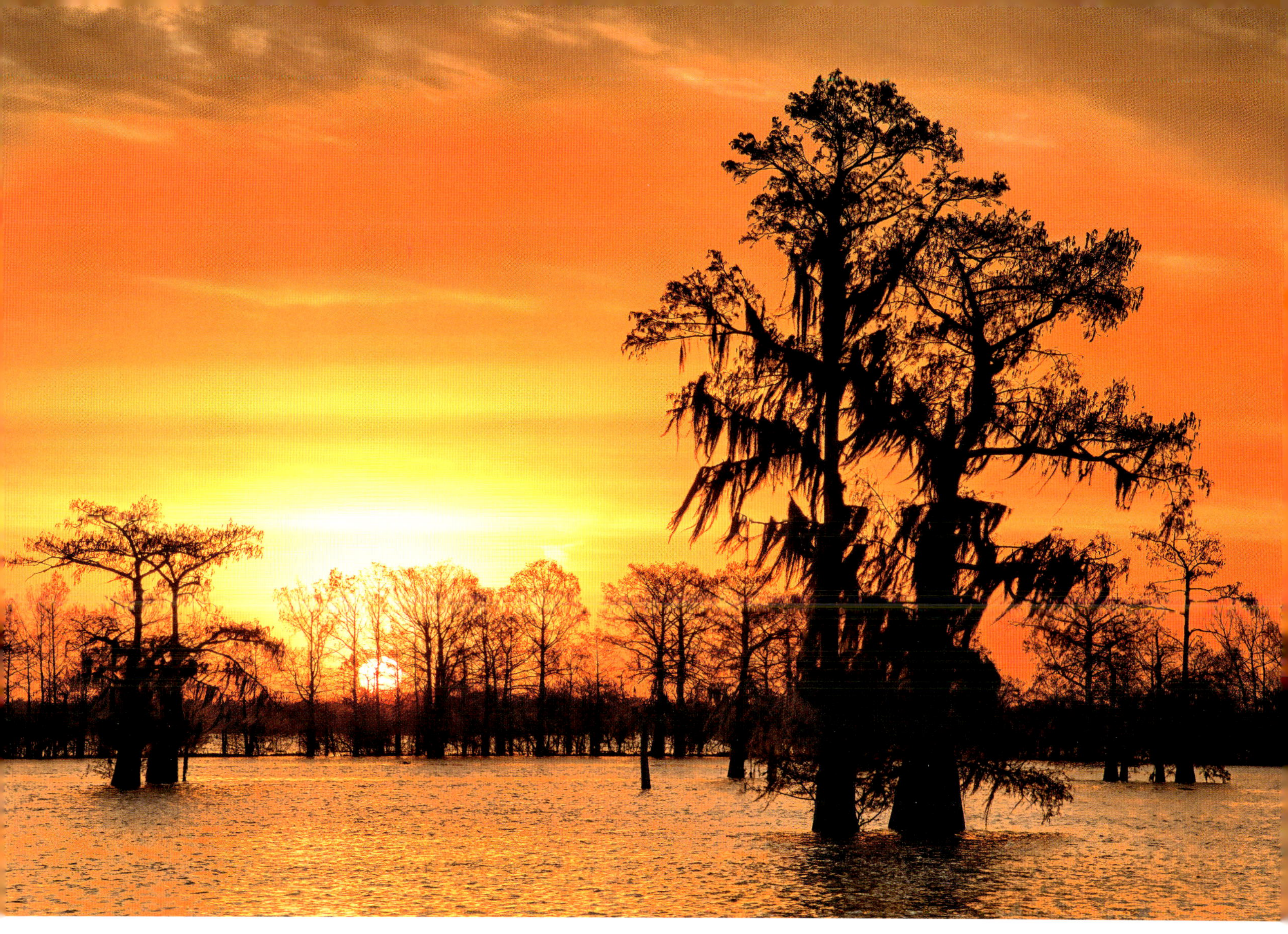

Opposite page: Watching the first golden light of day wash through a beautiful cypress tree is one of the reasons I love to paddle these wonderful swamplands. On this morning the light was simply exquisite, bringing out the amazing textures of this moss-draped tree.

Sunrises are wonderfully unpredictable. There are times when it seems so unlikely there will be any color, with heavy clouds blanketing the skies. And duds do happen, but all it takes is a small opening in the cloud base to allow the sun to cast golden light across the skies.

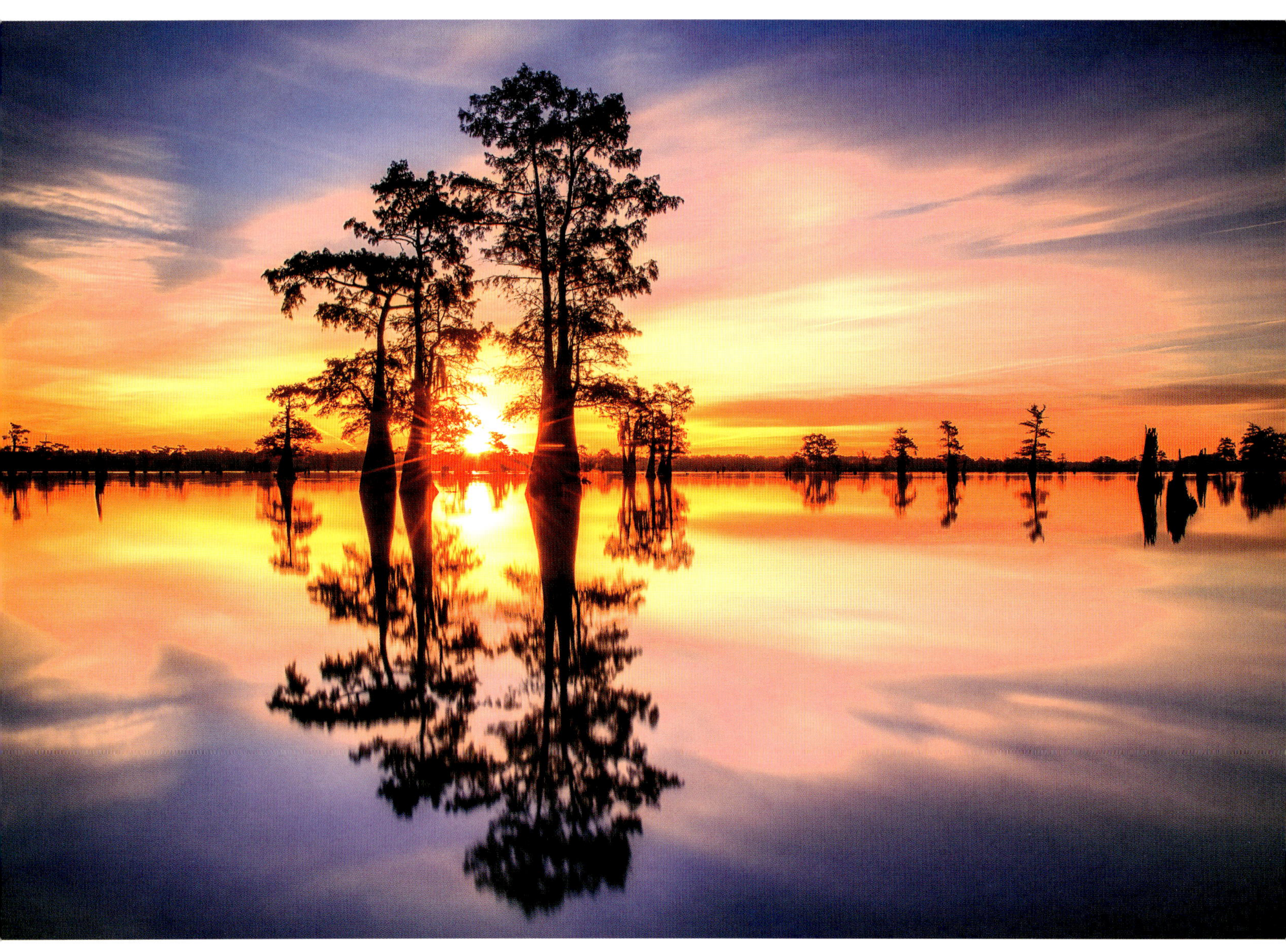

This was one of the calmest mornings I've ever spent in the swamps, with not a puff of wind to ripple the water or ruffle foliage. That allowed me to use a filter to slow my shutter speed and "drag" the clouds across the sky above. It truly was a special morning.

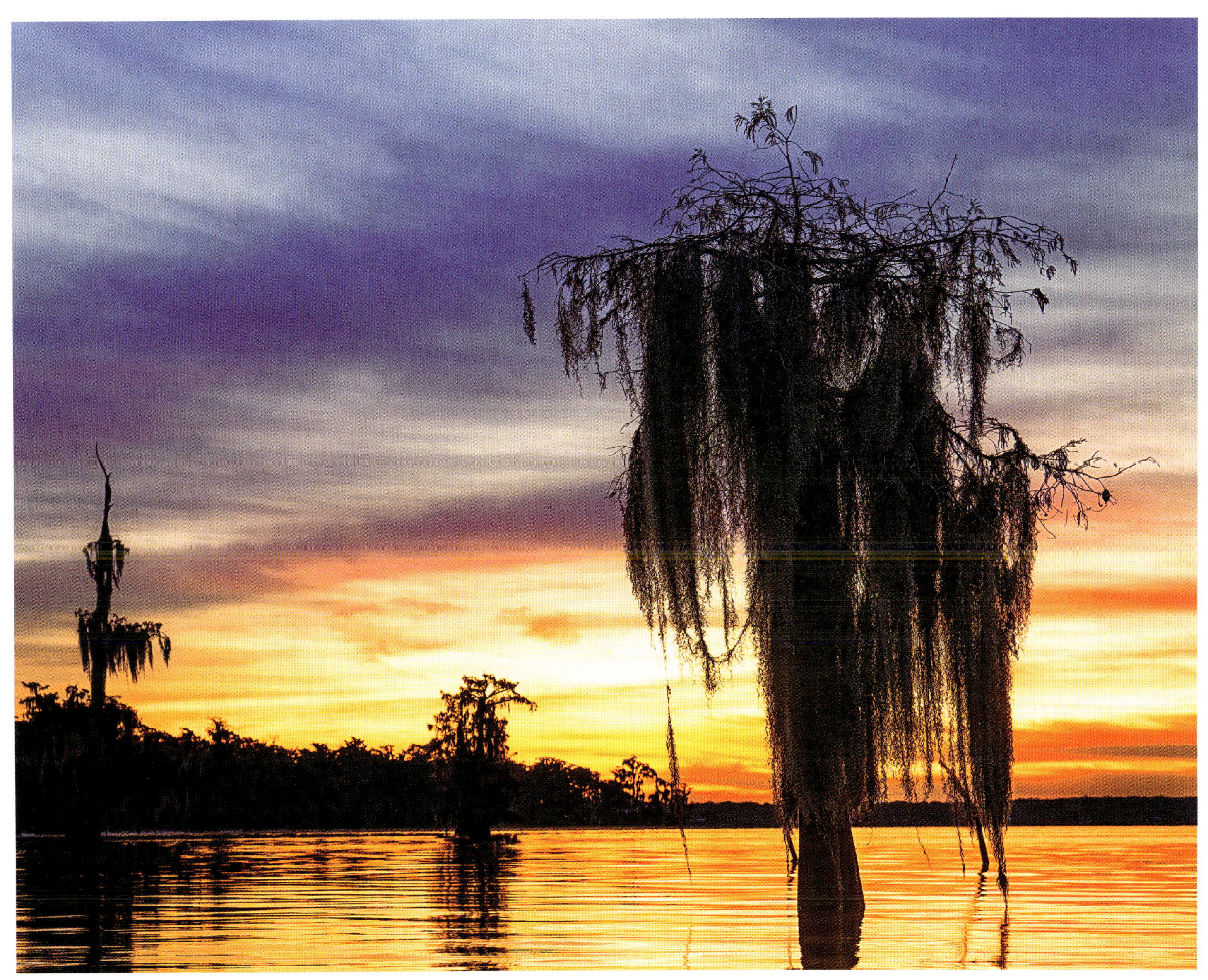

Lake Verret's beautiful cypress trees are covered with heavy coats of Spanish moss, and there's little more stunning than seeing one of those trees silhouetted by a gorgeous sunrise.

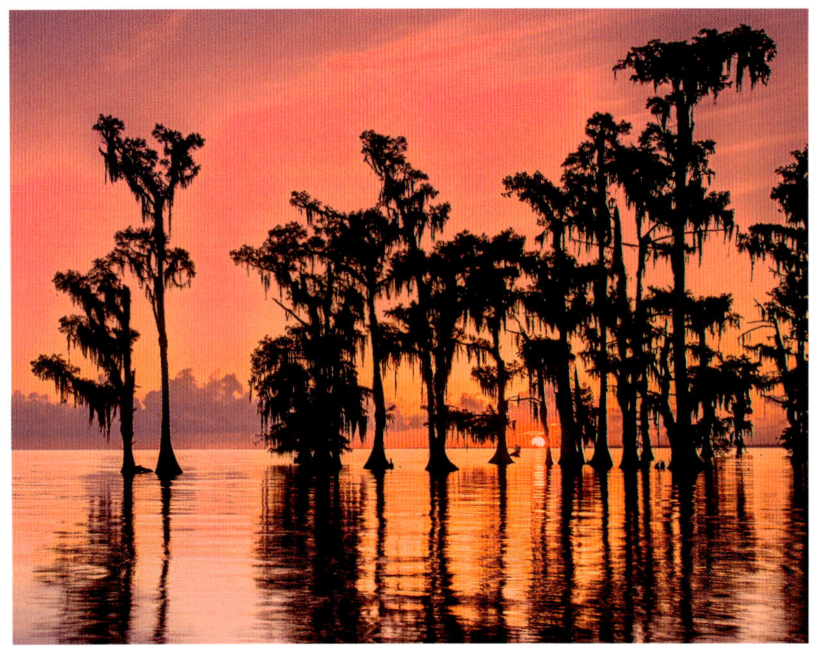

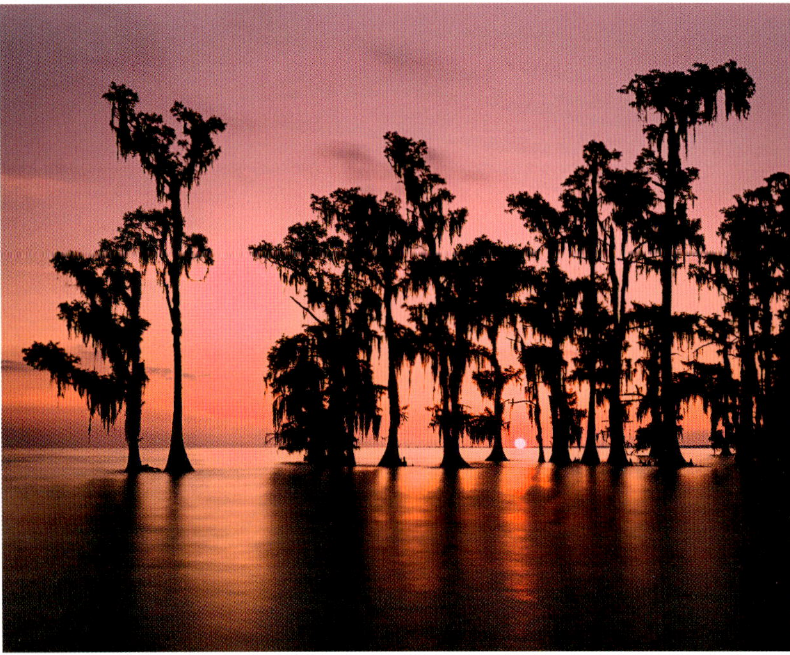

Every sunrise is different. This line of cypress trees on the edge of Lake Maurepas just west of New Orleans offers the perfect view of the sun burning through the clouds on the horizon while casting gorgeous colors ranging from yellow and orange to bright pink across the sky.

On this morning, I set up very early at the same location and used an app to determine exactly where the sun would rise through the group of Lake Maurepas trees. Hazy clouds turned incredible shades of purple and caused the sun to appear as a well-defined ball. I waited until the sun appeared to be resting on the eastern horizon to snap the shutter.

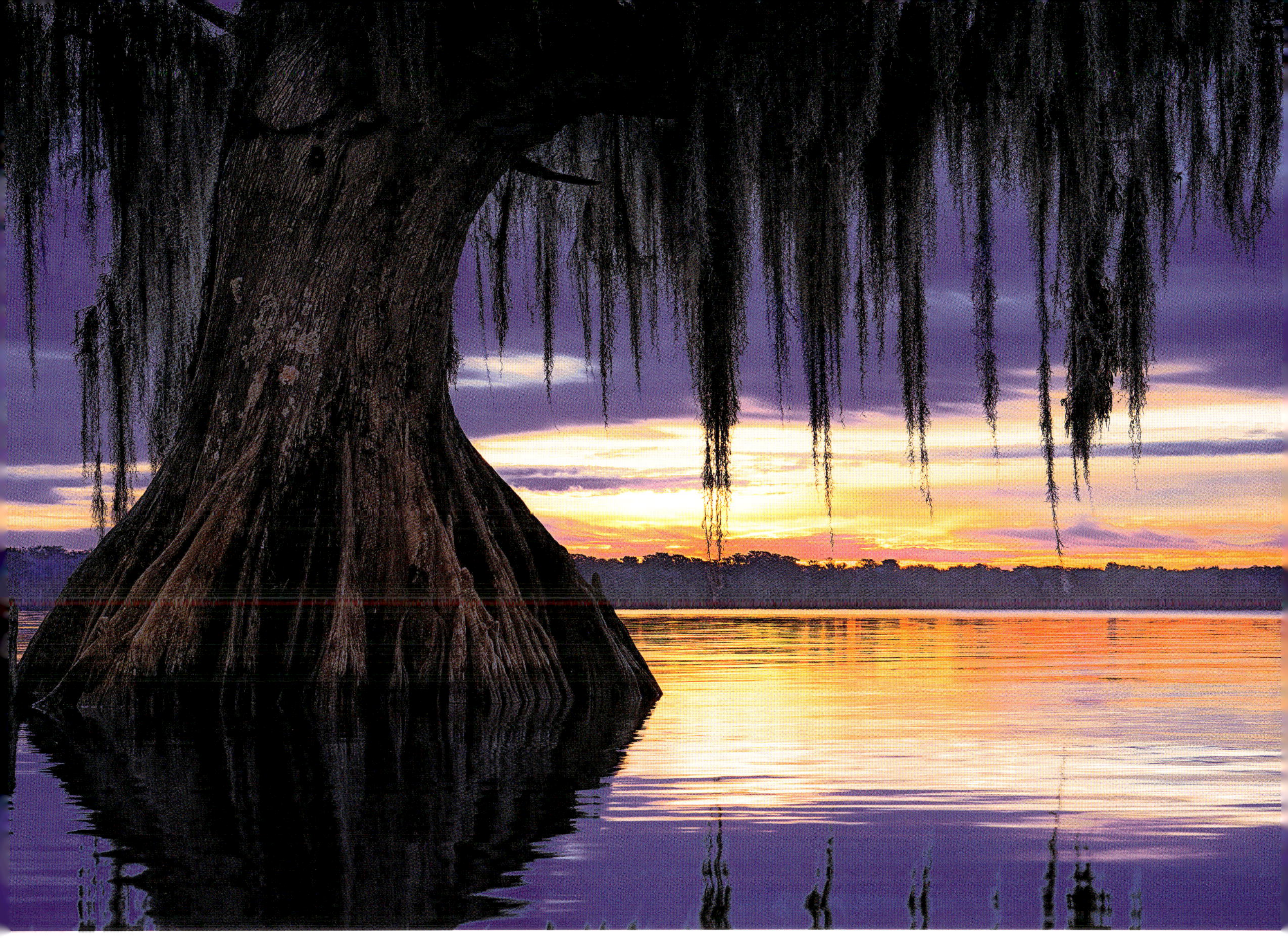

This is my absolute favorite cypress tree on Lake Verret. The old cypress has a character-filled trunk and thick veils of Spanish moss that made the perfect frame for this moody sunrise. It was such a beautiful morning, with thick clouds turning purple as the thinner areas blazed with light.

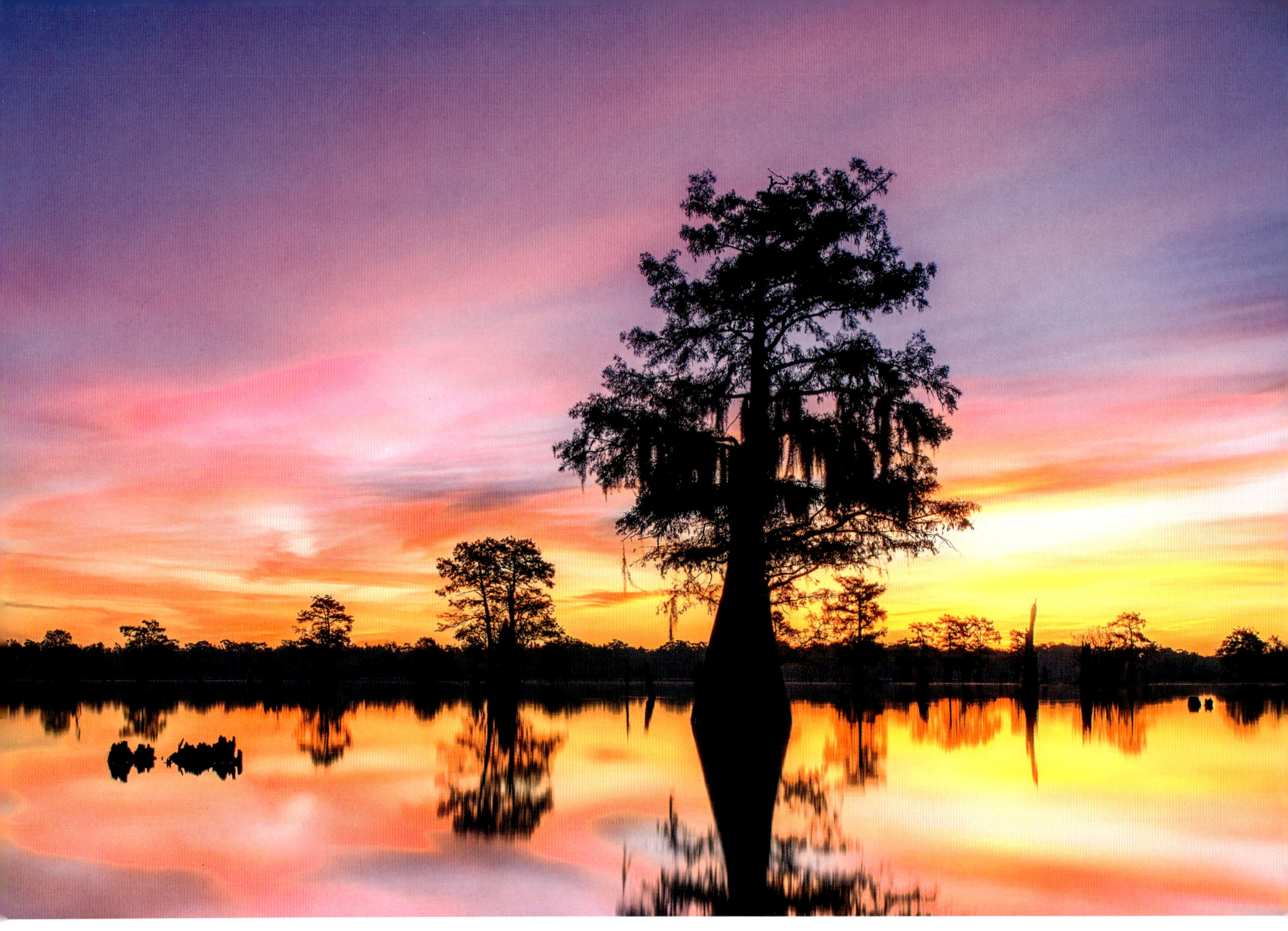

Glass-smooth water provides a perfect reflection of the sky, and on this day I used a neutral-density filter to emphasize the already calm waters. That created a mirrorlike effect that glowed with the incredible colors of sunrise.

The lakes in the swamps turn to glass on calm days. On this day, I set up under thick blankets of low clouds to highlight the expanse of Lake Palourde, using a single tree standing well out from the banks as the focal point. I was convinced the clouds would snuff all color from the sunrise, but golden light blossomed across the sky as the sun rose invisible on the horizon.

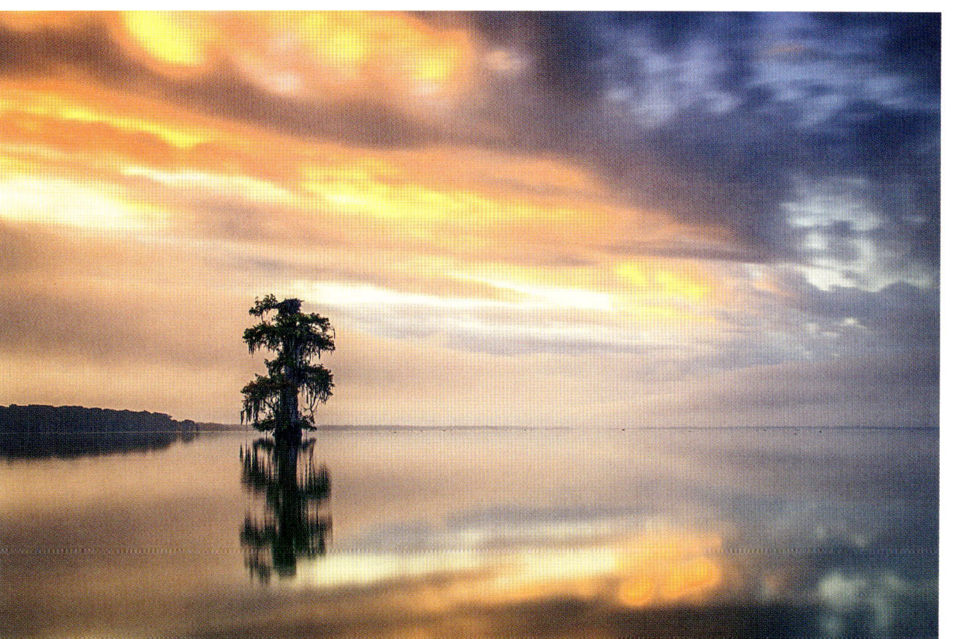

The graceful arch of this cypress tree's trunk and limbs, along with the mass of Spanish moss, make it stand out from the crowd. On this morning, amazing sunrise colors provided the perfect opportunity to use it to frame the clouds and the main forest beyond.

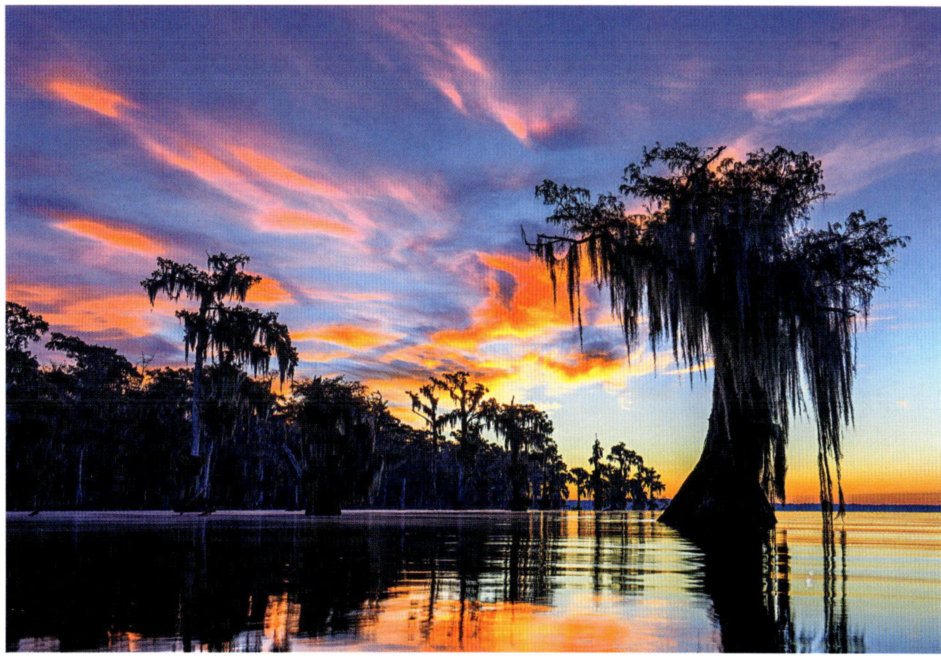

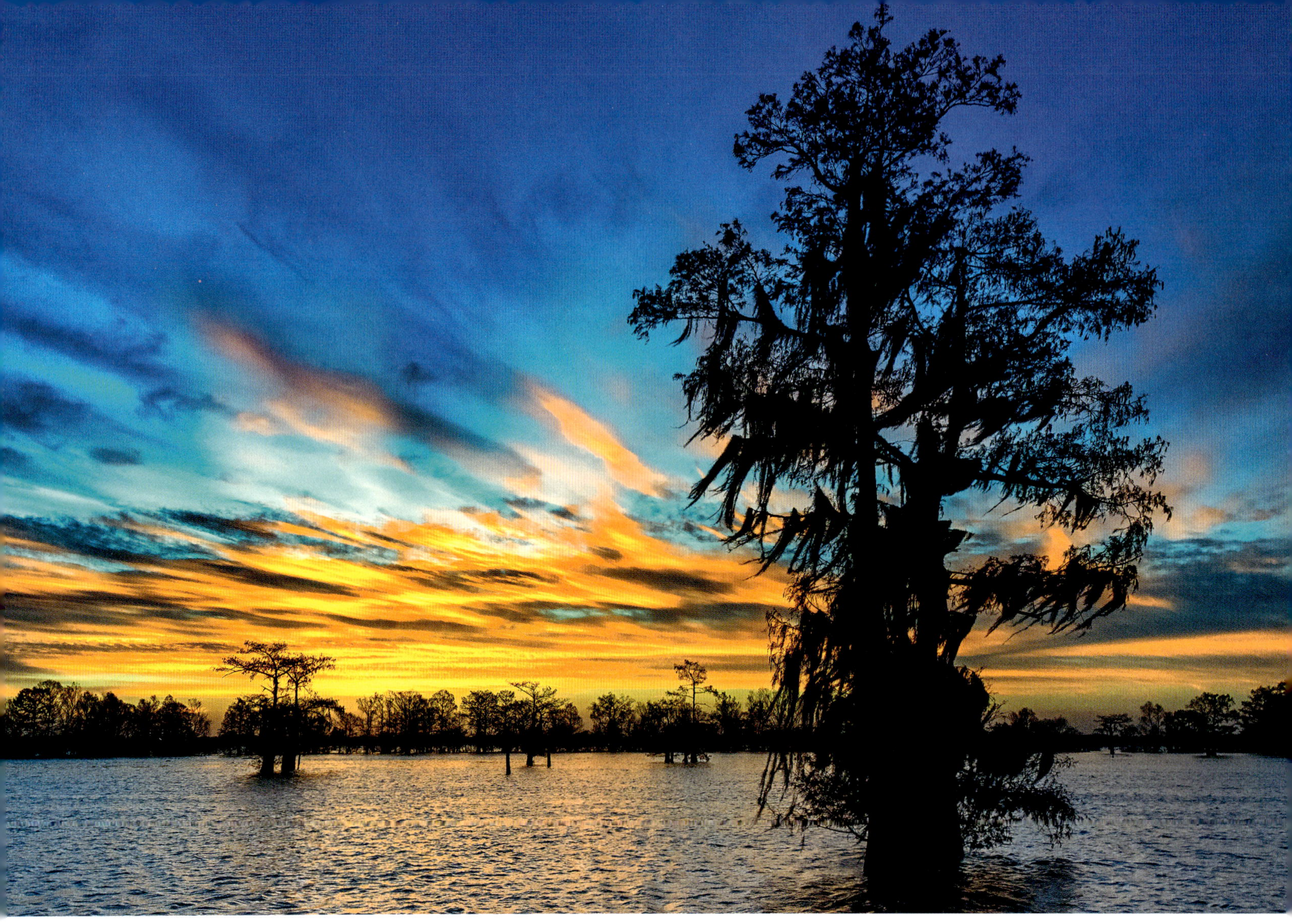

It's always incredible to watch how a scene changes as sunrise progresses. I was set up in Henderson Swamp on this day, well before light bled over the horizon. Incredible color blossomed across the undersides of the clouds a few minutes before official sunrise. The clouds behind the silhouetted trees add interest to the final photo.

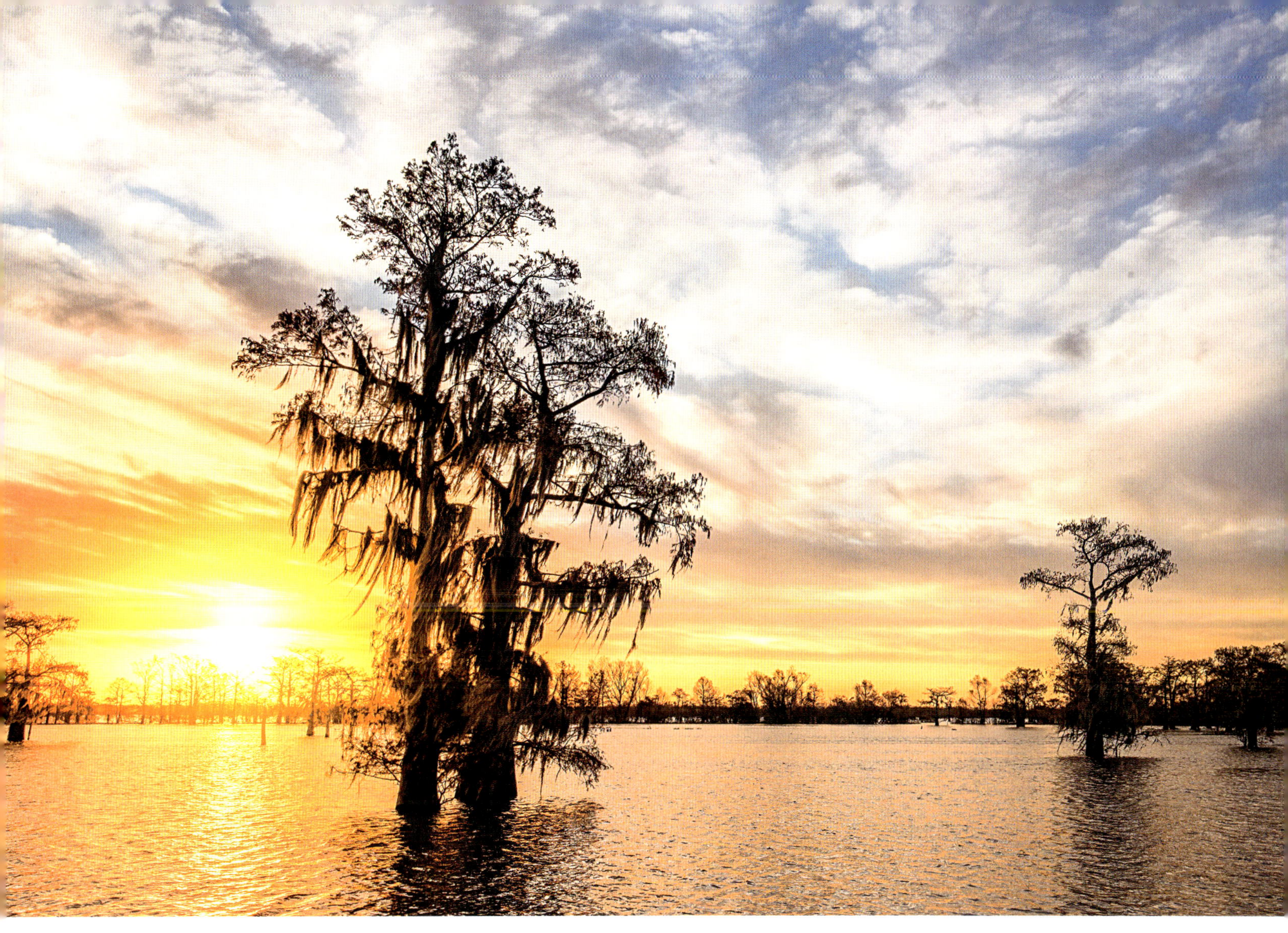

I stuck around to watch the rest of the sunrise, and soon amazing golden light was cast across the rippled waters of the swamp and lit up the trees. The blue in the sky peeking through the clouds added wonderful contrast to the scene.

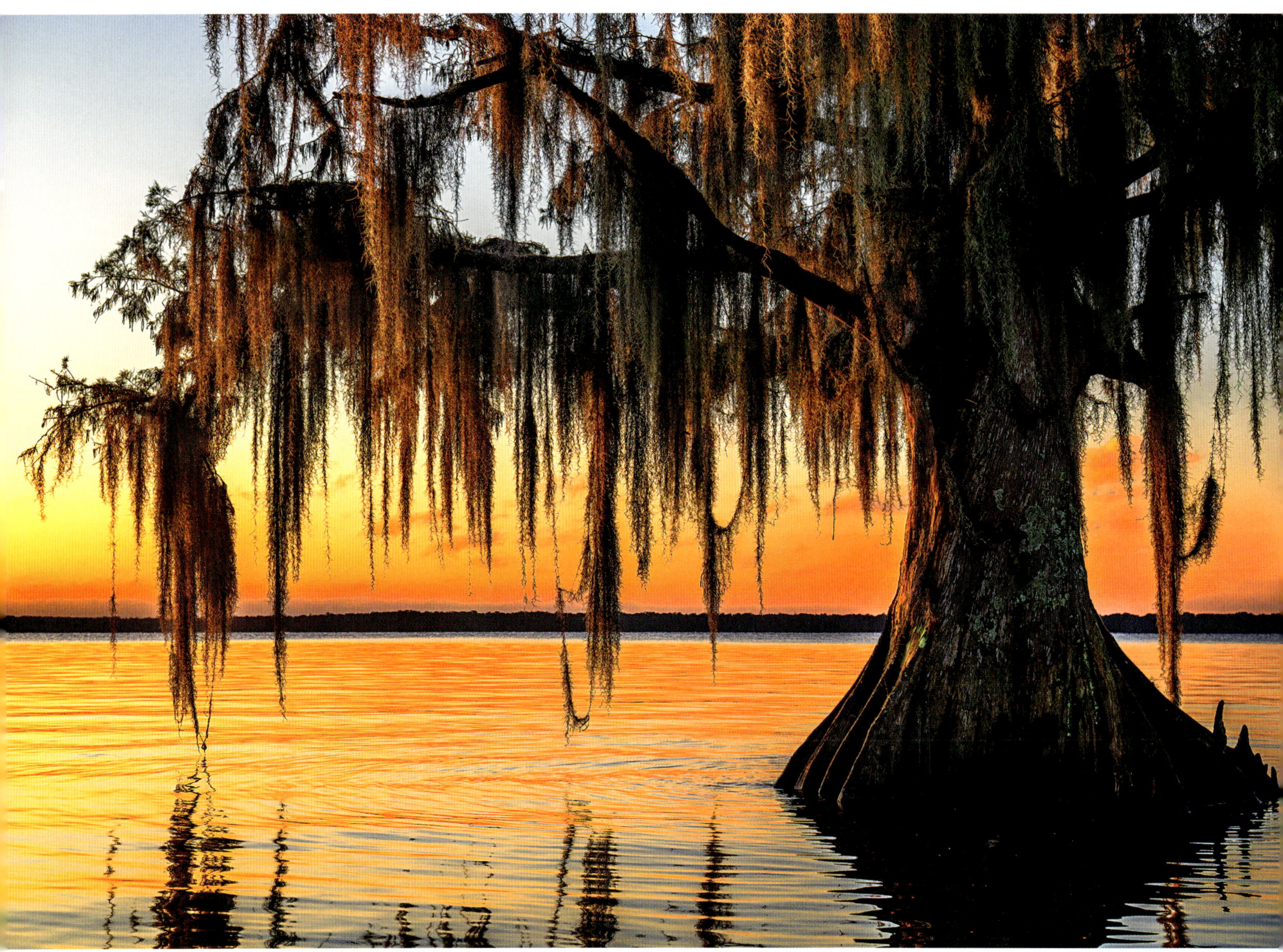

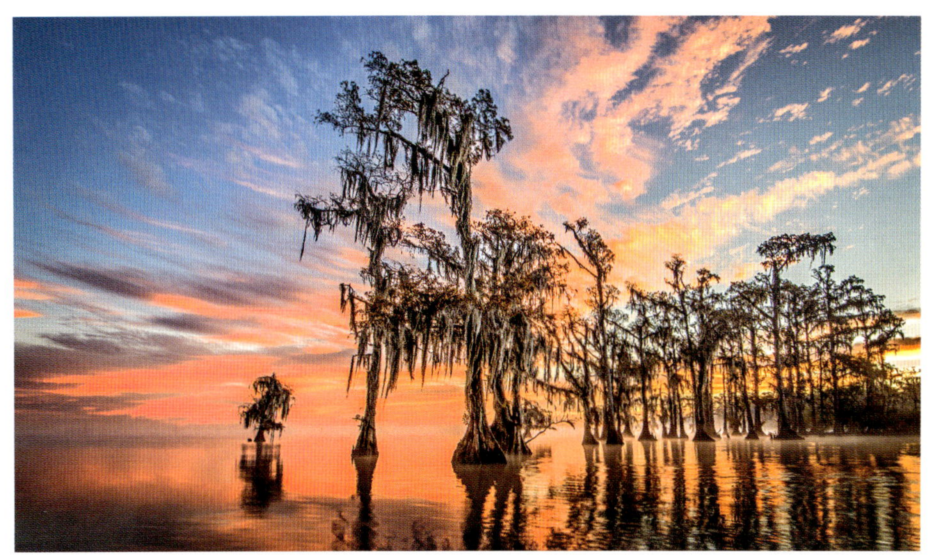

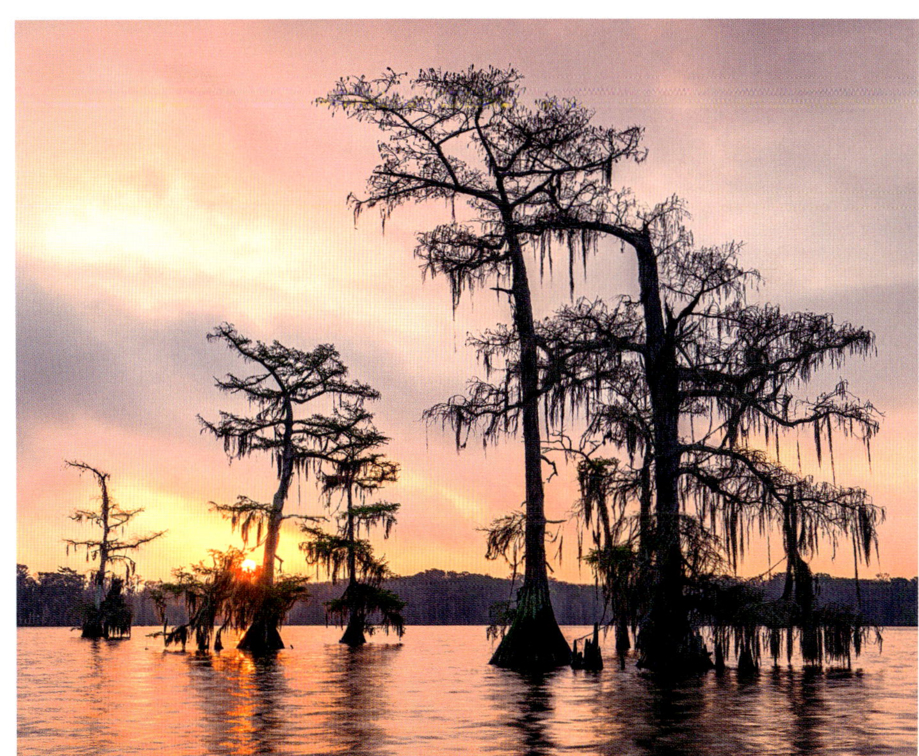

Some mornings are simply surreal. I was standing waist deep in Lake Maurepas on this morning when the rising sun absolutely set the sky on fire.

Cypress trees grow in harsh environments, and that seems to generate such character-filled scenery. Trees twist; they grow crookedly; tops get blown out. And that fact is often shown best when most leaves have fallen off for the short winter we experience in the Deep South.

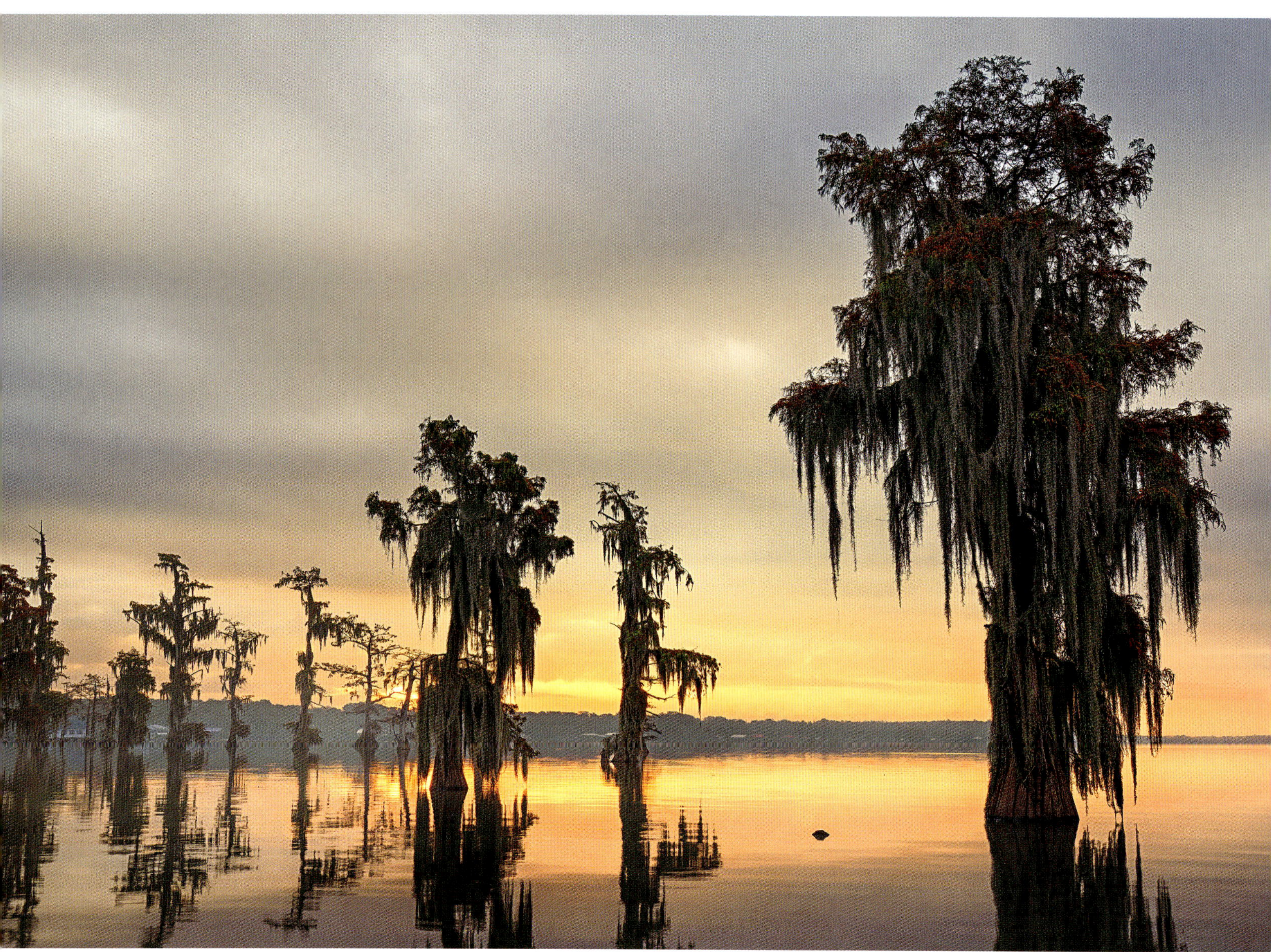

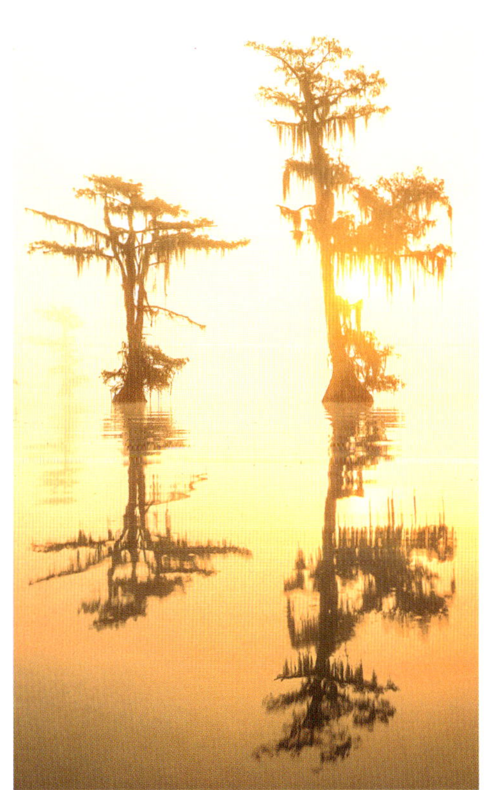

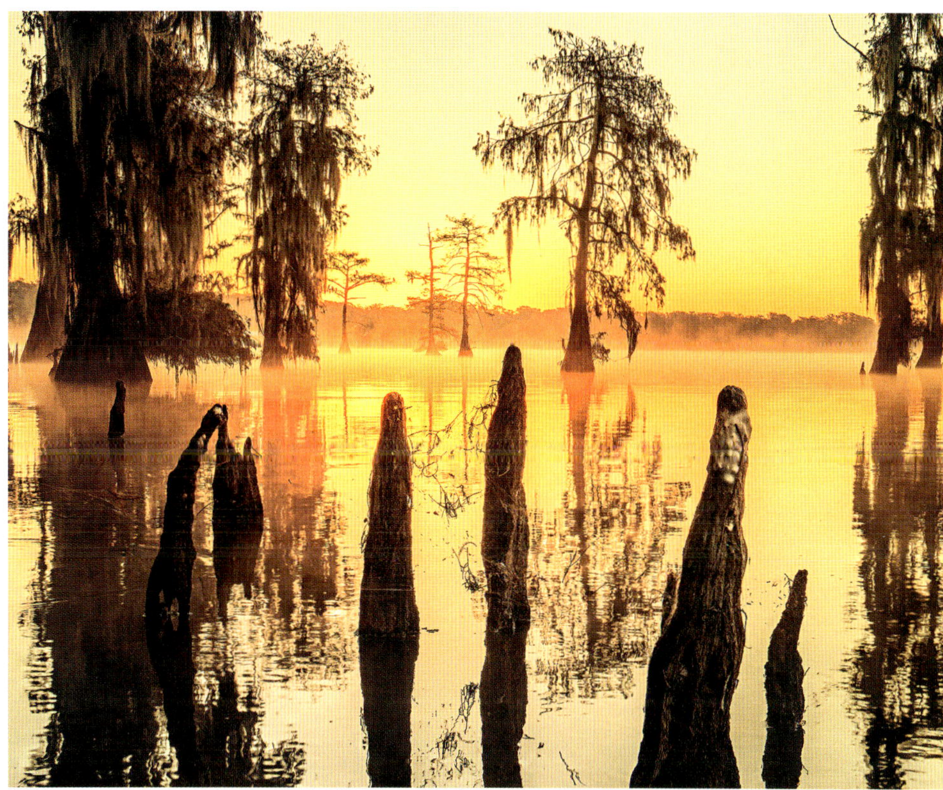

Opposite page: There's never a bad sunrise over the swamps. They are all so different and offer individual beauty. This is a great example of how even a muted sunrise can be otherworldly. I was floating in the Lake Verret swamp, and the rising sun was able to push the barest bit of golden light through the thick clouds, but the upside was that the light was diffused and lit up more detail in the trees.

Fall days often present the opportunity for fog to form in the swamps, and that can combine with sunrise to add incredible mystery to the already beautiful scenery. I tucked behind some cypress knees, positioning my camera almost at water level, to create this image of golden fog hanging just above the water in the background.

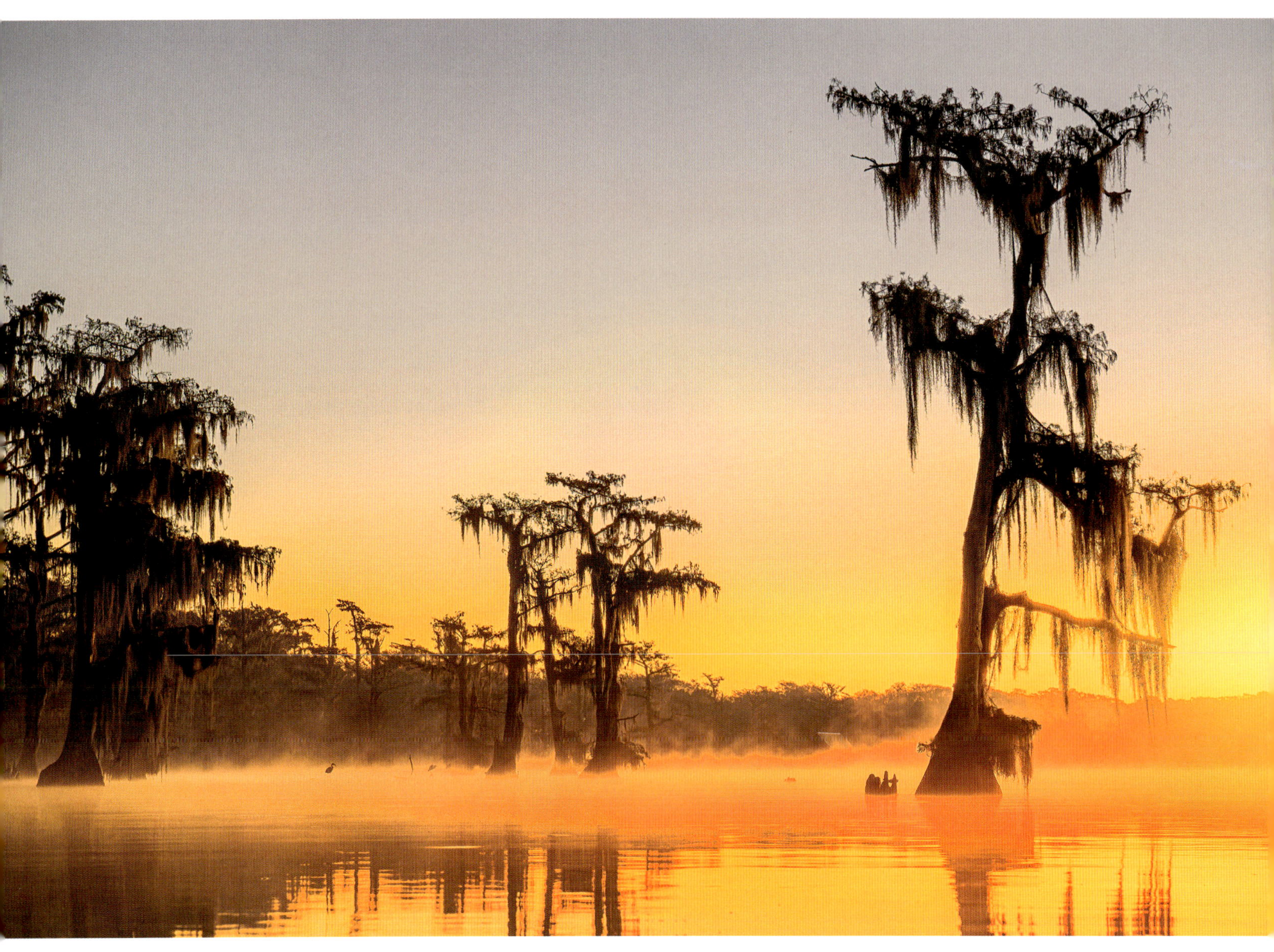

It's always fun to watch fog form and then light up as the sun breaches the trees. Add a couple of feeding herons to the mix, and the result is an iconic view of the Louisiana swamp.

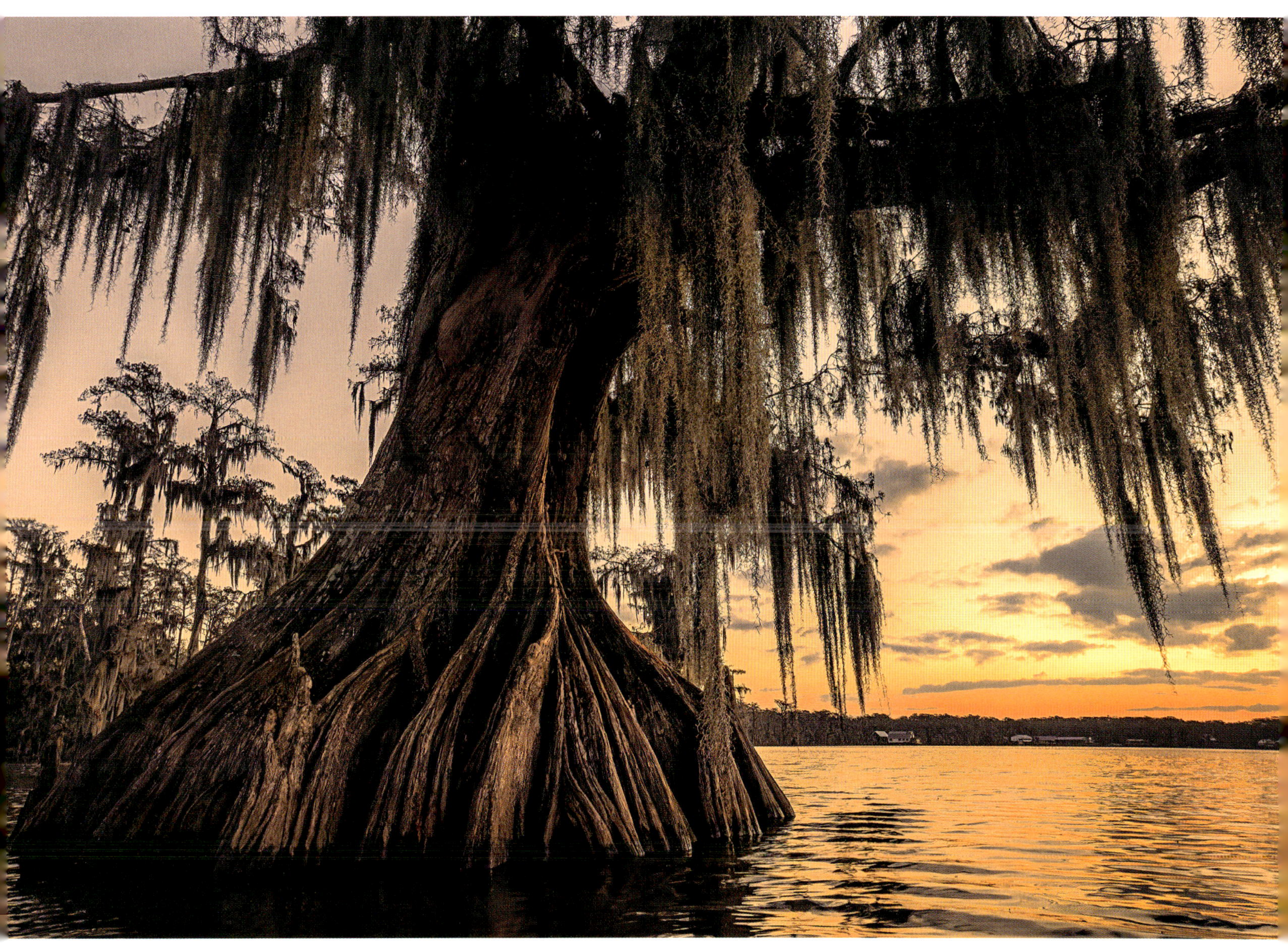

This Lake Verret tree seems to draw me back for another photograph every time I paddle that part of the lake.

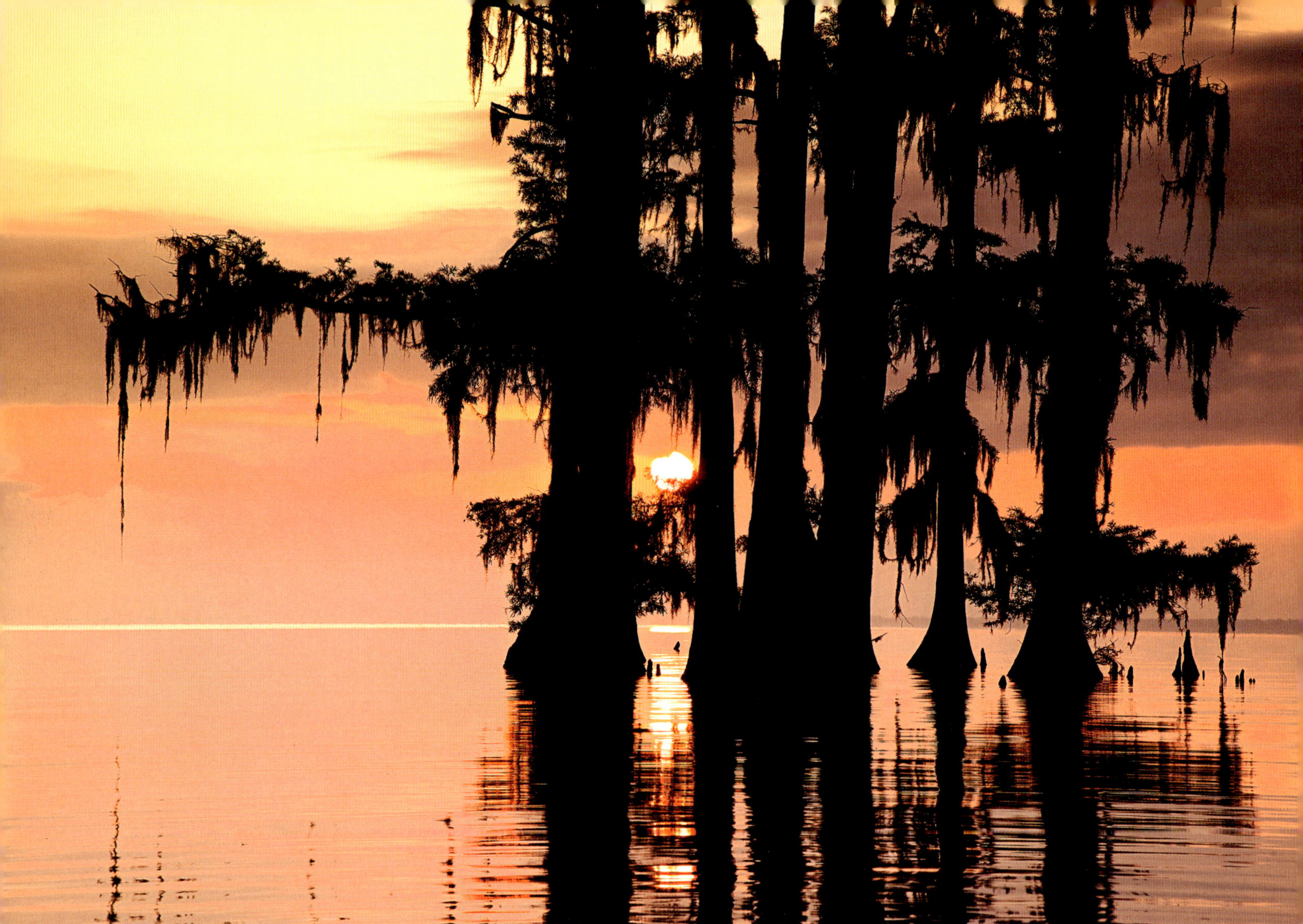

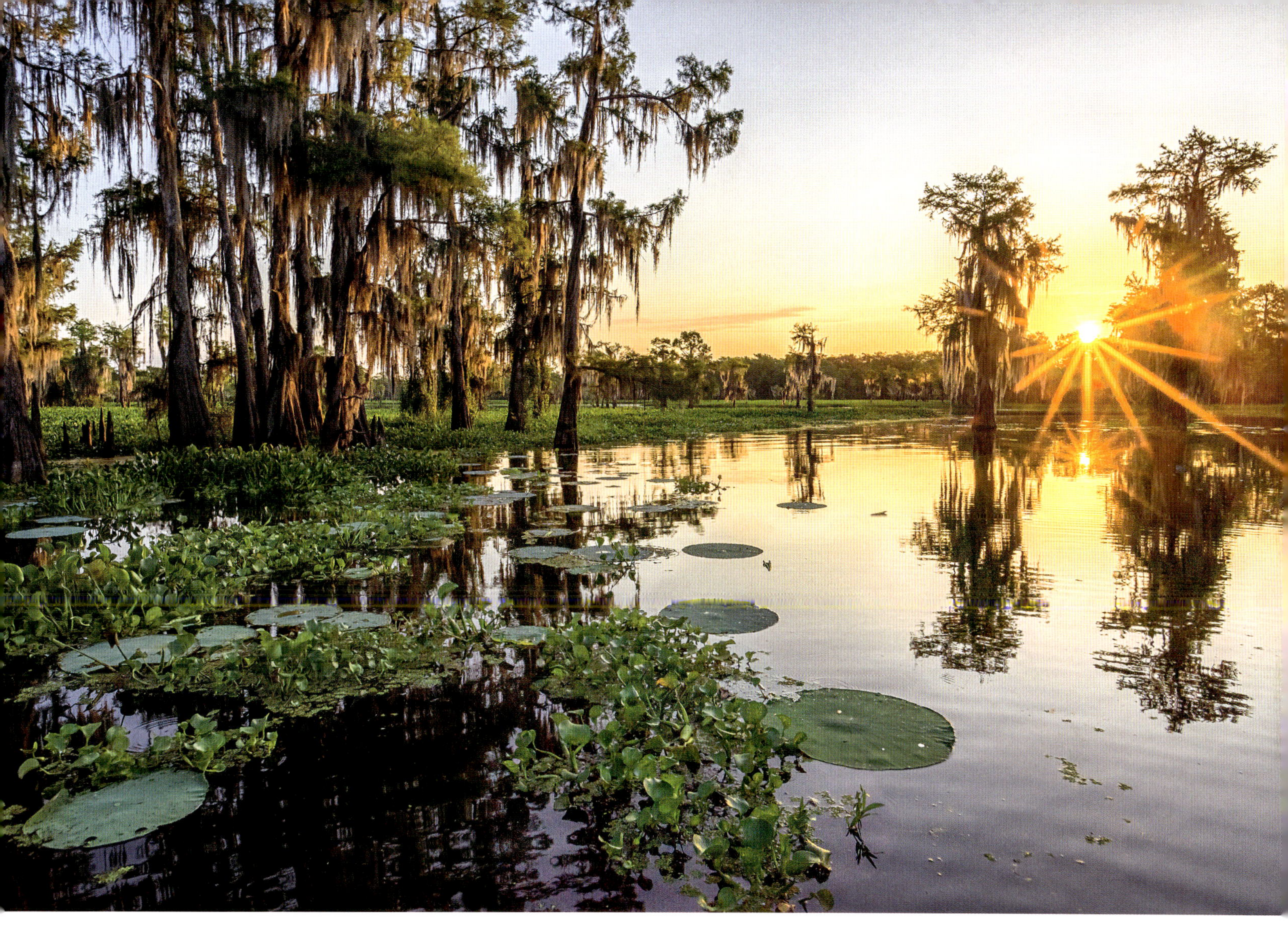

There's little more amazing than watching the sun burst over the horizon and send that first soft light of day over the flooded swamps deep within the sprawling Atchafalaya Delta. This beautiful scene is just off Duck Lake, one of several natural lakes on the southern end of the largest river swamp in the United States.

CHAPTER TWO

LUSH BEAUTY

Black water the color of coffee grounds seeps through the flooded forests that make up the South Louisiana swamps. Bayous wind through these most wild of American landscapes, Spanish moss dangling from cypress trees in curly tendrils growing into thick gray mats that contrast wonderfully with rich green foliage.

Civilization fades, leaving only the calls of myriad birds, the croaking of frogs, the growling of alligators, and the splashing of fish. It's a harsh, dynamic environment that resists modernity.

These wetlands cover vast areas of South Louisiana. The Atchafalaya Basin alone is approximately 20 miles wide by 150 miles long, covering more than 1 million acres. Mostly accessible only by boat, the swamps are impervious to development. So they are largely left alone.

These wetlands are irresistibly beautiful, beckoning any nature lover to explore the twisting bayous and rivers. They serve as refuges from the busyness of modern life. Certainly, small communities and towns are built on the edges of these swamplands, but the heart of the swamp remains undeveloped.

Cypresses often form wide, ribbed bases that send out large root systems designed to increase stability in the muddy bottoms. Their knees jut out eerily from the inky water, creating obstacle courses for boats and wildlife.

Ridges, known locally as cheniers, provide dry ground here and there. Gorgeous live oaks take advantage of these high spots, spreading branches out over the water and creating a bit of diversity. Of course, Spanish moss usually hangs from these trees.

It's a severe world that doesn't suffer weakness. Tropical storms blow through, breaking off treetops or uprooting whole trees. Lightning strikes scar or kill trees. Floods inundate forests that normally have a few inches of water and sometimes dry out altogether. Humidity hangs in the air, often bringing with it the pungent scent of decay.

Entering these waterlogged mazes can be intimidating to the uninitiated. To those who know the swamps, however, these are places of refuge that reconnect us to a distant past and offer unsurpassed natural beauty.

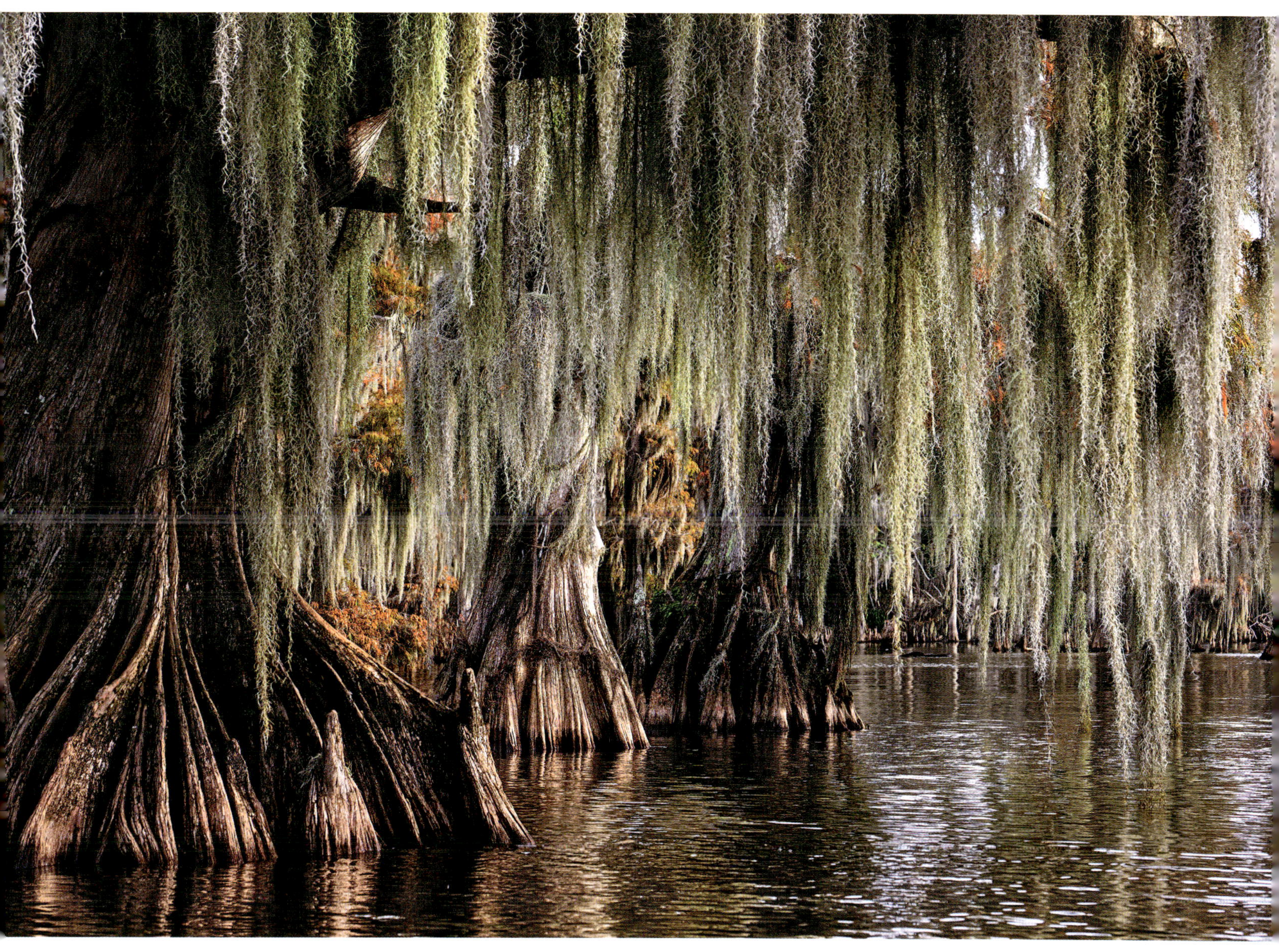

South Louisiana's swamps are primal places of incredible beauty that seem immune to the passage of time. Largely inaccessible except by boat, they offer refuge from the daily grind of the modern world.

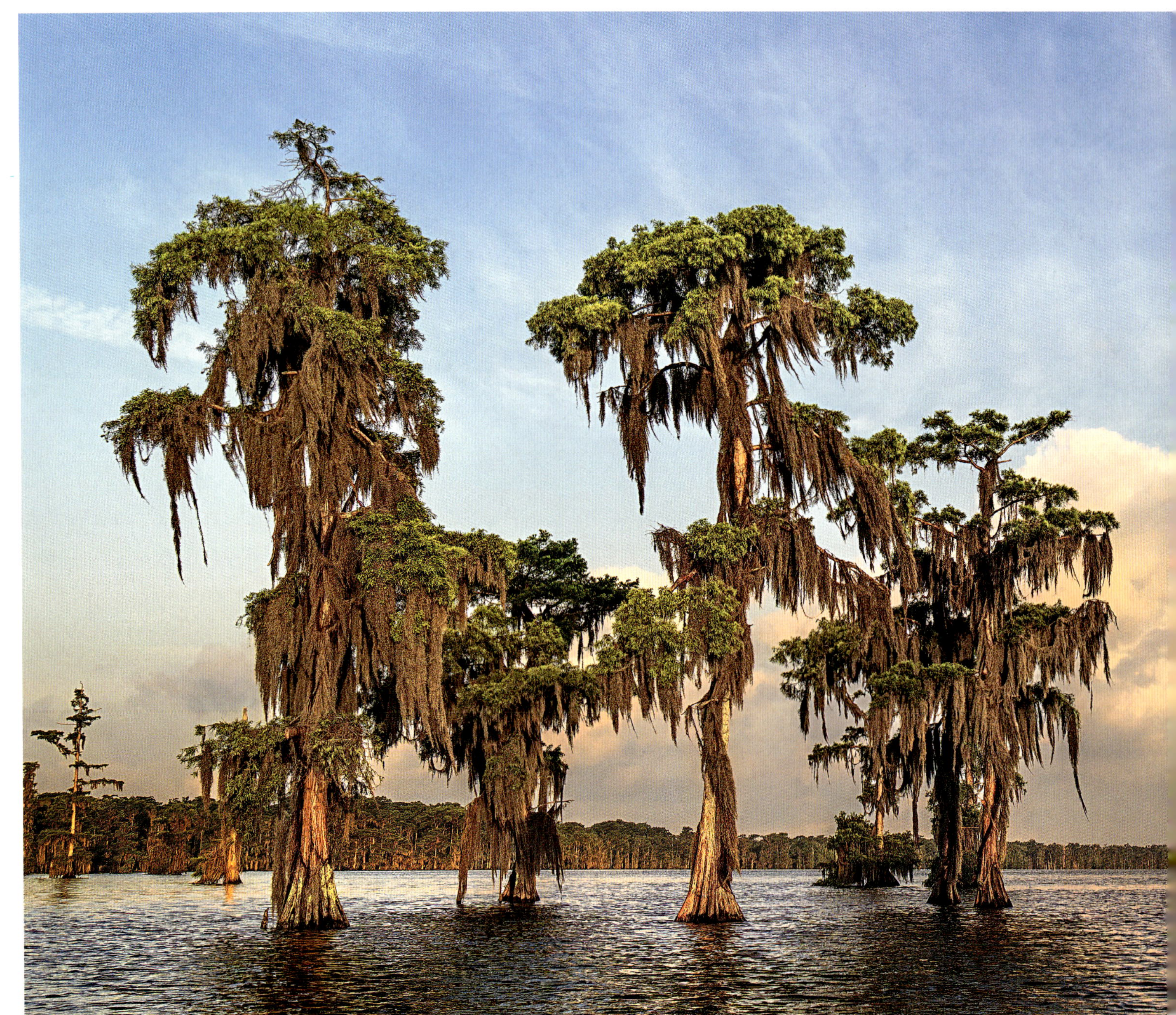

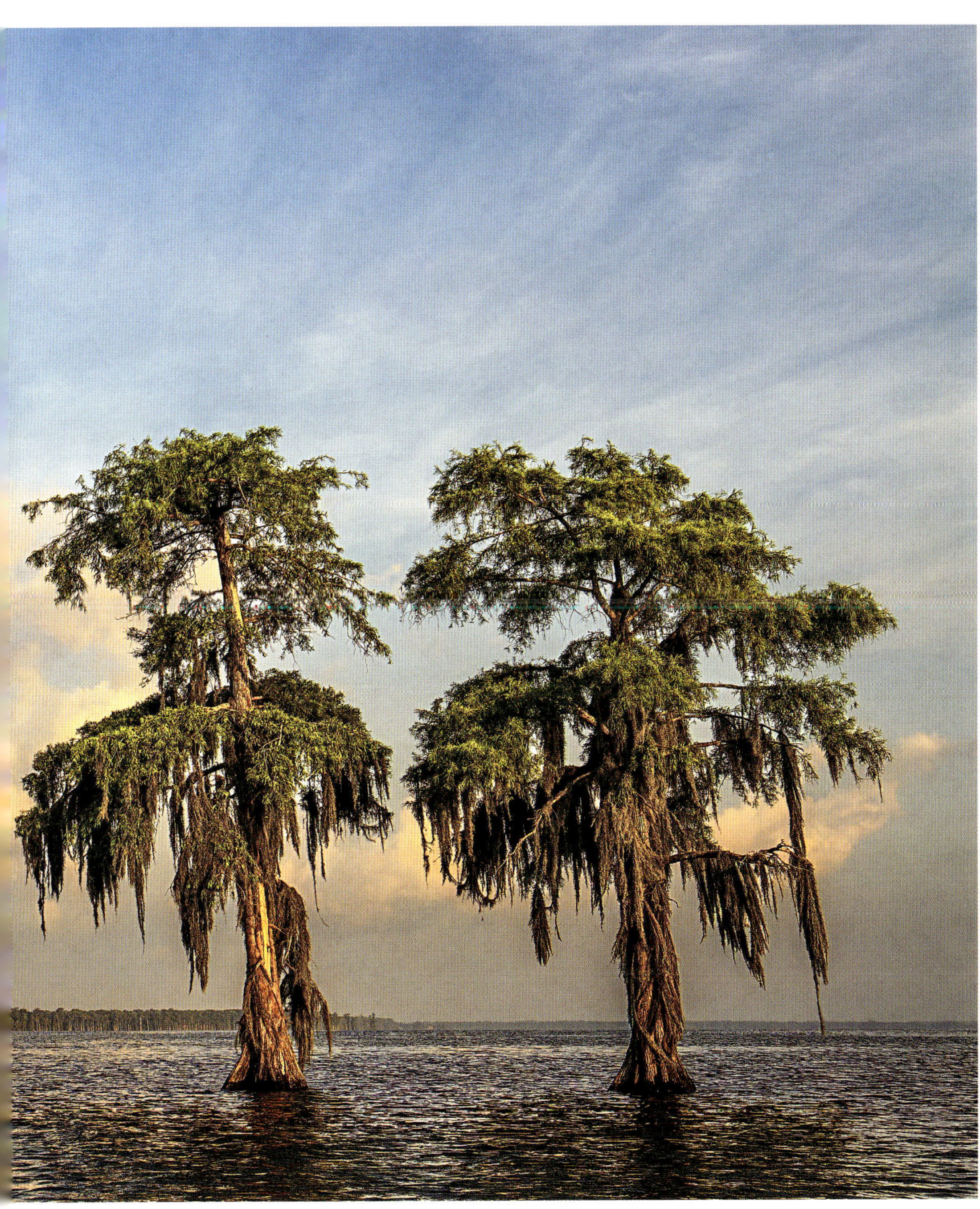

Spanish moss is ever present in the swamps, decorating the trees and offering wonderful contrast to the lushness of the foliage. This moss doesn't harm the trees; it's rootless and draws sustenance from the air and rainfall. In fact, it's not moss at all. Rather, the stringy tendrils are part of the pineapple family.

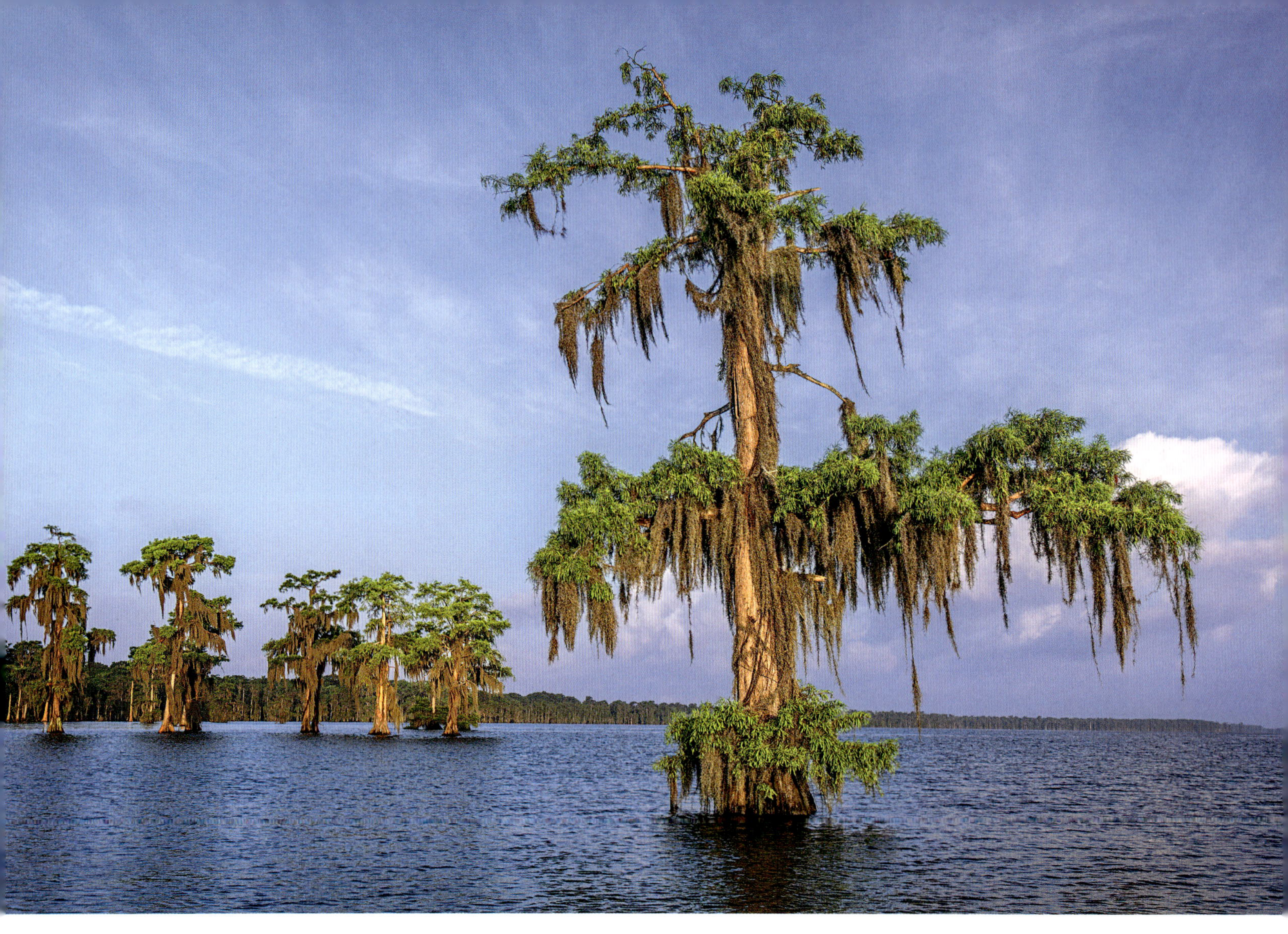

Cypress trees can have a ton of character, with gangly branches sprawling away from the trunk and offering purchase for Spanish moss and birds alike.

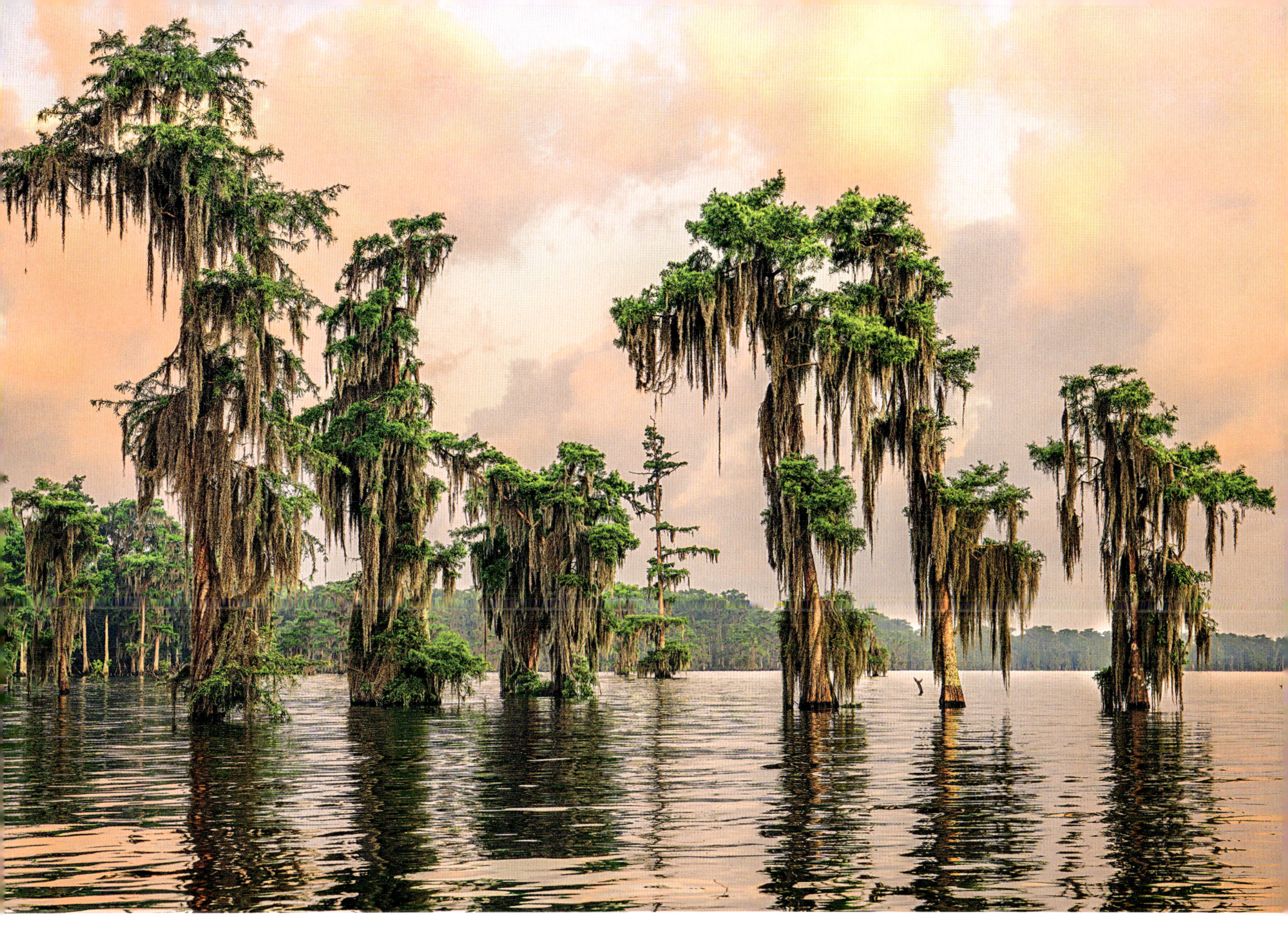

The lushness of the swamps is stunning, especially as the new growth of spring brings color back to the landscape. Add the pastel tinting of clouds just after sunrise and the combination is magical.

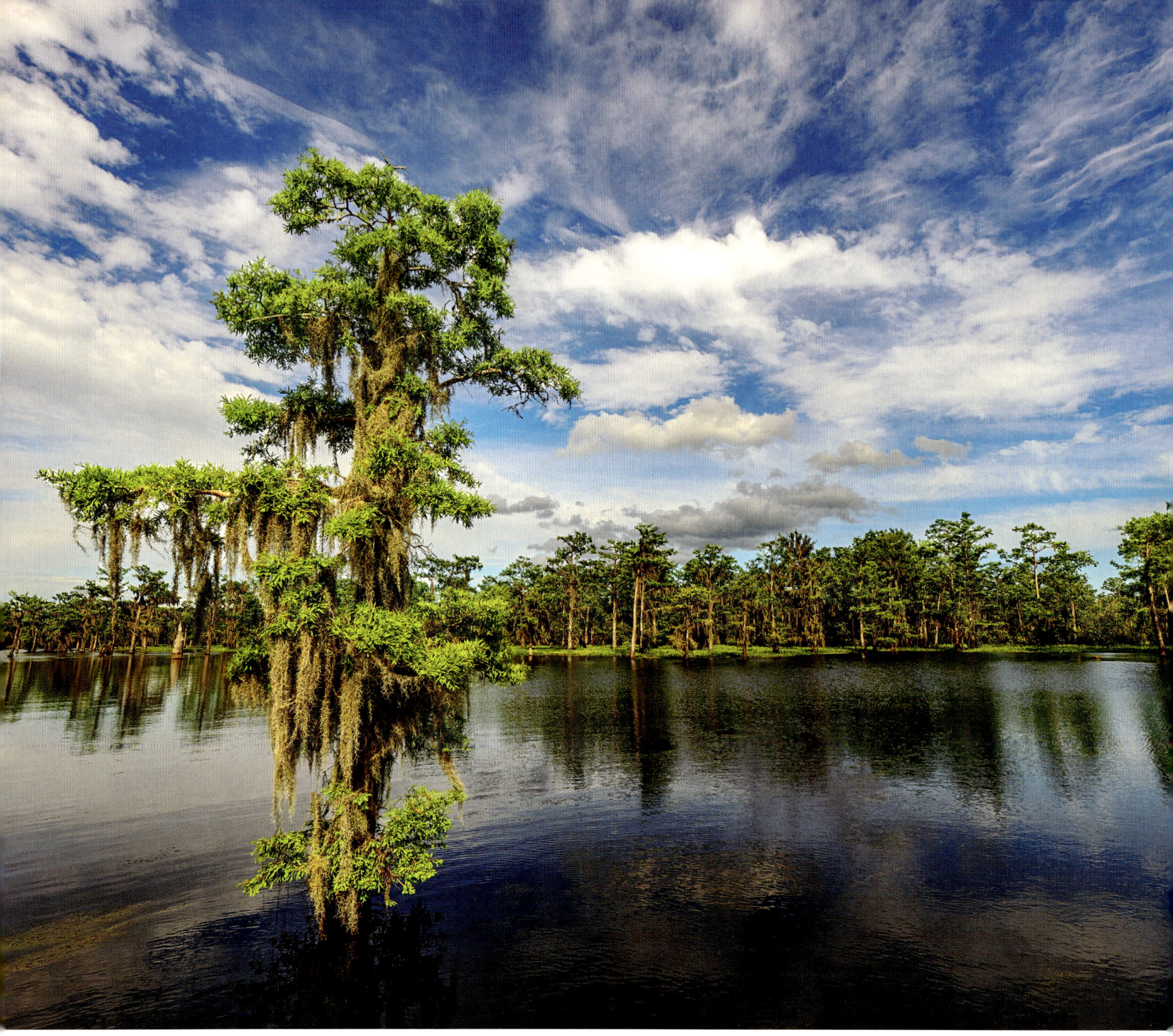

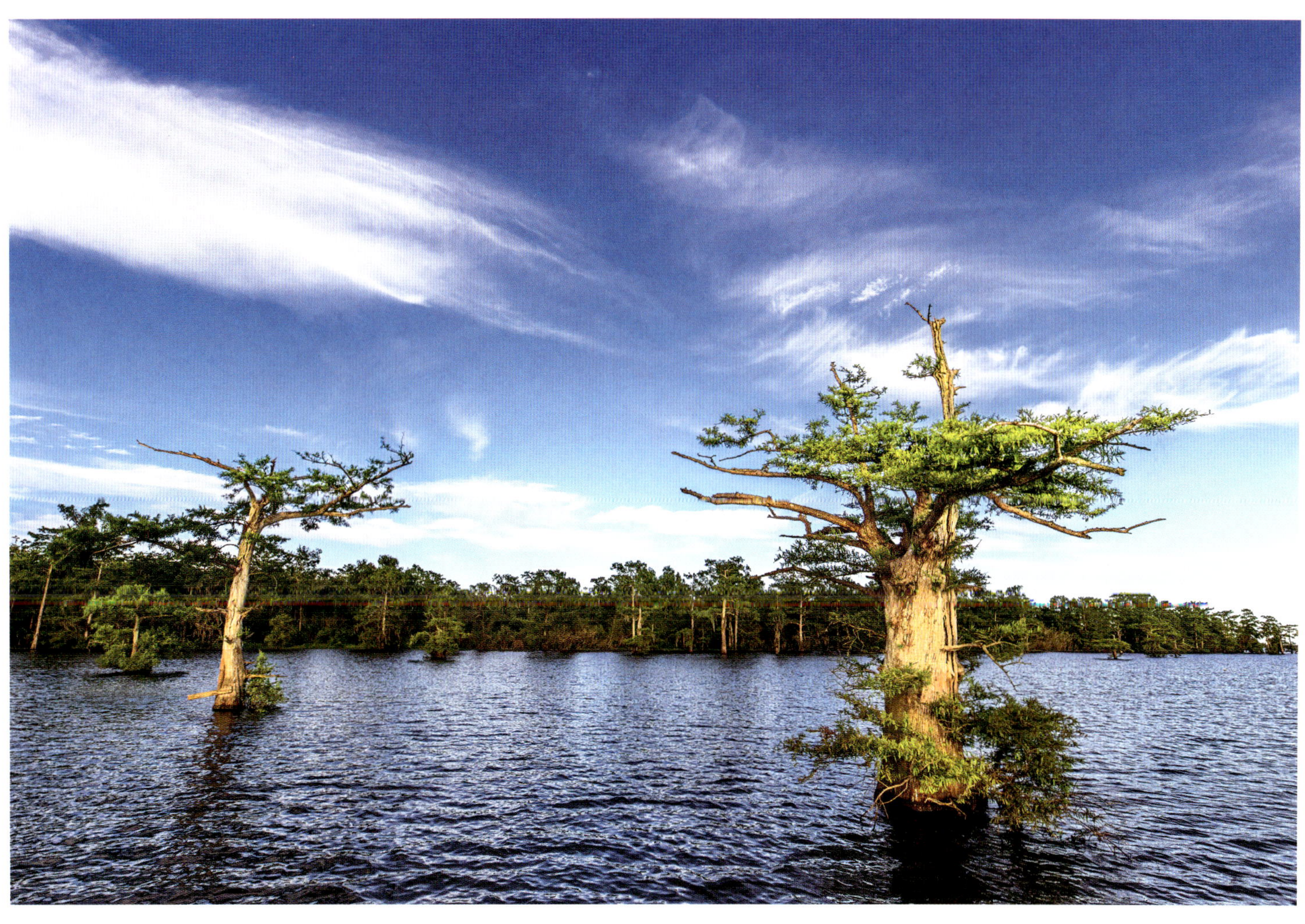

Opposite page: The vividness of the swamps can be striking, as the bright greens of the flooded cypress complement the intense blue of the skies above.

Storm-torn trees illustrate the harshness of the Louisiana swamps. Nature perseveres, however, and damaged cypress trees often push out new growth on the remaining trunks.

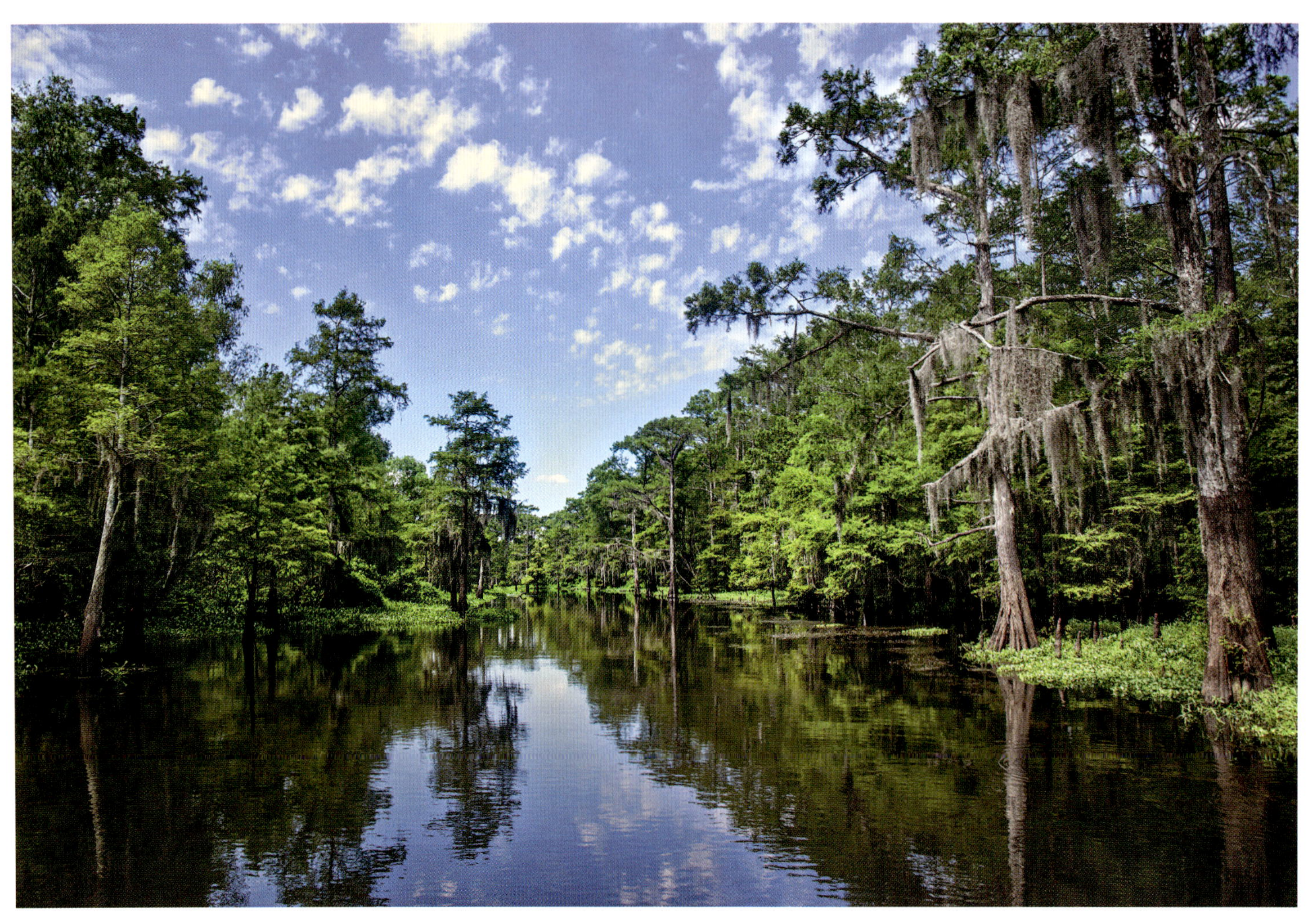

Bayou Chevreuil is one of the scenic routes winding through the lush, flooded cypress forests of the Atchafalaya Basin.

Opposite page: Dead snags are common along the bayous, testifying to the dynamic nature of the South Louisiana swamps. These dead trees offer housing for woodpeckers and other wildlife.

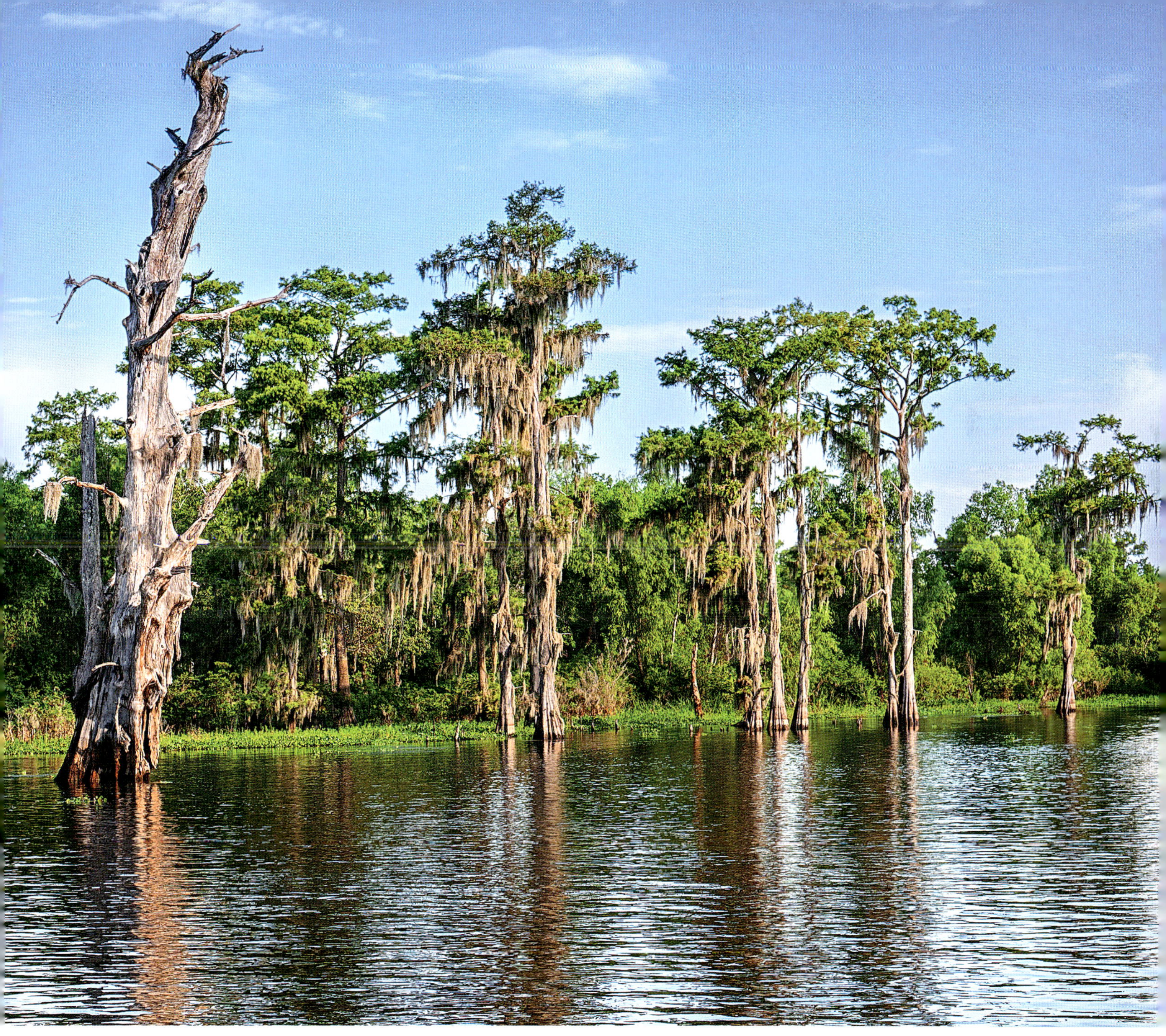

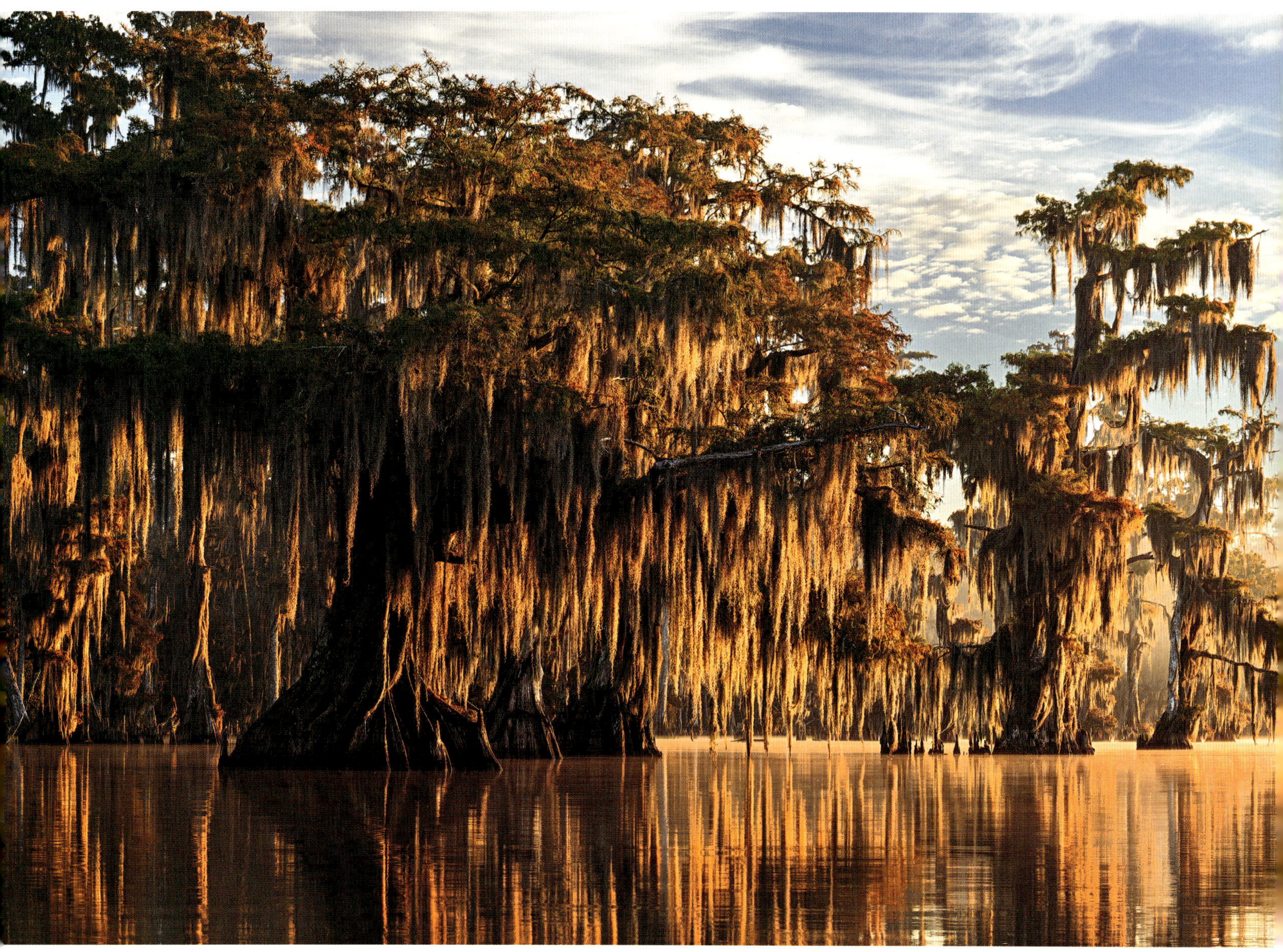

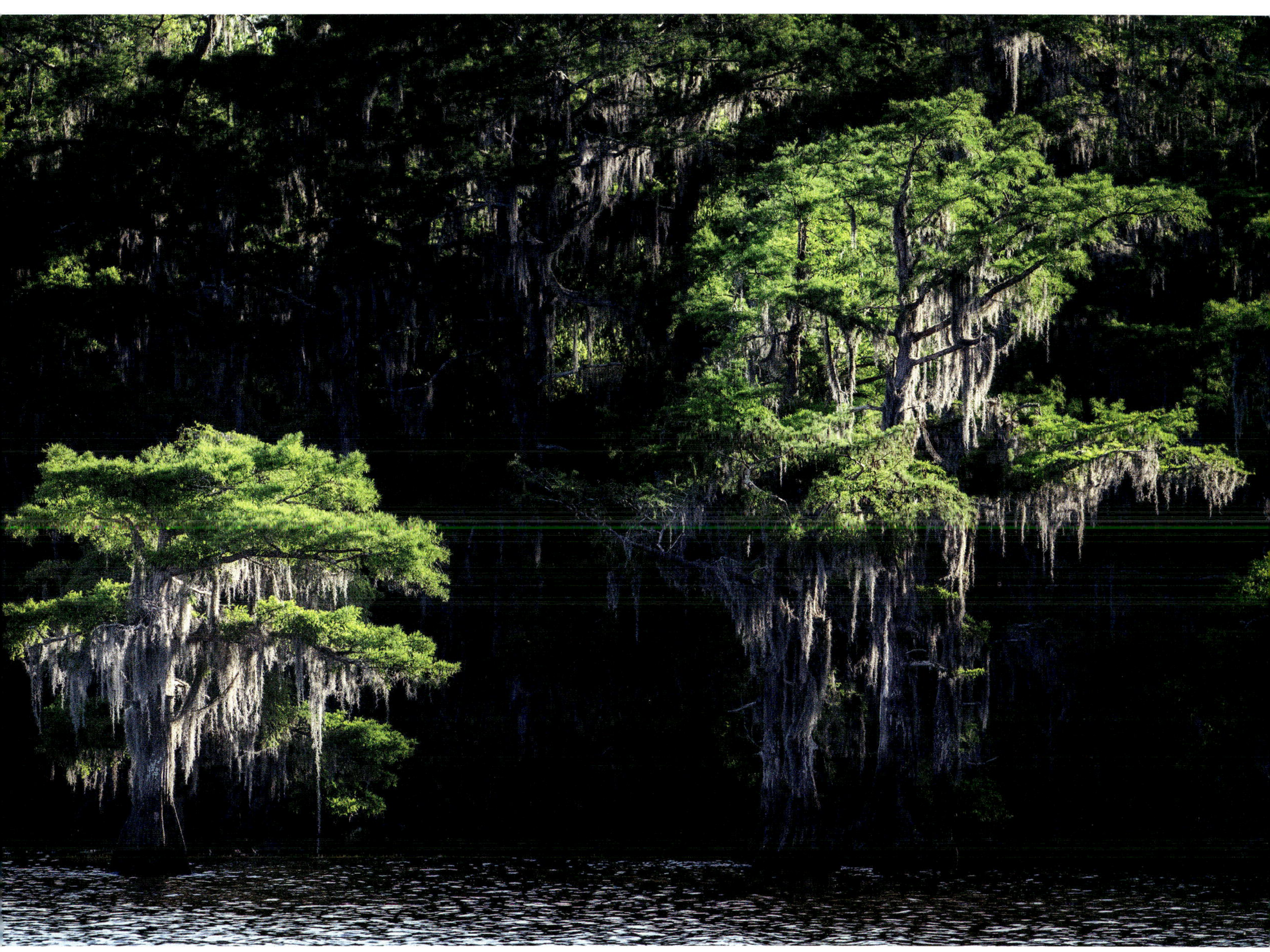

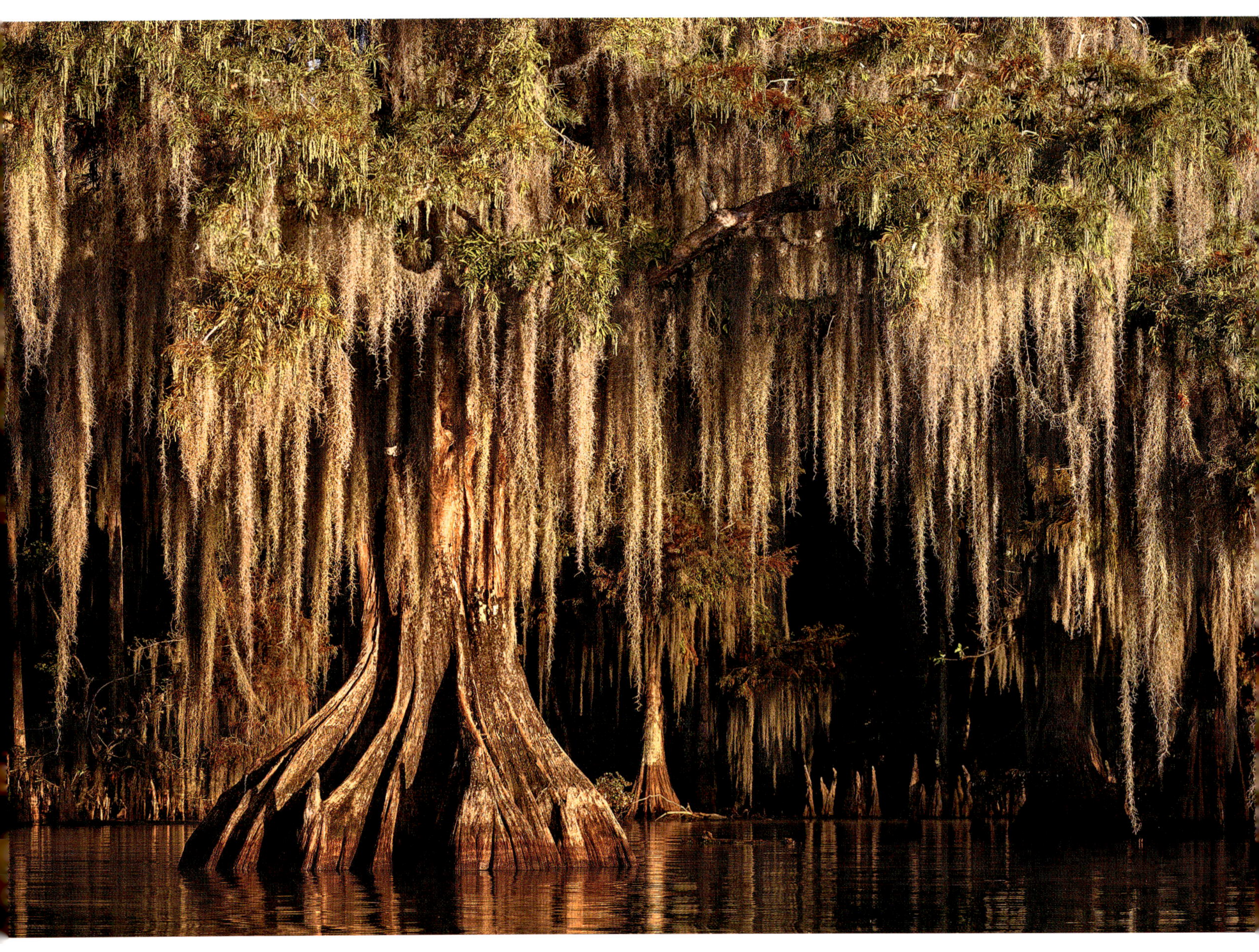

The first light of day hangs in the sheets of moss dangling from one of the cypress trees standing on the edge of Lake Verret.

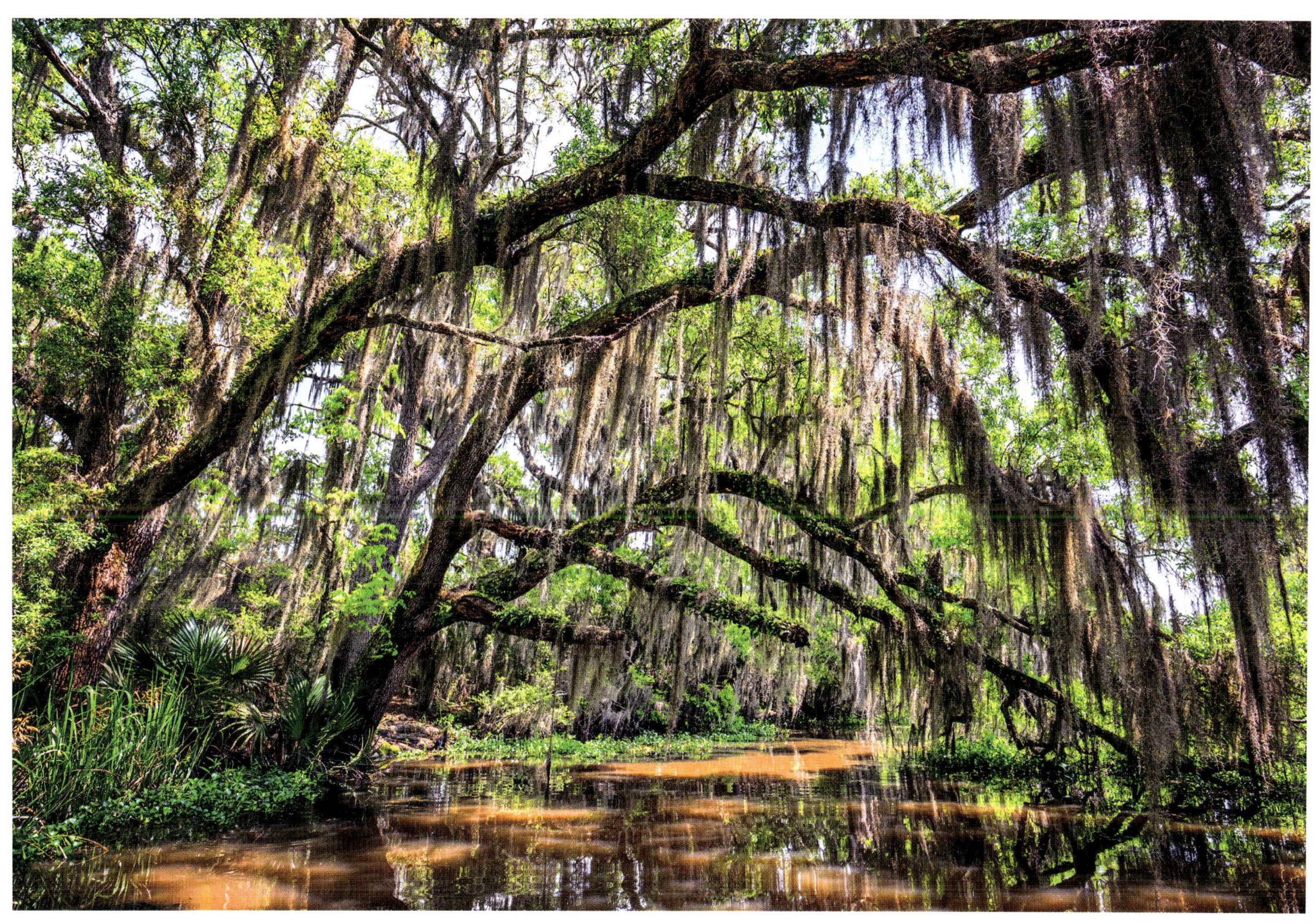

Live oaks growing along bayous and canals often send out arching branches that create canopies over the water. This scene near Bayou Teche National Wildlife Refuge reminds me of a vaulted cathedral.

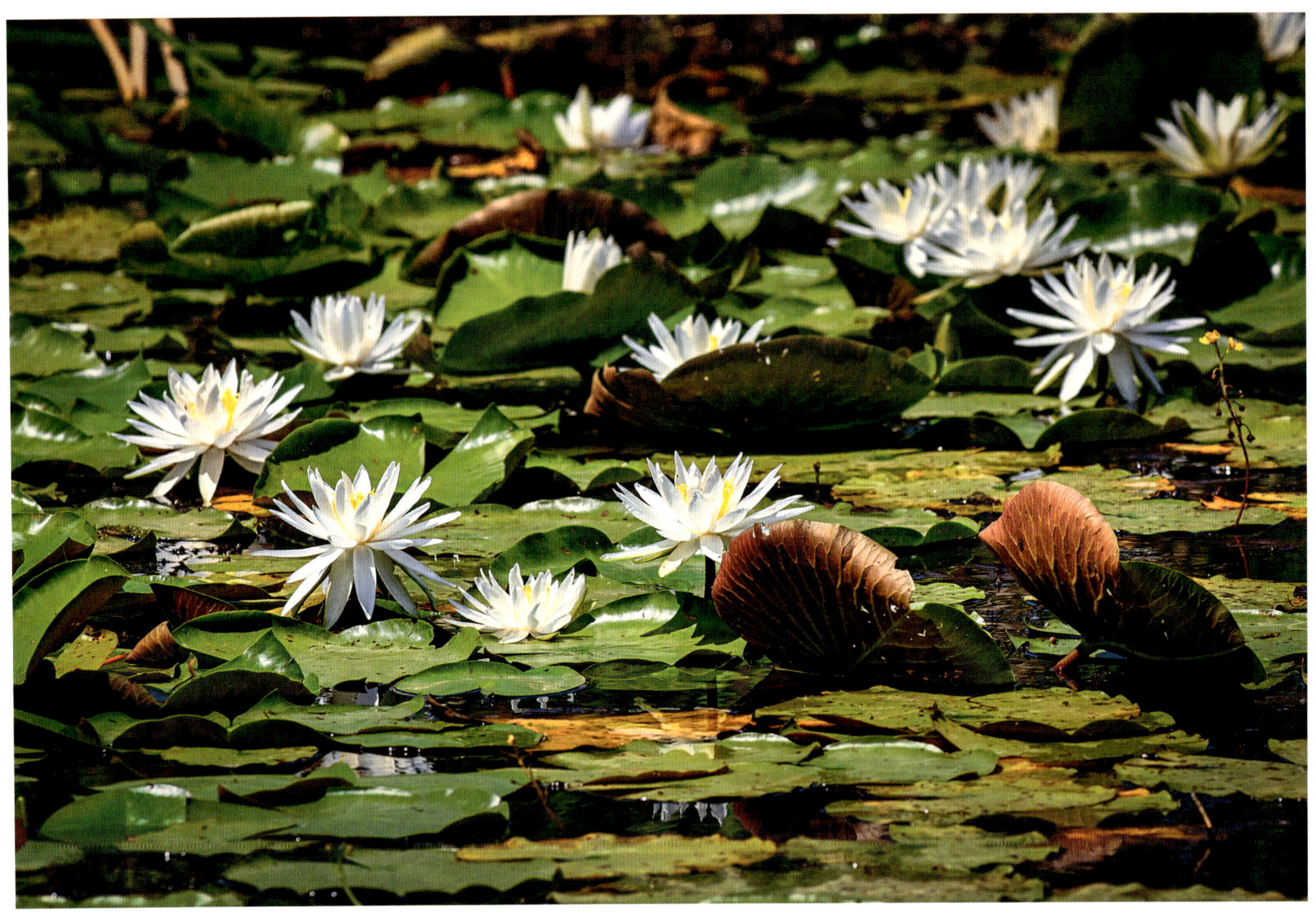

Fields of American lotus often cover shallows along the edges of lakes and bayous. These flowering lilies are known colloquially as "graine à voler" and produce edible seeds once the flower dies.

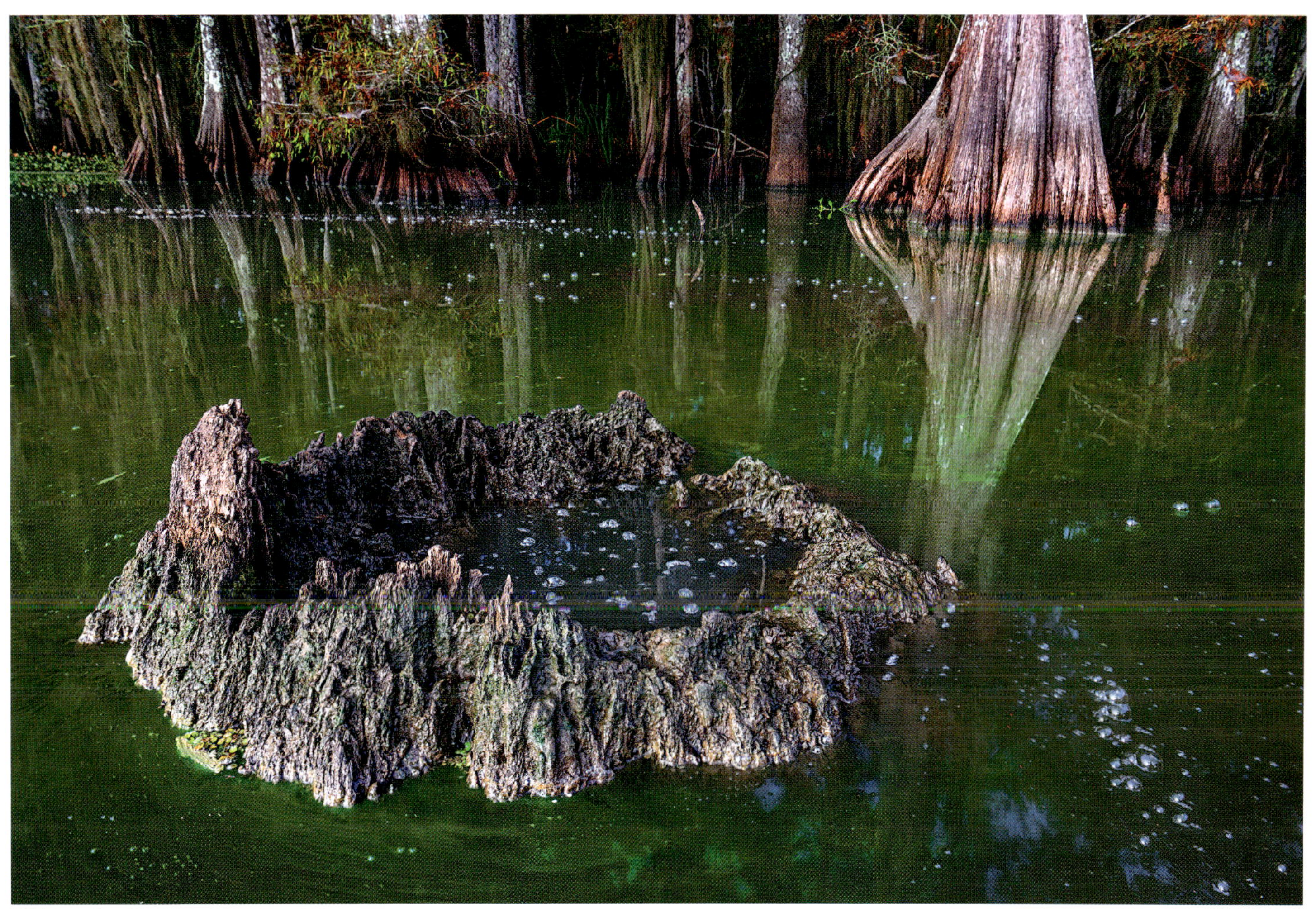

Traces of the past are everywhere in the swamps. Stumps mark where grand old trees once stood. This stump stands near the edge of the main swamp surrounding Lake Dauterive.

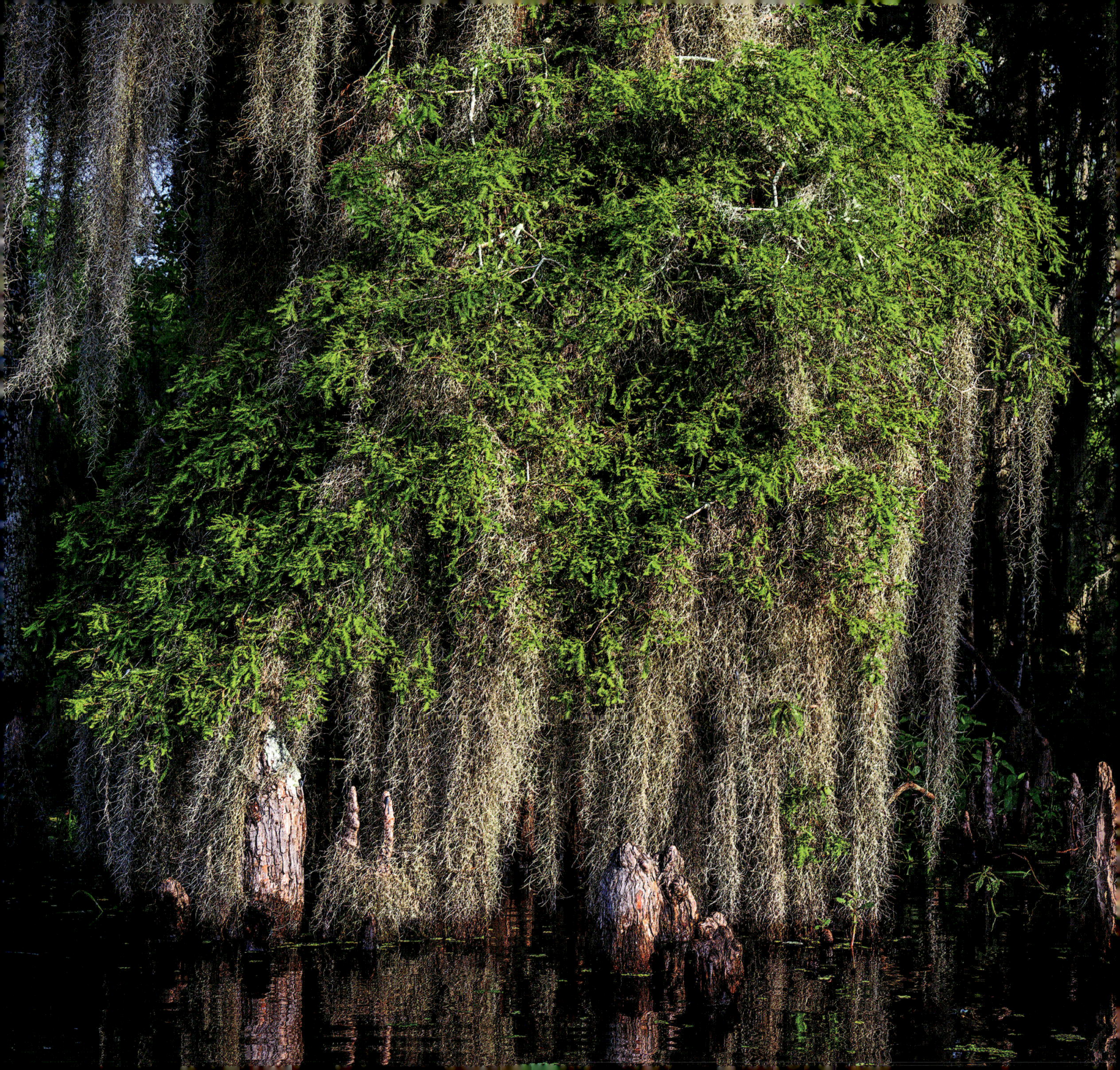

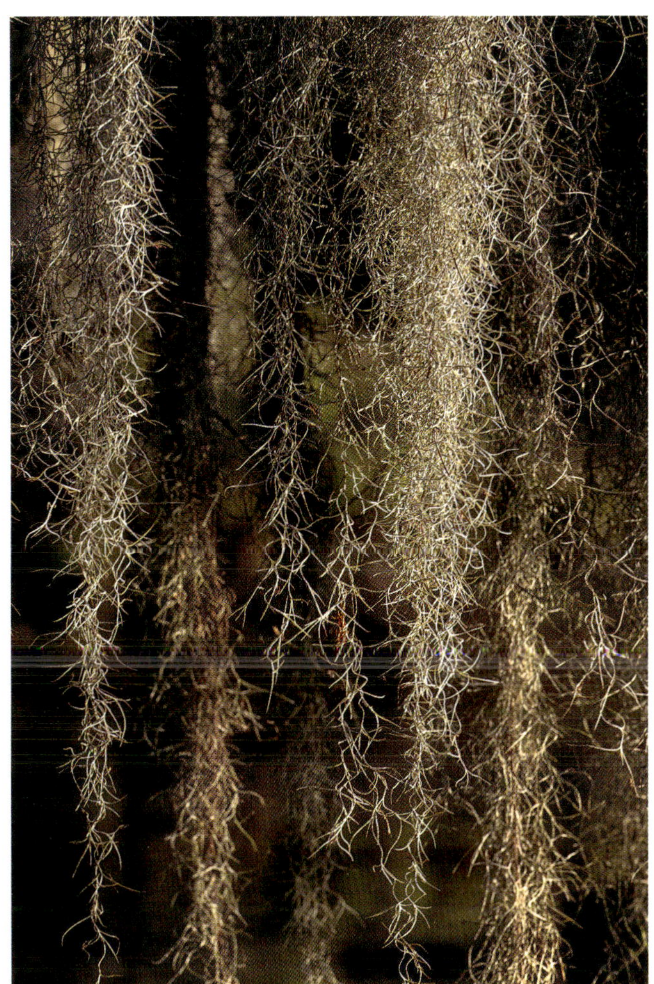

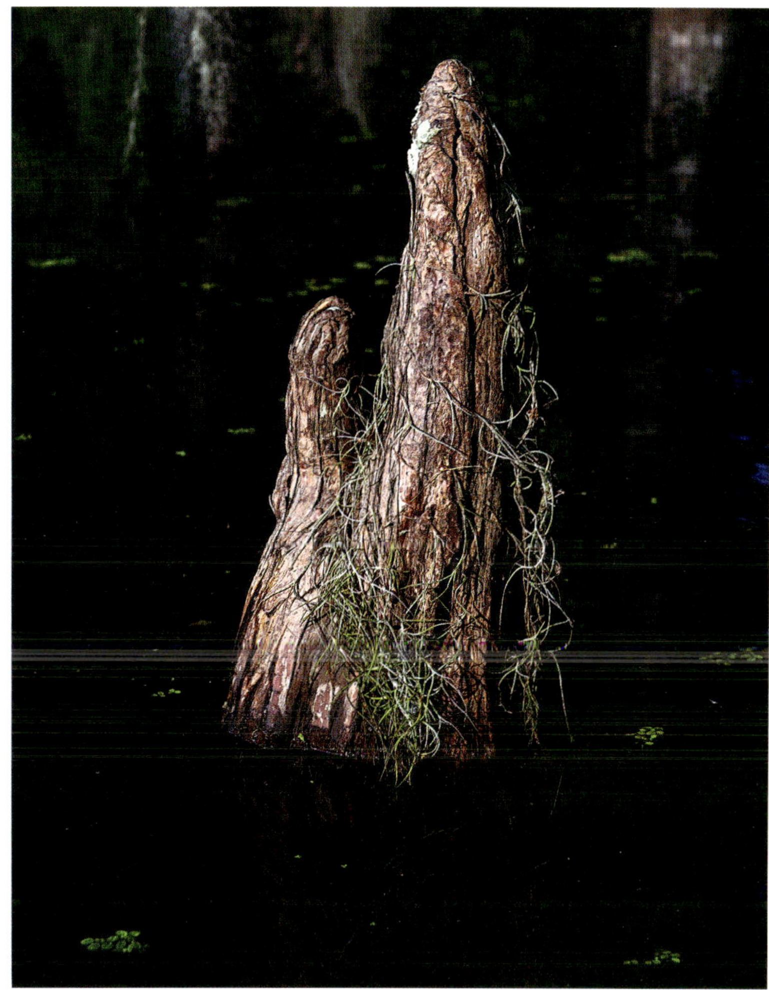

Spanish moss is formed from individual, viny tendrils. Part of the Bromeliaceae family, this moss was once the source of a thriving industry in which locals harvested it for use as mattress stuffing.

With no roots, the stringy vegetation grows wherever it's blown from trees, even on cypress knees.

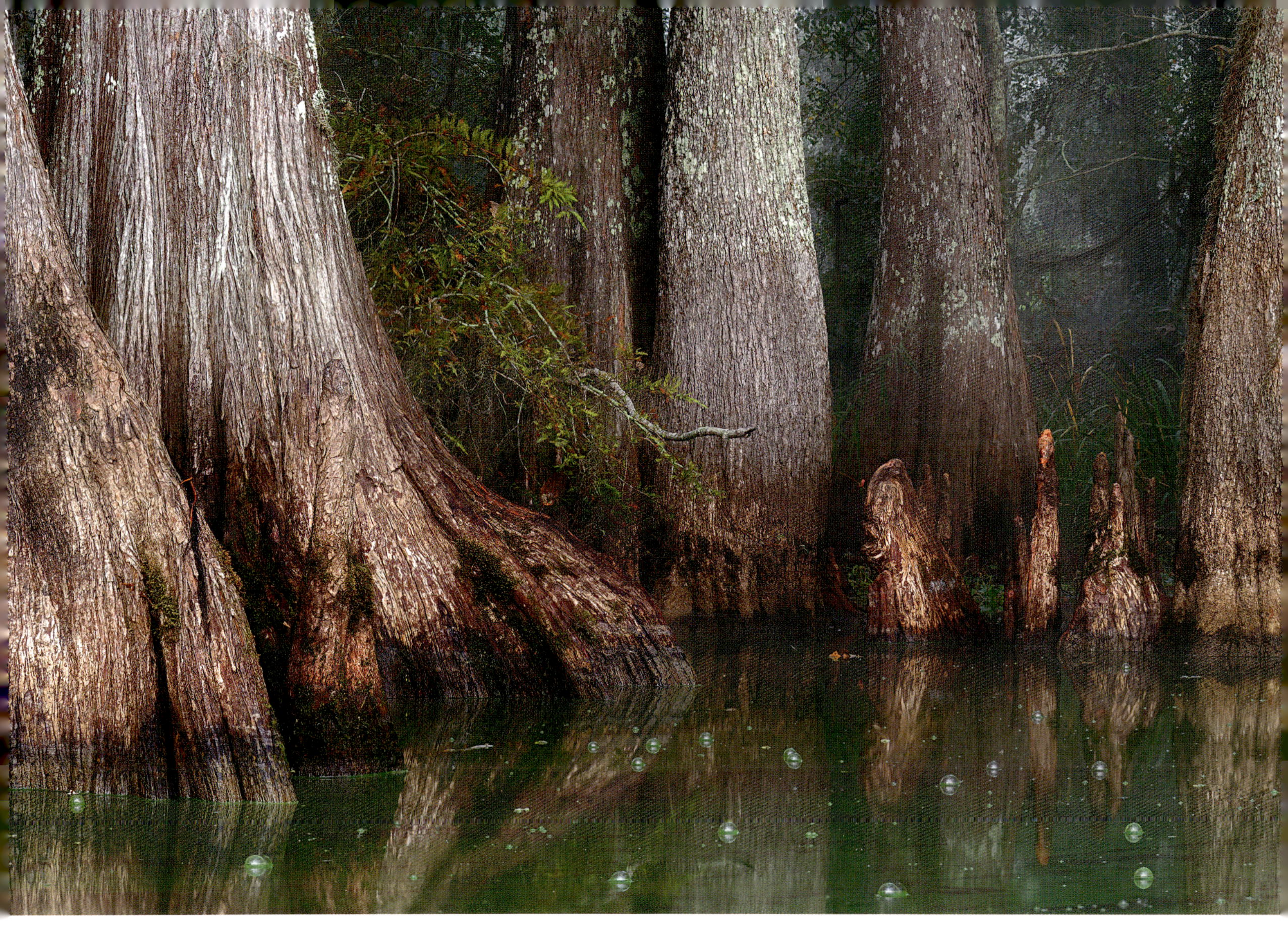

Cypress and tupelo trees form the basis of a rich, watery landscape that often seems impenetrable. This nearly solid line of trees stands on the edge of Lake Dauterive, around which spreads miles of boggy swamp.

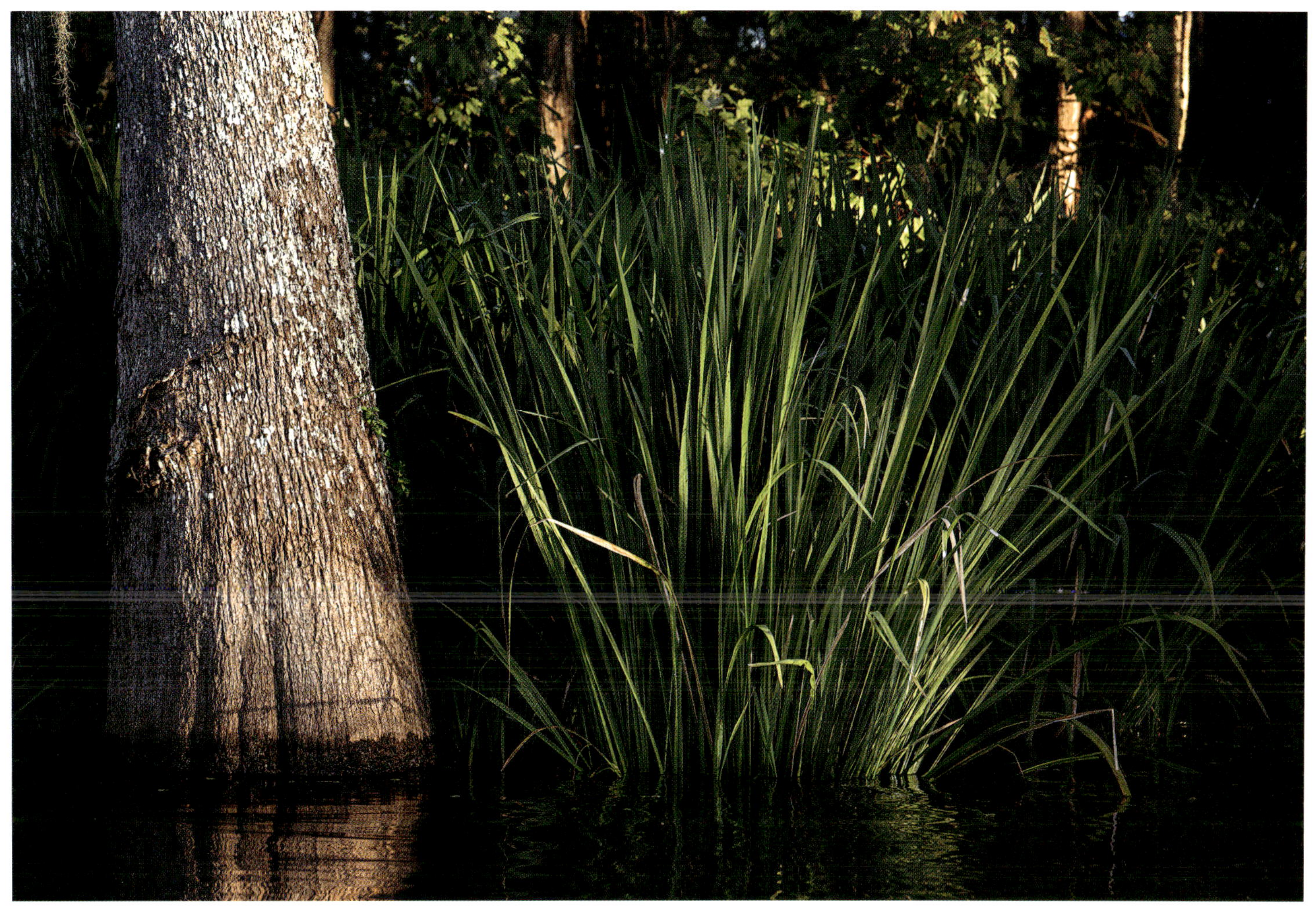

Reeds are common along the edges of the swamp, filling in gaps between trees and offering refuge for fish and all manner of insects. This contributes to the food chain of the fertile wetlands.

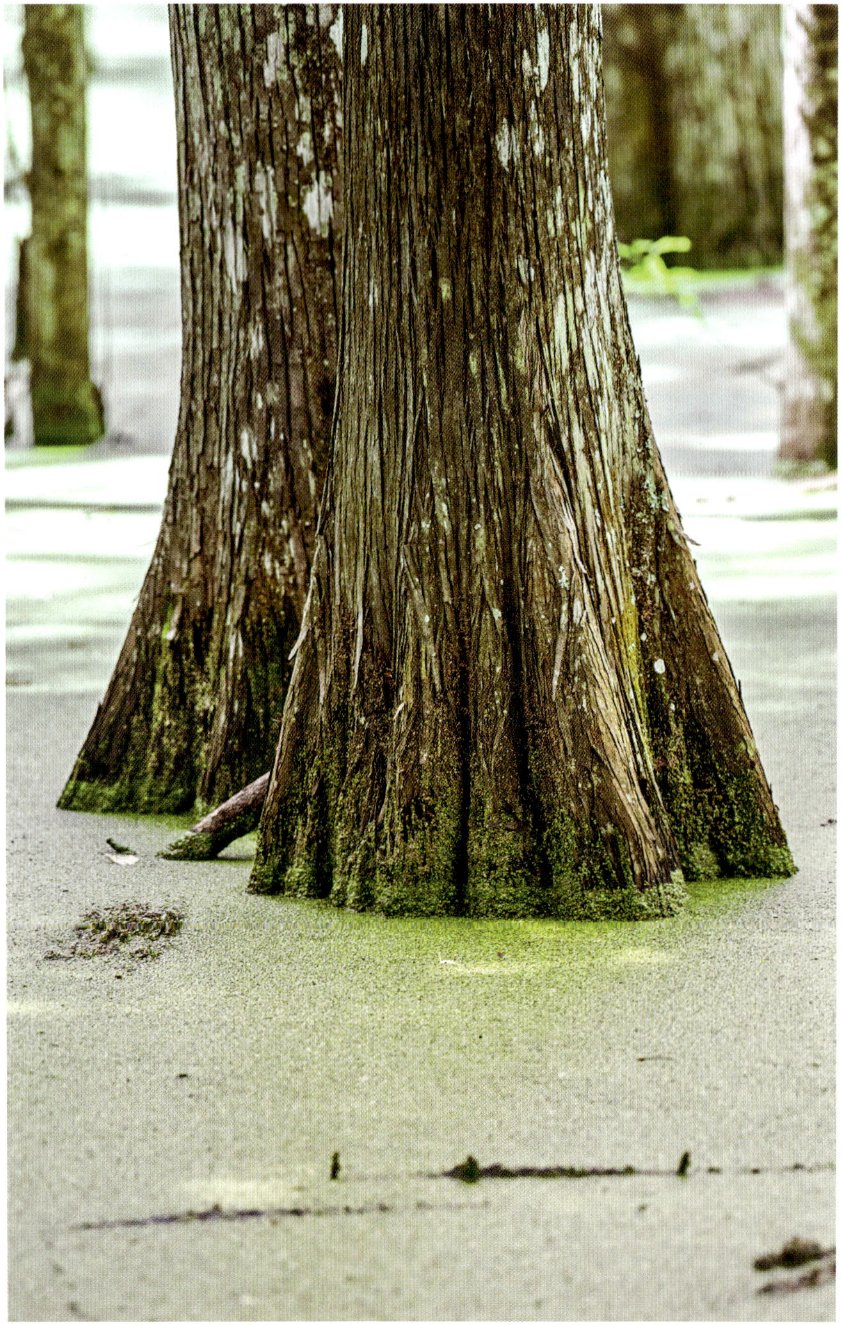

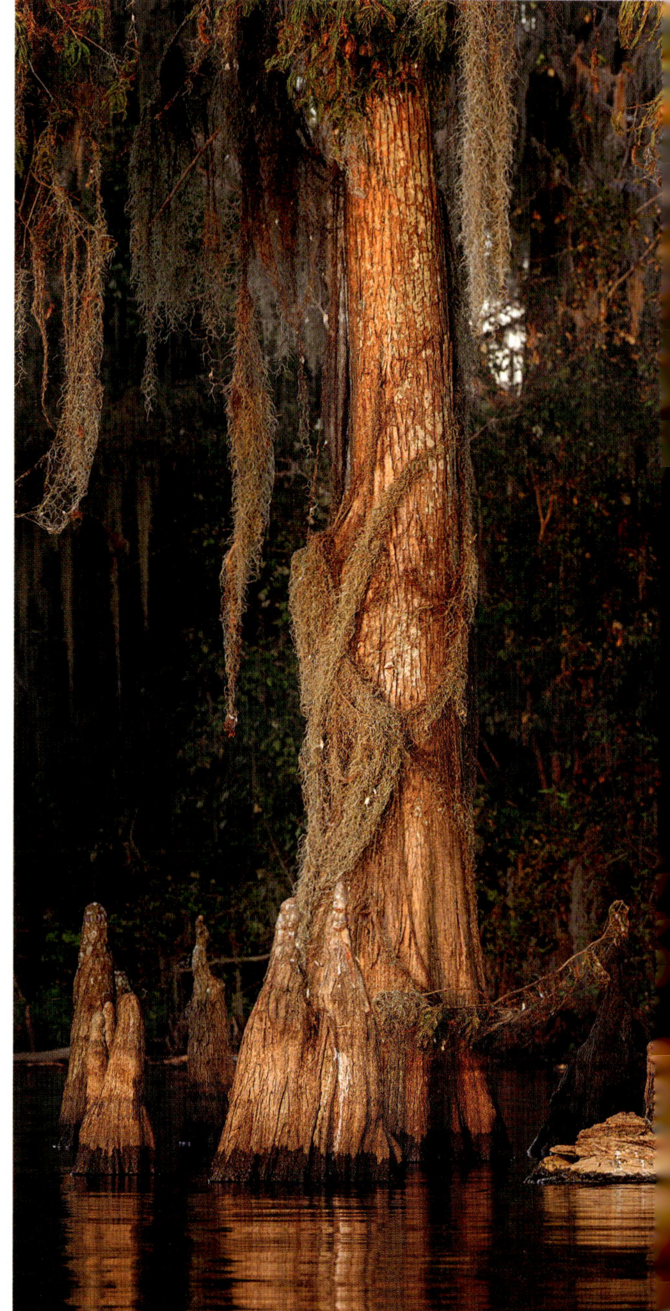

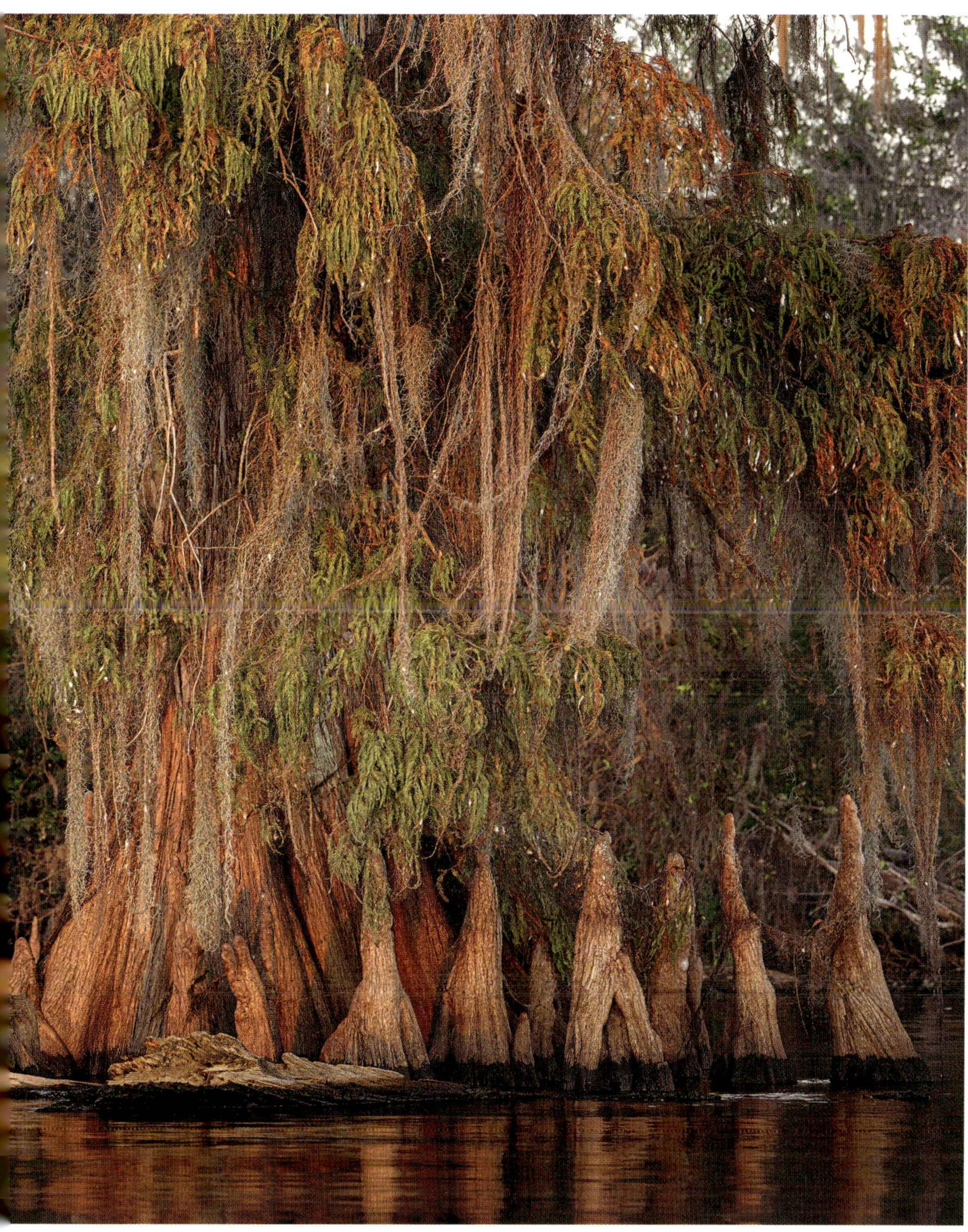

Opposite page: Duckweed often covers large areas of water in the depths of the swamp, attracting insects and serving as an important food source for fish and waterfowl. This tiny floating plant is native to the United States, but it can be problematic in confined areas, where it can form thick mats that block out sunlight needed by other aquatic plants.

Cypress trees support massive weight, especially when moss grows thickly among its branches, so trees send out expansive root systems that surround the trunks and provide stability. The "knees" growing above the water are part of those roots.

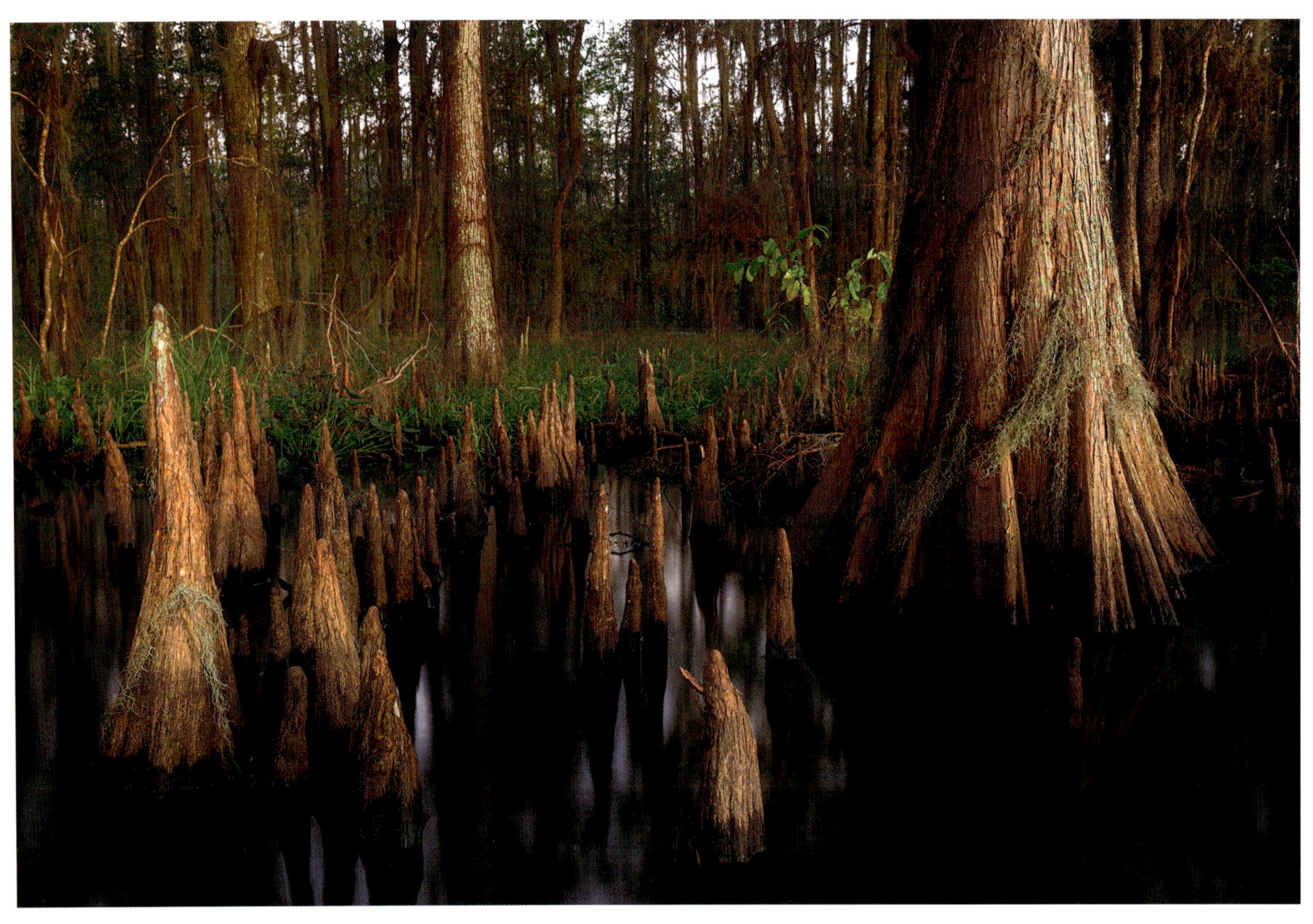

Cypress knees sprout from cypress trees' root systems, illustrating just how large a footprint these trees need to remain standing.

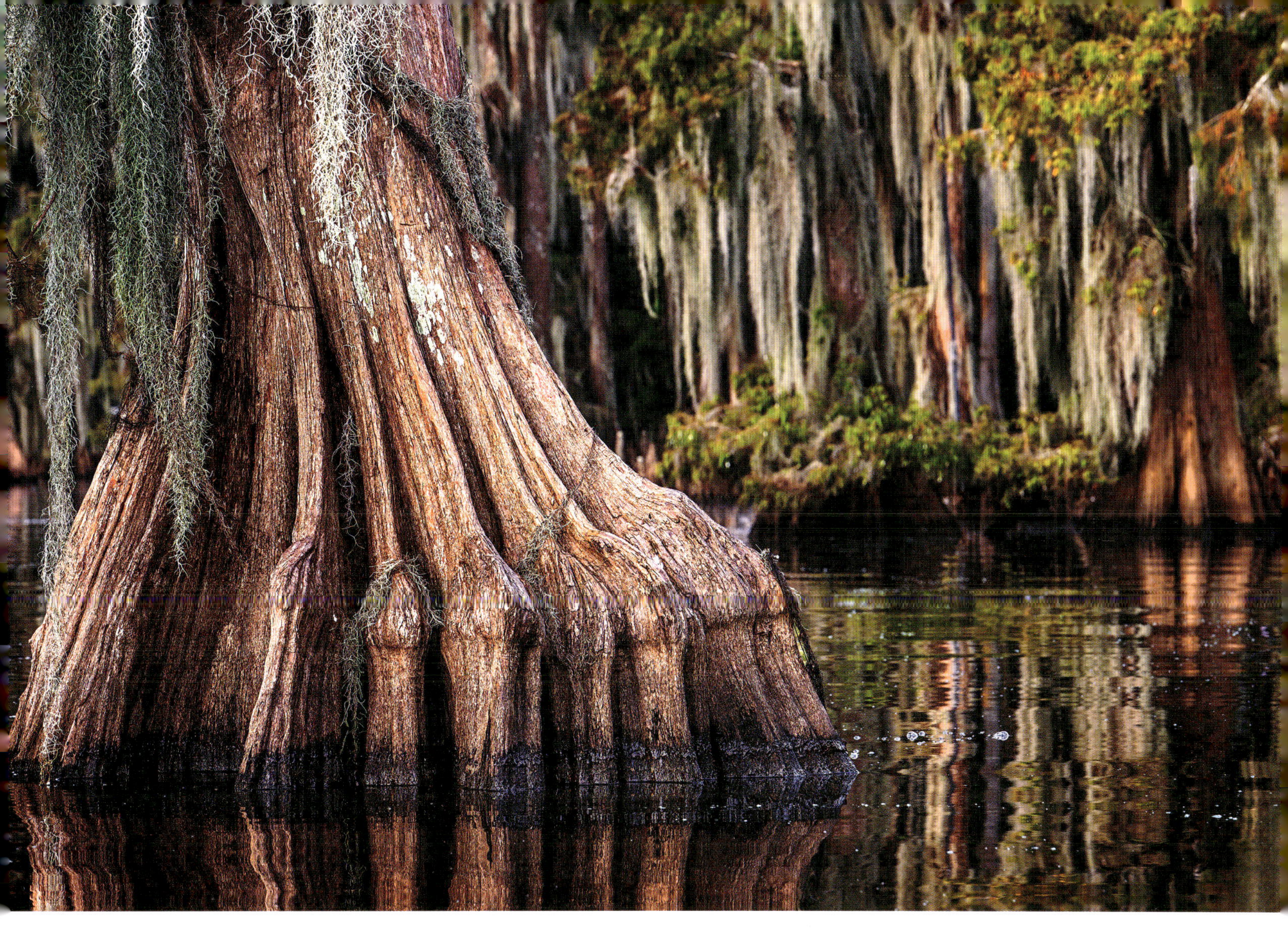

Cypress trees often have such incredible character to their trunks. This old tree formed ribs in its root system, stabilizing its weight.

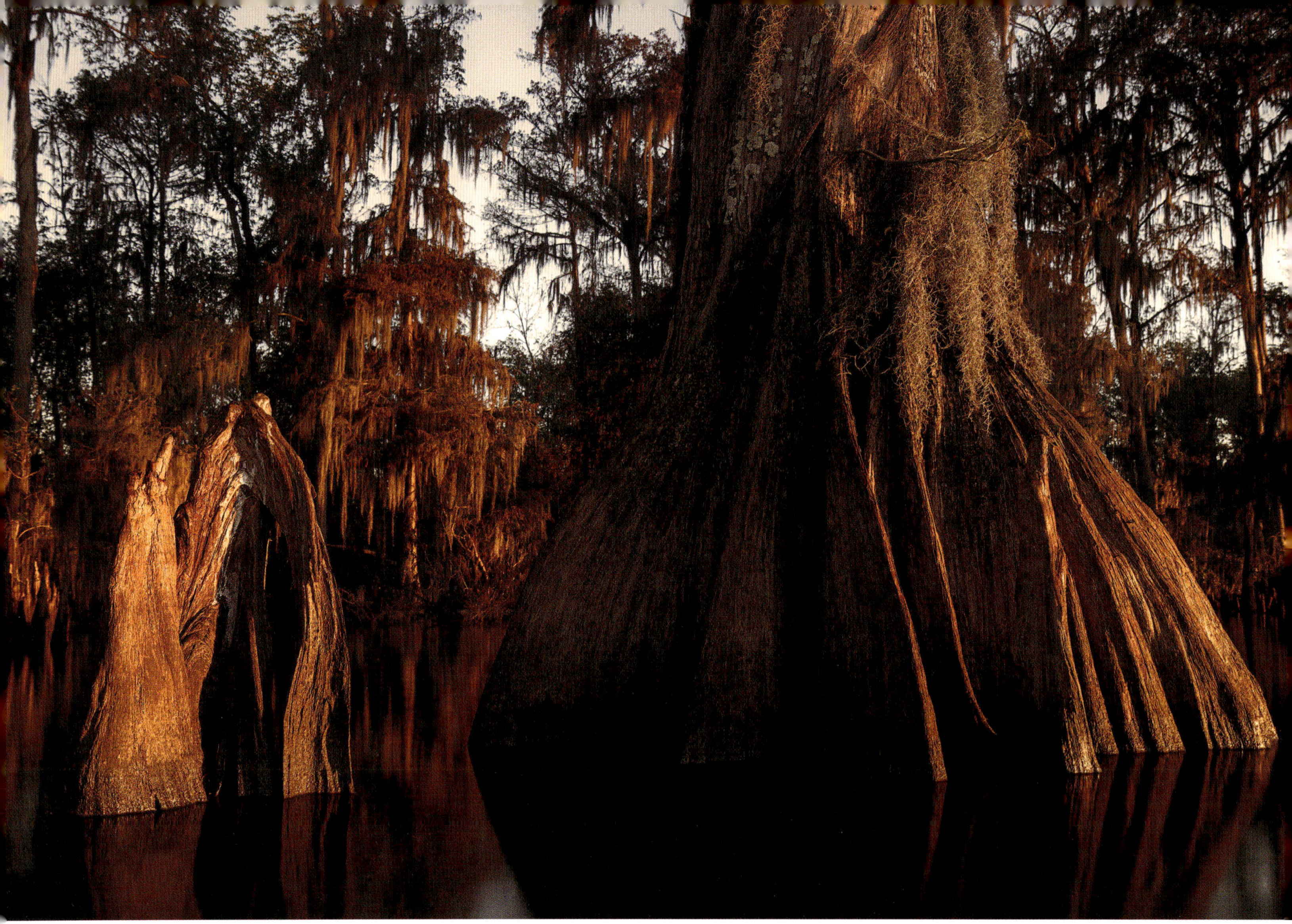

Early morning light brings out the wonderful character of cypress trees and their associated knees. This tree has amazing ridges along its trunk that form a large footprint in the muck below the inky waters of Lake Verret.

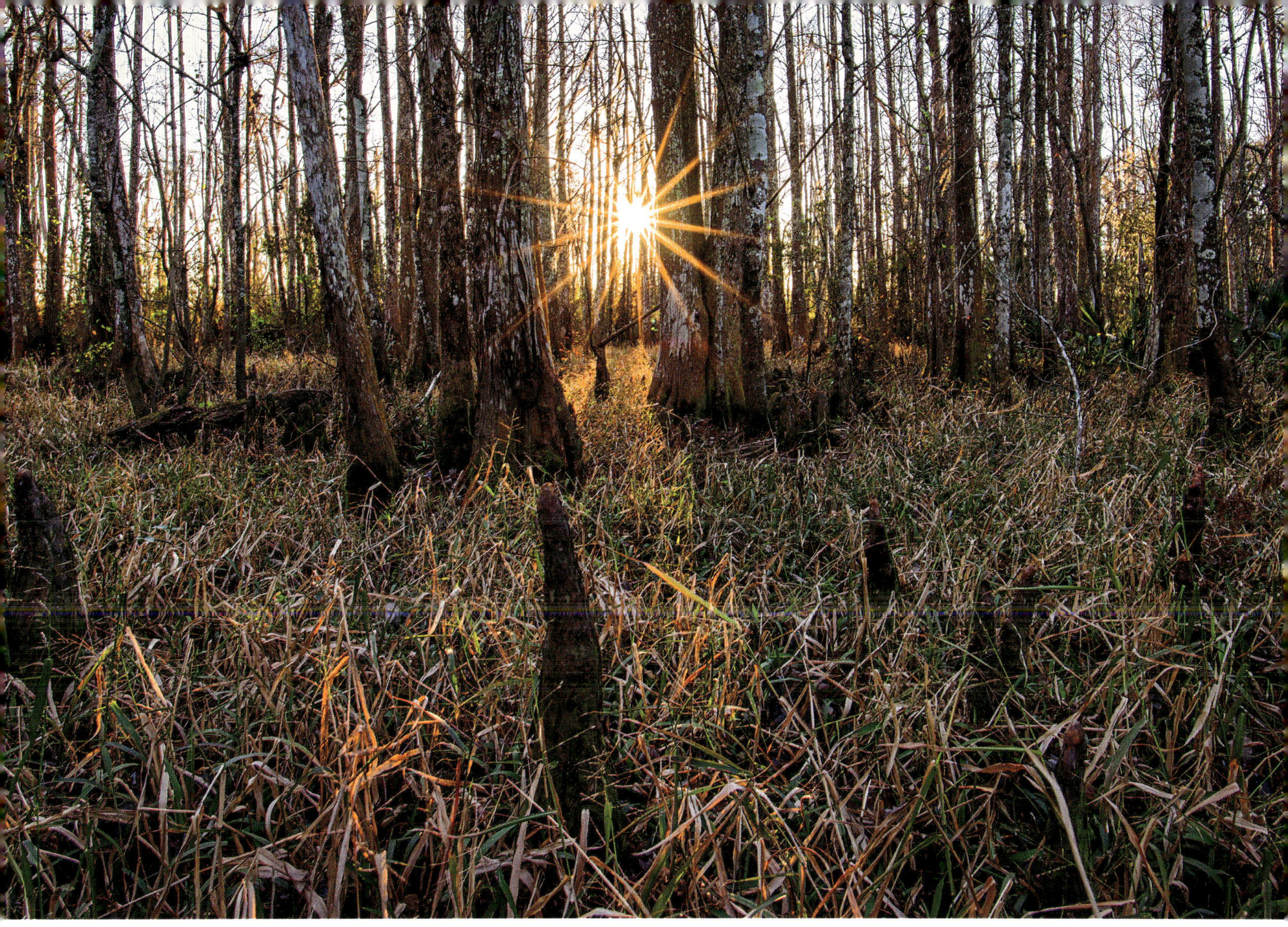

Not all swamps are inundated with water on a day-to-day basis. Some, like this area along the Tchefuncte River, are flooded only during high-water periods.

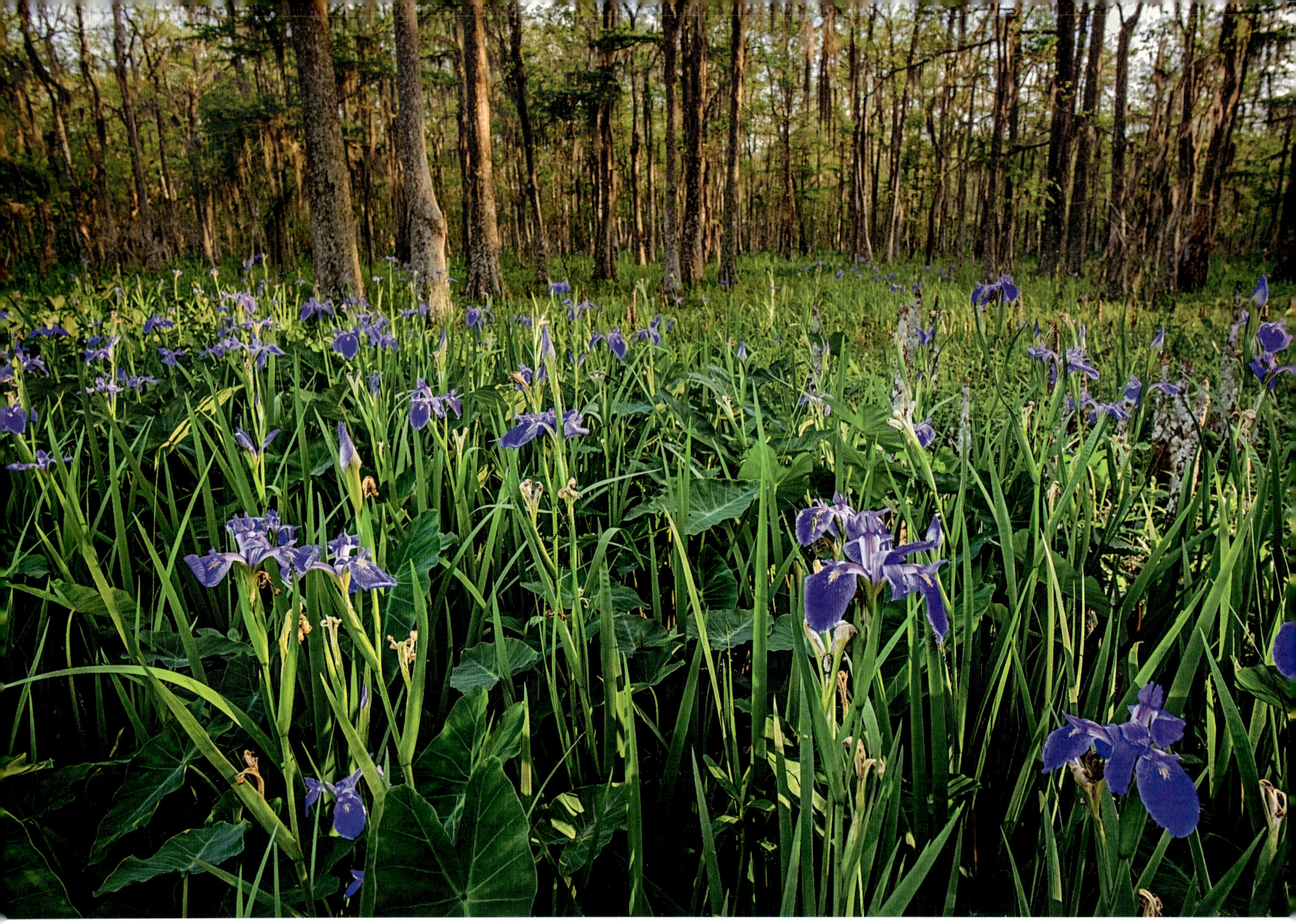

Purple irises add amazing pops of color for a couple of weeks each spring. These flowers create carpets of beauty, preferring boggy areas not completely inundated with water. This field is located along Bayou Magazille just off Lake Verret.

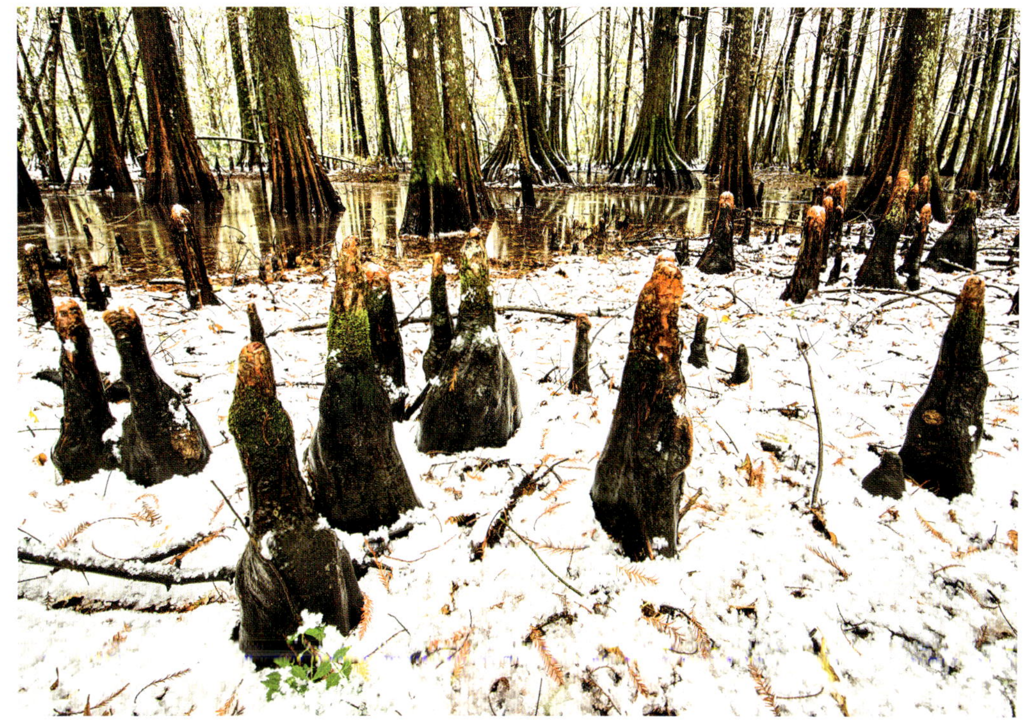

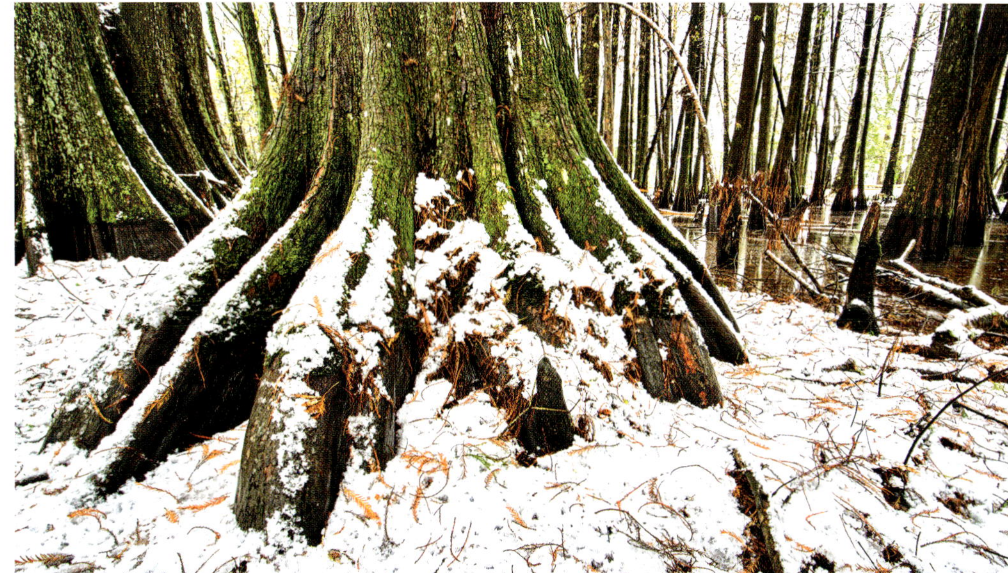

Snow is rare in South Louisiana, but a thick layer of fluffy snow coated the swamps in 2017. Snow covered the mud around the water, making the cypress knees really stand out. I loved how snow also collected on the craggy trunks of the largest trees in the background.

The trunk of this old cypress tree seemed to be clawing at the surrounding snow. Fallen cypress leaves added wonderful color to the scene.

CHAPTER THREE

WILDLIFE

What is the first animal that comes to mind when you think of the Louisiana swamp? My bet is that an image of an American alligator just popped into your head. There's a good reason for this. The swamps are loaded with this apex predator. Even when the species was listed as threatened by the federal government, those reptiles were anything but rare in our waterways.

However, gators aren't the only wildlife found in these wetlands. The flooded forests teem with an incredible amount of other animal life. Nutria, egrets, herons, ibises, roseate spoonbills, and the occasional wood stork are just a few of the species you'll find prowling the Louisiana swamps. Raptors including owls, hawks, osprey, and bald eagles add to the feathered life. River otters, deer, raccoons, and even bears join the mix. And then there are the many fish species.

In short, Louisiana's swamps are a wildlife lover's paradise.

You just never know what you'll find swimming, flying, or resting as you move through the swamps. It's an added bonus to the beauty of the South Louisiana swamps to watch the many bird species flying about, see that gator slip from a log, or spot an otter dragging a fish out of the water.

Come along on a visual tour of some of the swamp's creatures.

Opposite page: Alligators are known for their armored bodies, but one of the coolest features can be their eyes. Eye color ranges from darkest black to speckled gold. This alligator was slipping through the dark waters near my kayak, watching me with golden eyes.

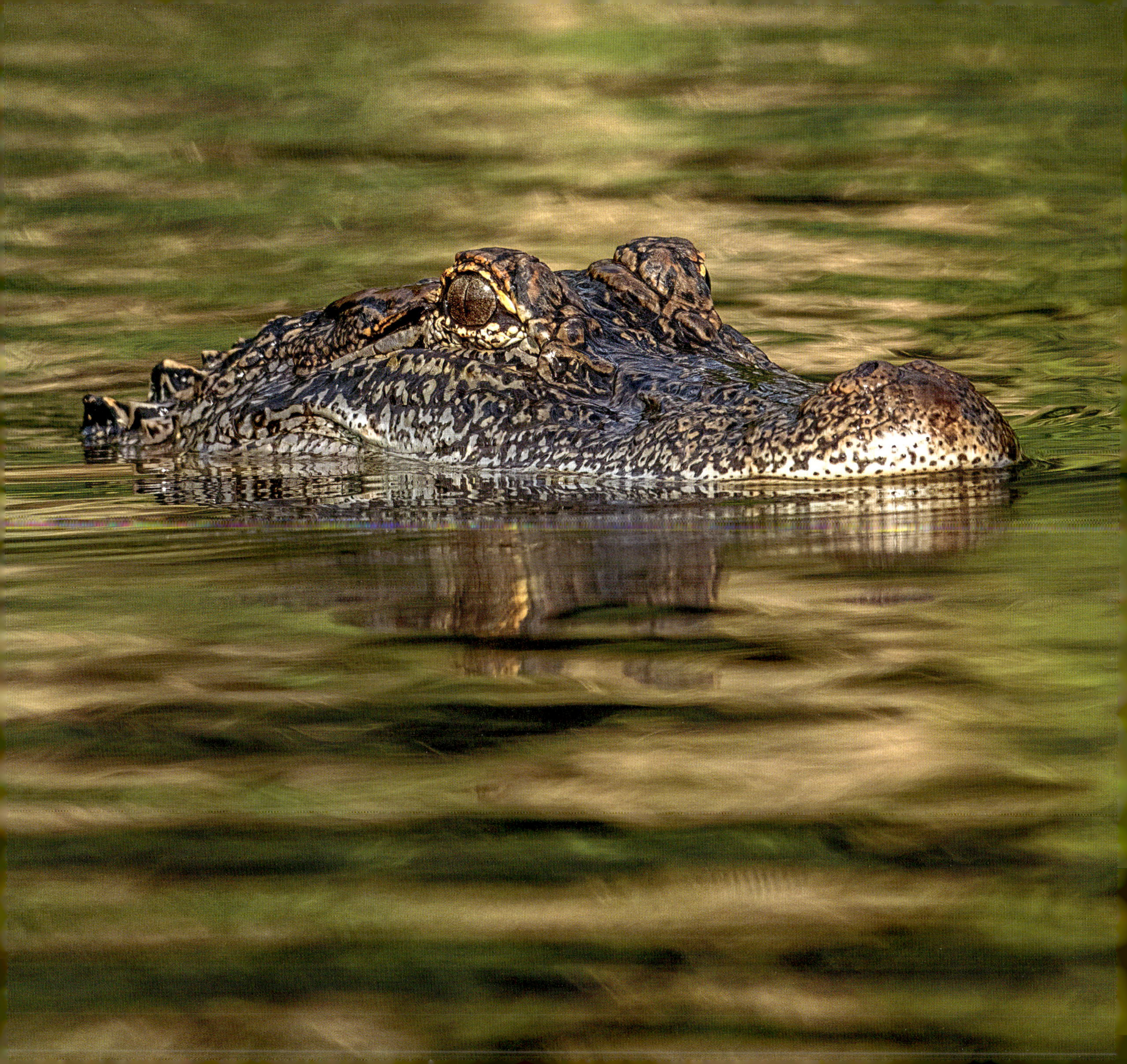

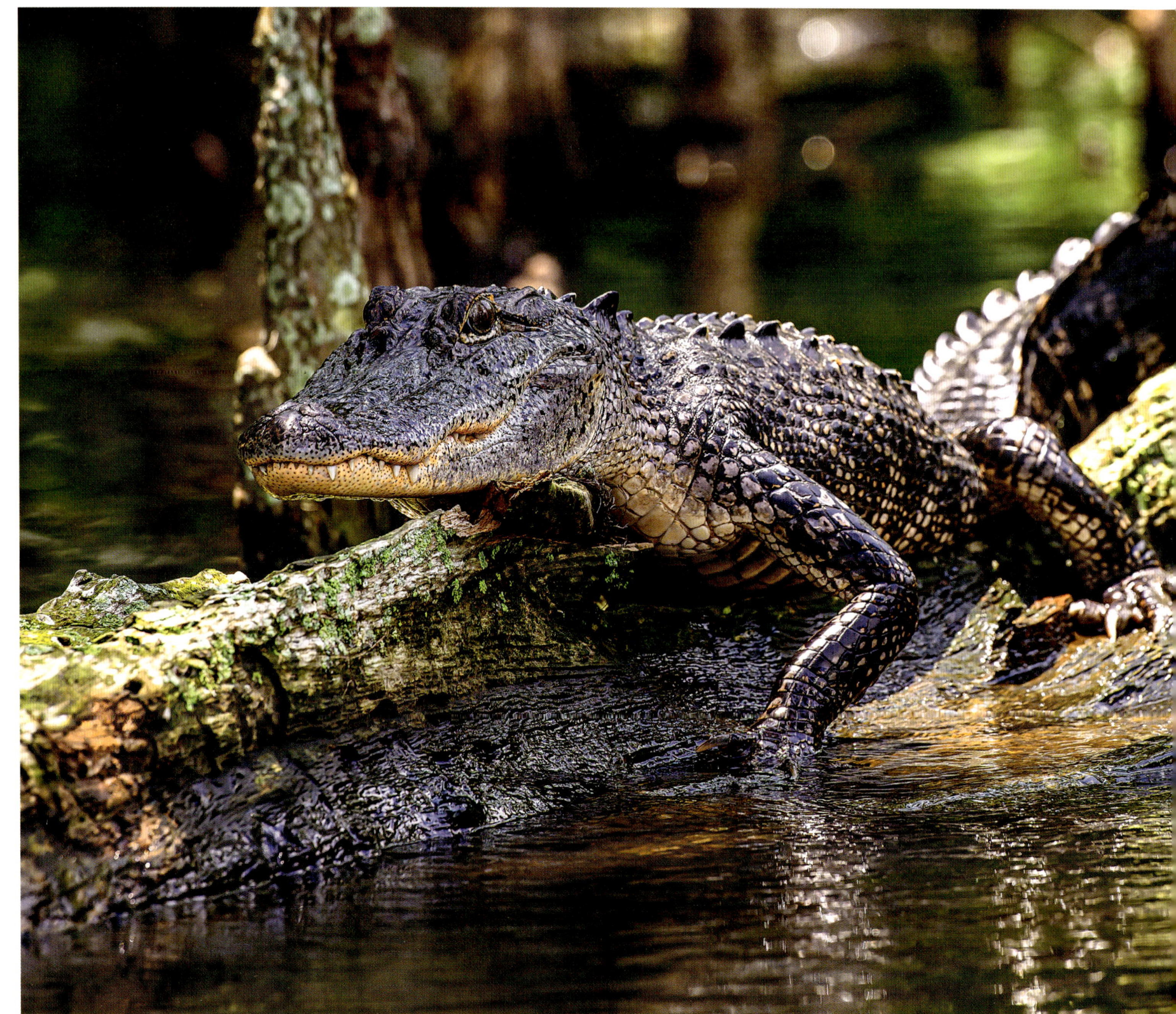

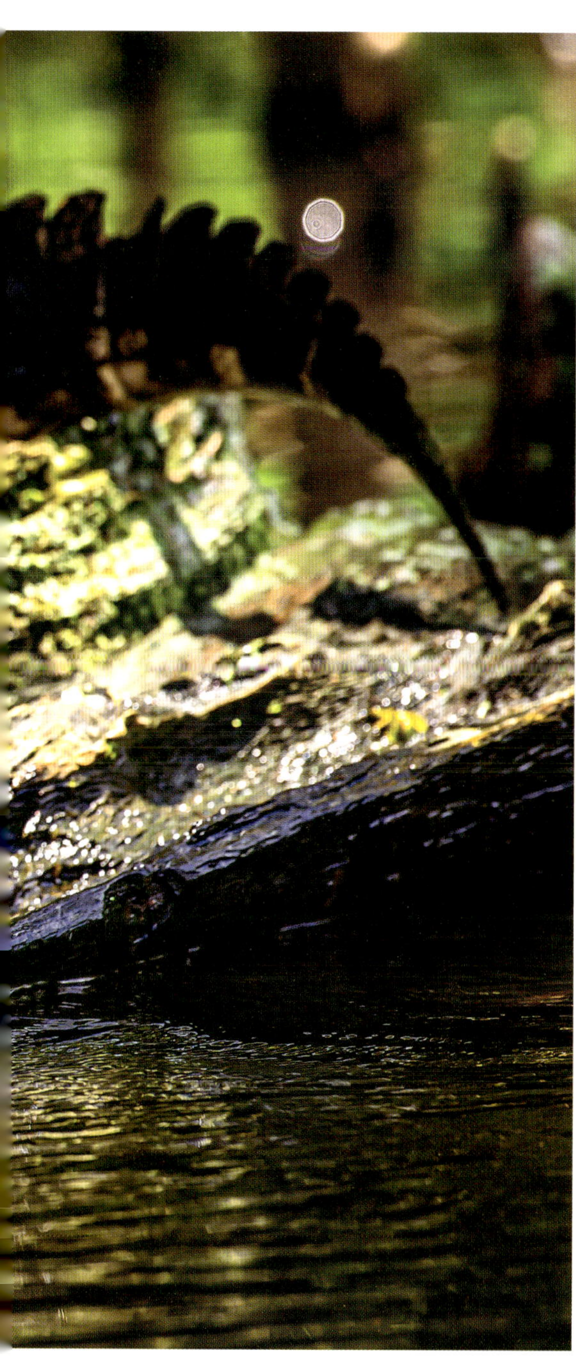

Louisiana's gators aren't overly aggressive, but it's still best to keep your distance. I was paddling through the flooded cypress of Lake Verret when I spied this medium-sized alligator relaxing on a log. It might look like I'm right next to it, but I used a long lens to create this image.

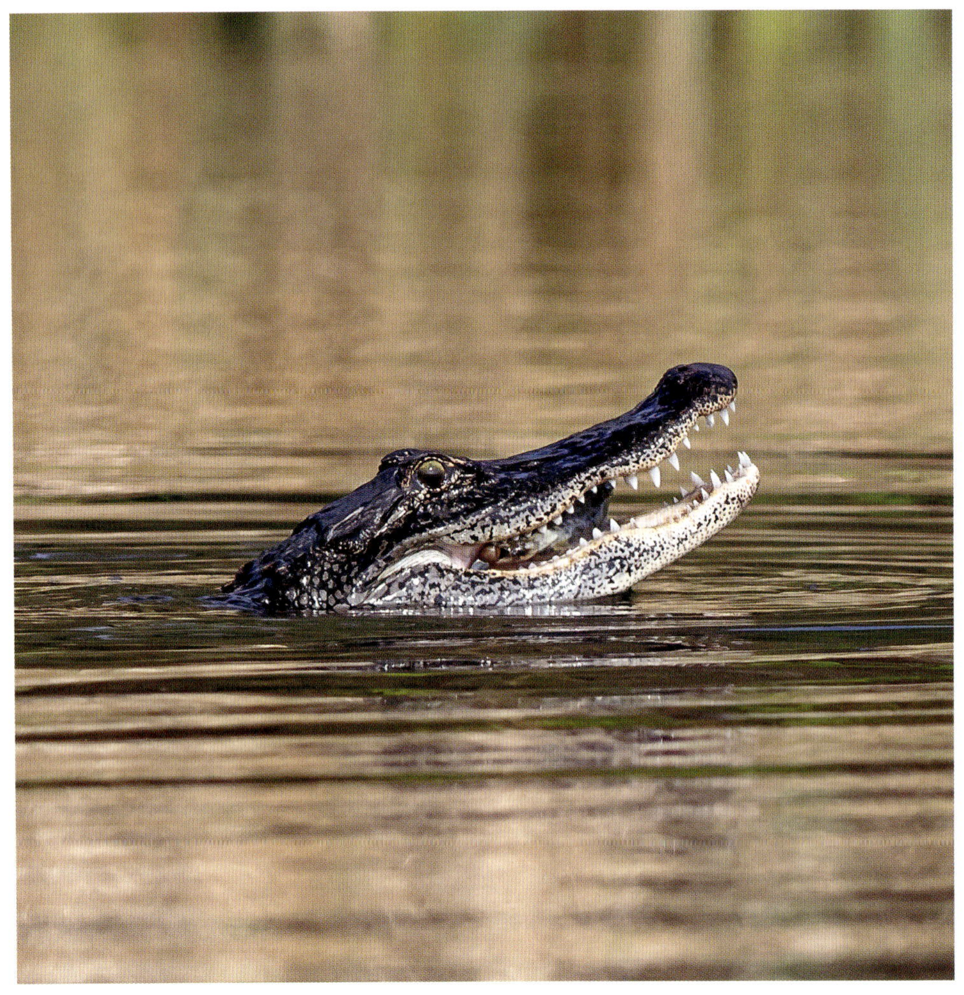

These gators sport huge, sharp teeth that mark them as apex predators. This large alligator crunched a dead fish floating in the swamps near Morgan City.

Opposite page: These reptiles rely on stealth for hunting success, so often only their eyes and snouts are visible. I found this large gator slithering off a canal bank, eyeballing me across the water.

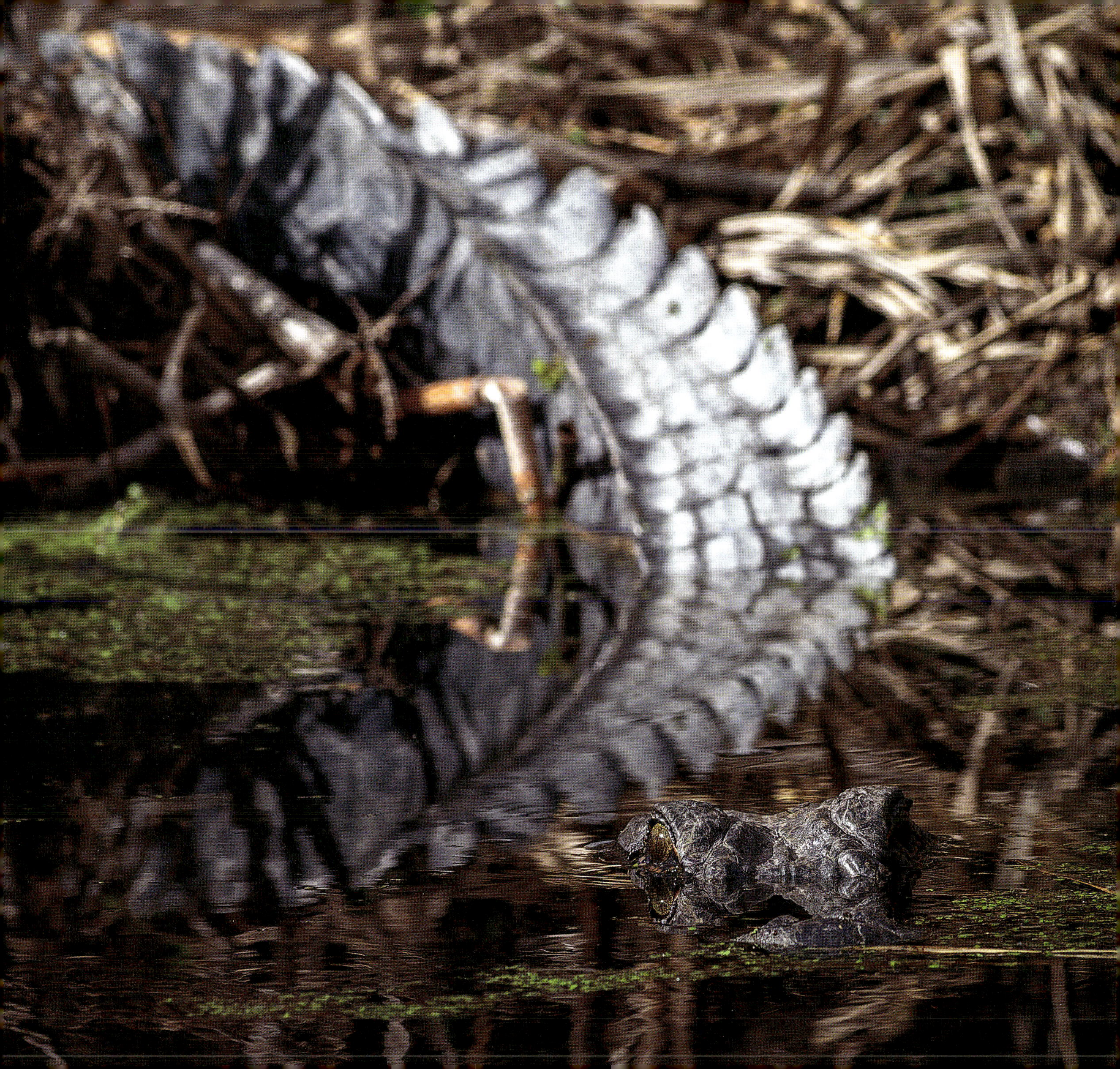

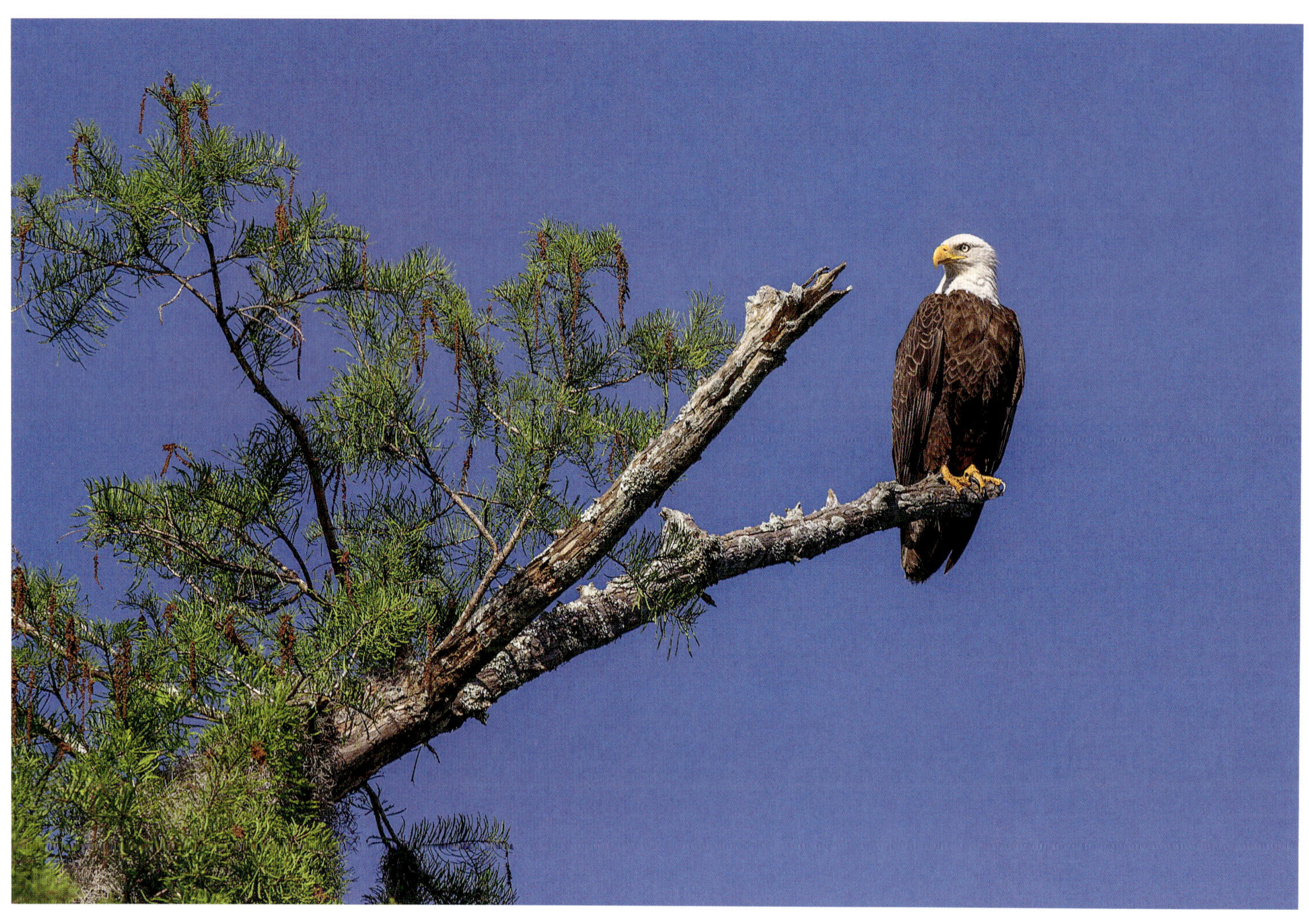

Bald eagles are just one of the raptors found throughout Louisiana's swamps, but they are definitely among the coolest. This beautiful eagle was perched atop a tall cypress tree overlooking Blind River between Baton Rouge and New Orleans.

Opposite page: Seeing an eagle spread its wings as it launches into the air is always a treat. Their wingspan can reach more than 7 feet, and those talons are made for grabbing onto prey.

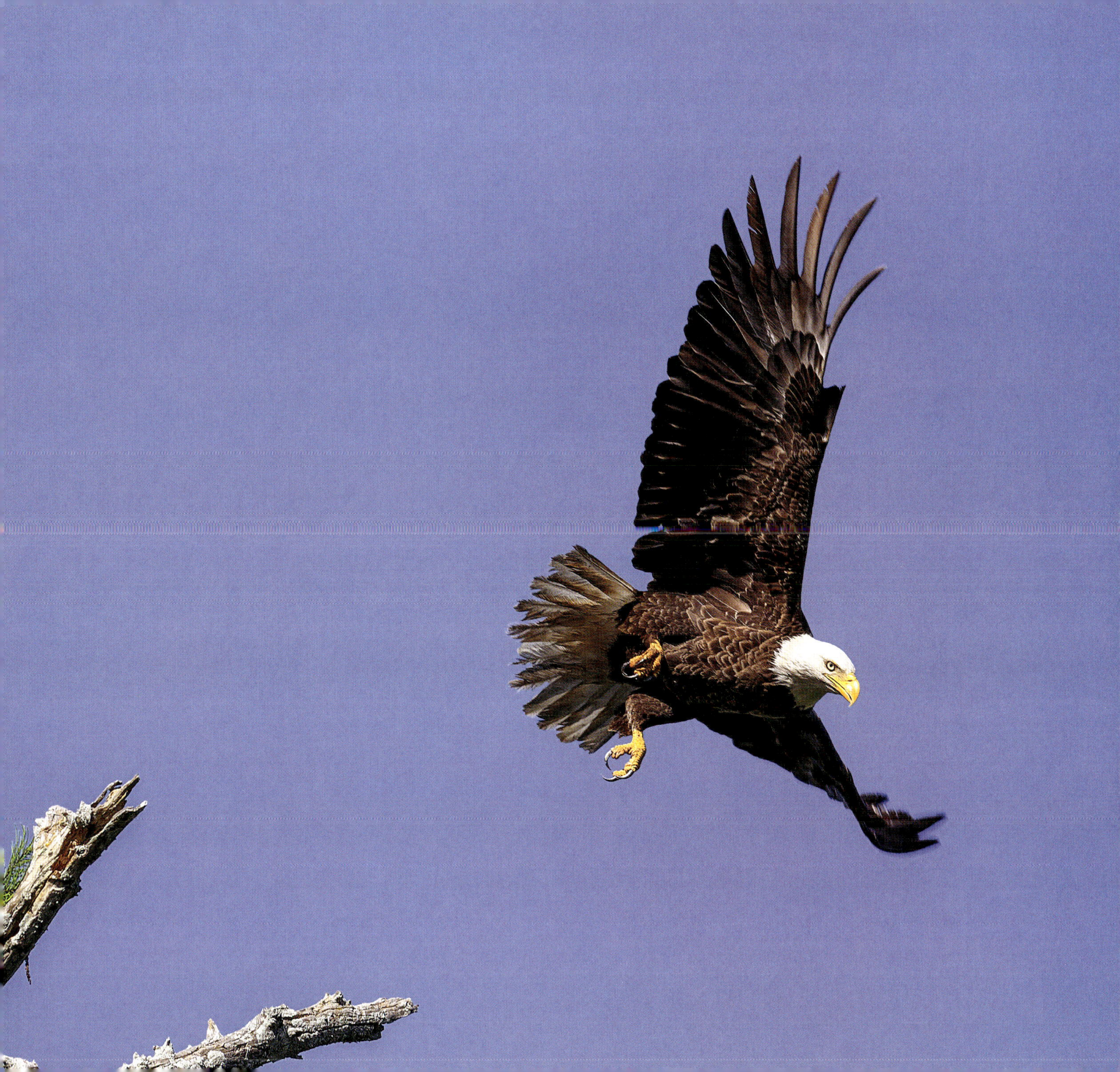

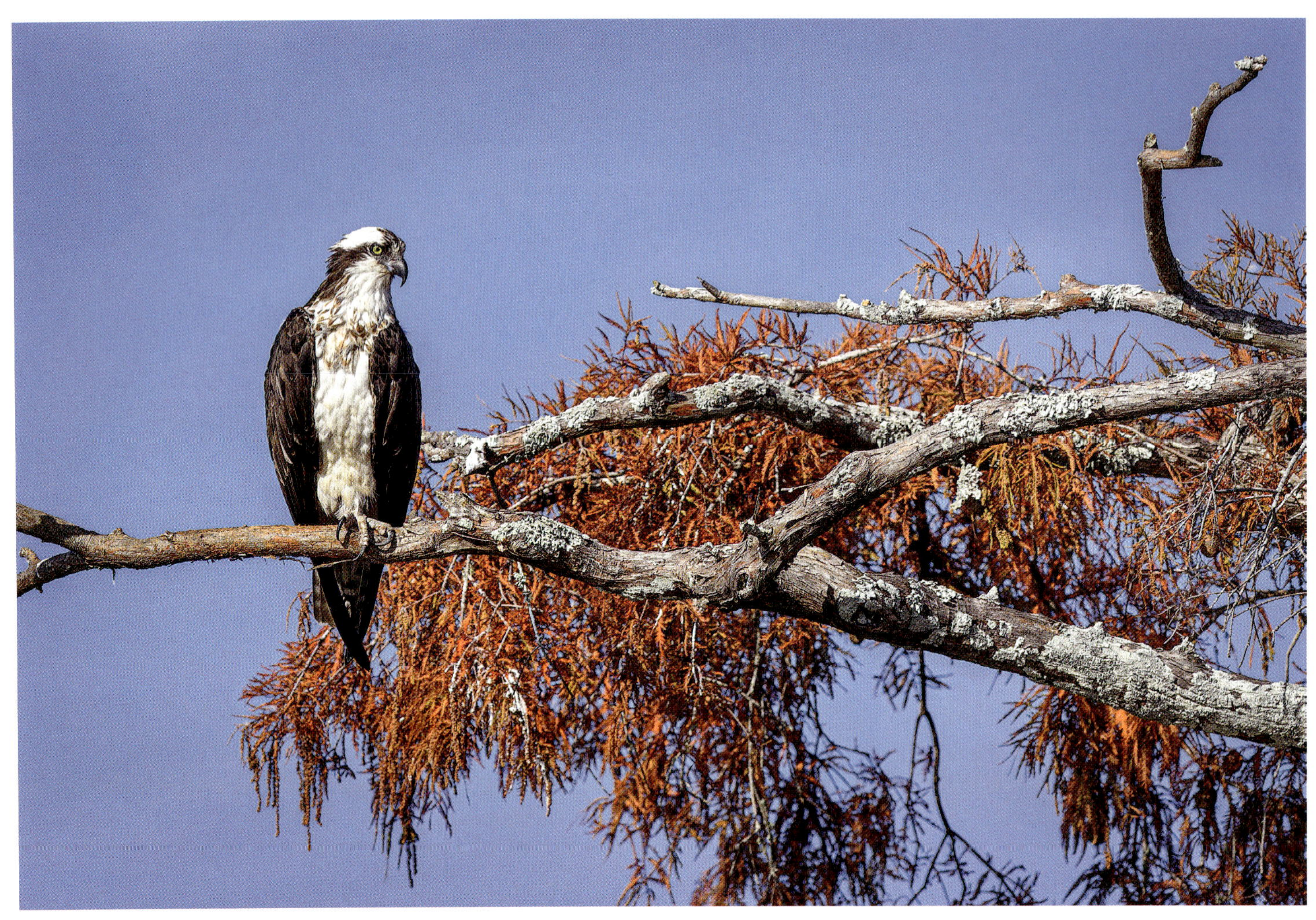

Osprey also ply these wetlands, hunting for fish and nesting in cypress trees. These raptors are my favorite, being accomplished hunters and overall mean customers known to pick fights with the much larger bald eagle.

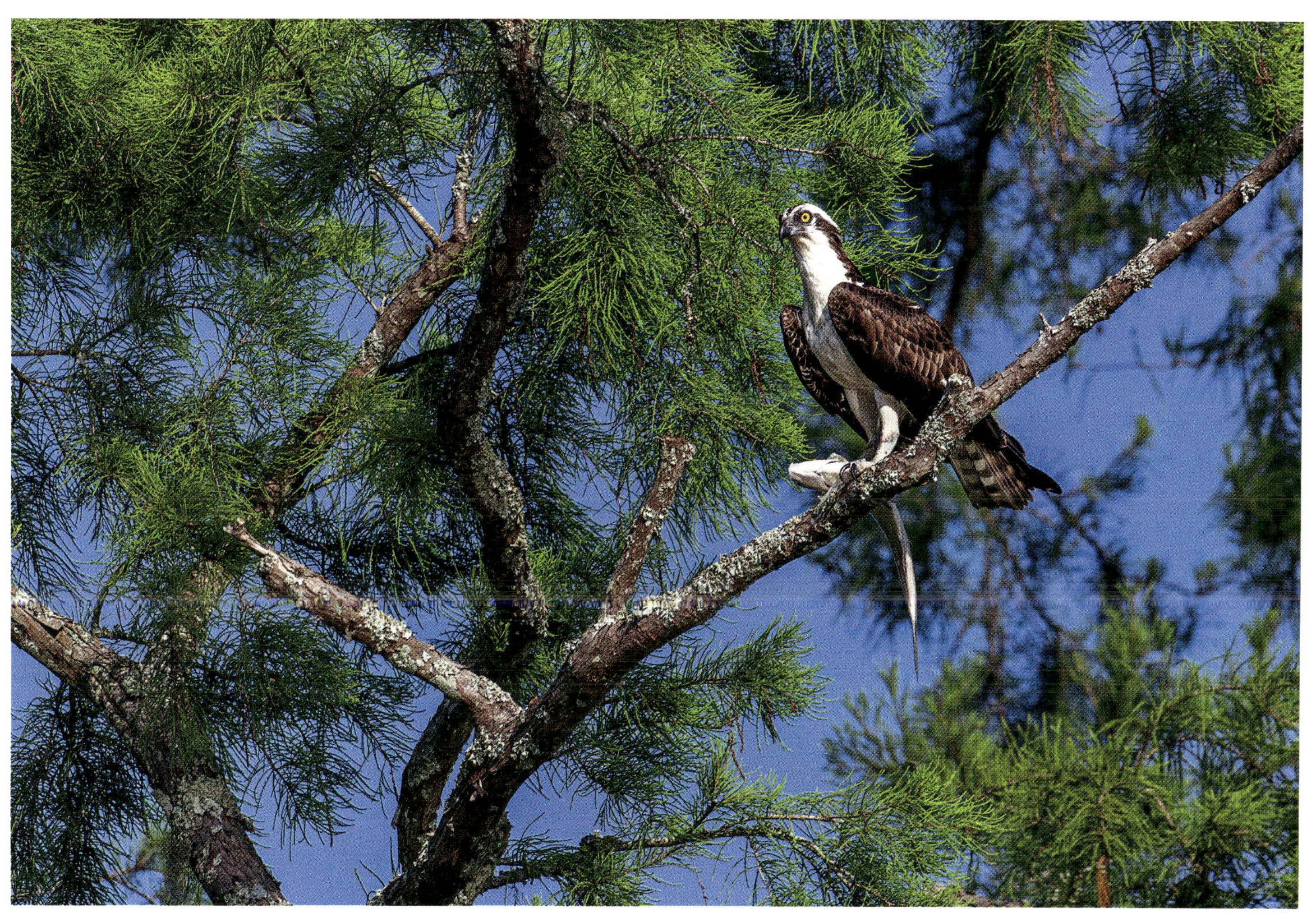

Unlike eagles, osprey don't normally eat carrion. They prefer their meals fresh. It's not uncommon to see an osprey fold its wings and plummet feet first into the water to grab a meal.

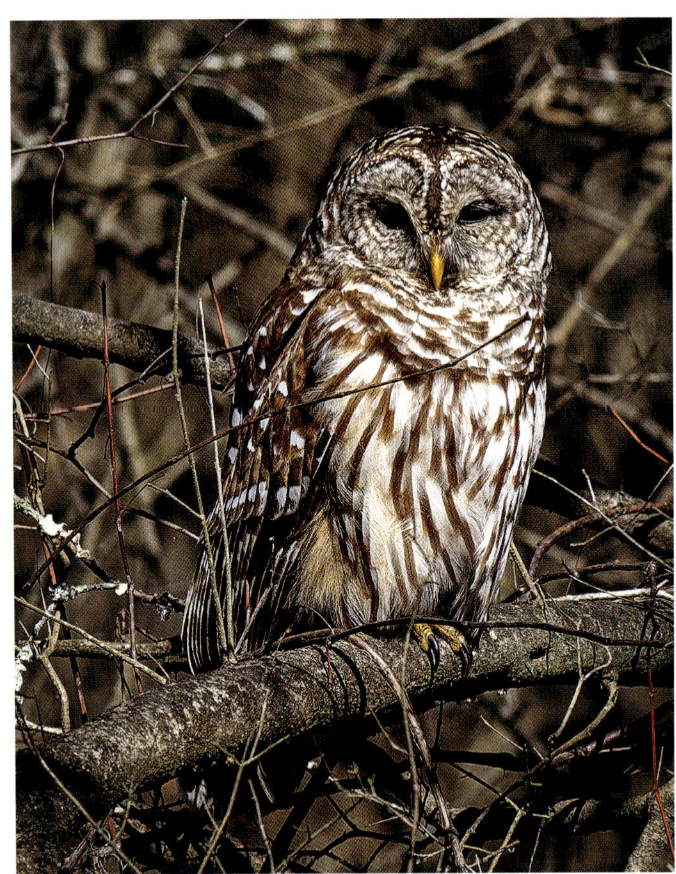

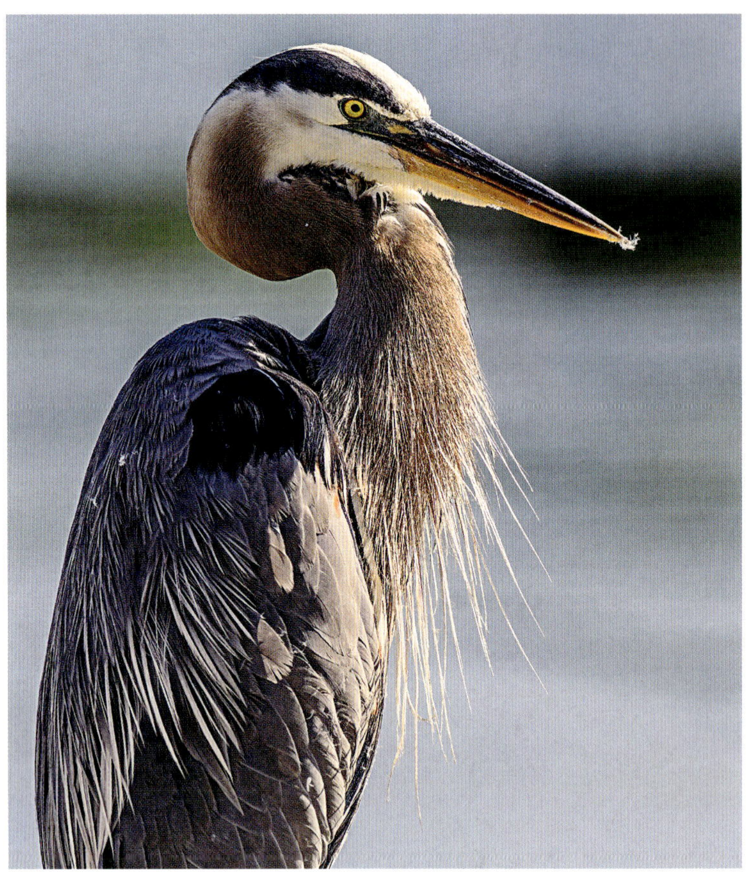

The hooting calls of barred owls echo through the swamps. Most active at night, these masters of camouflage can be difficult to spot. This one landed nearby after flying right by me without a sound while I was walking in the swamps of Cat Island National Wildlife Refuge.

The great blue heron is a beautiful bird found anywhere there is water. Once prized for their plumage by the millinery industry, which nearly hunted it to extinction, it is now a protected species.

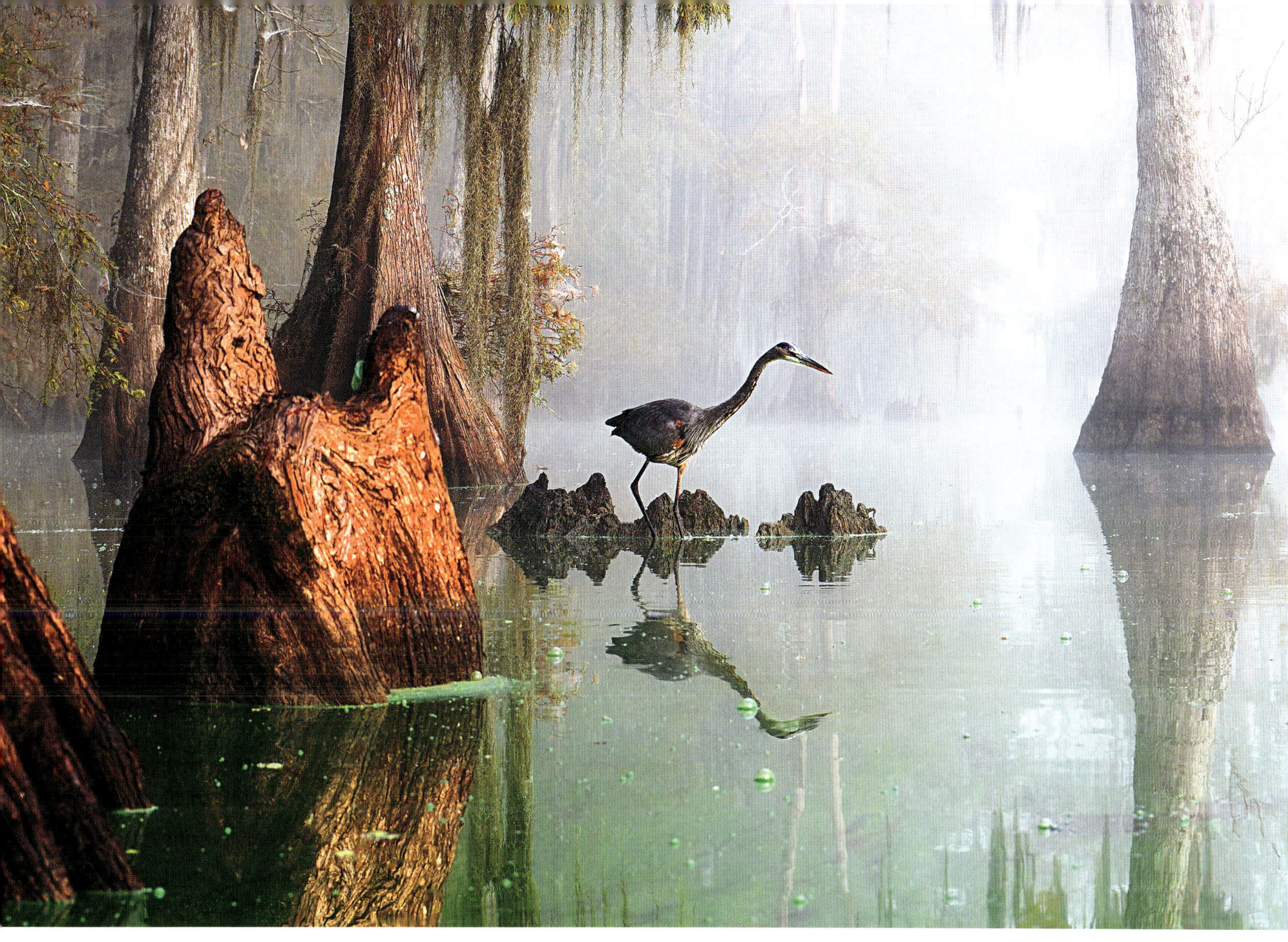

Great blue herons often have favored hunting locations, where they can pick off small prey swimming or washing by in the current. This heron was using an old cypress stump on one of my morning paddles on Lake Dauterive, and it returned time and time again.

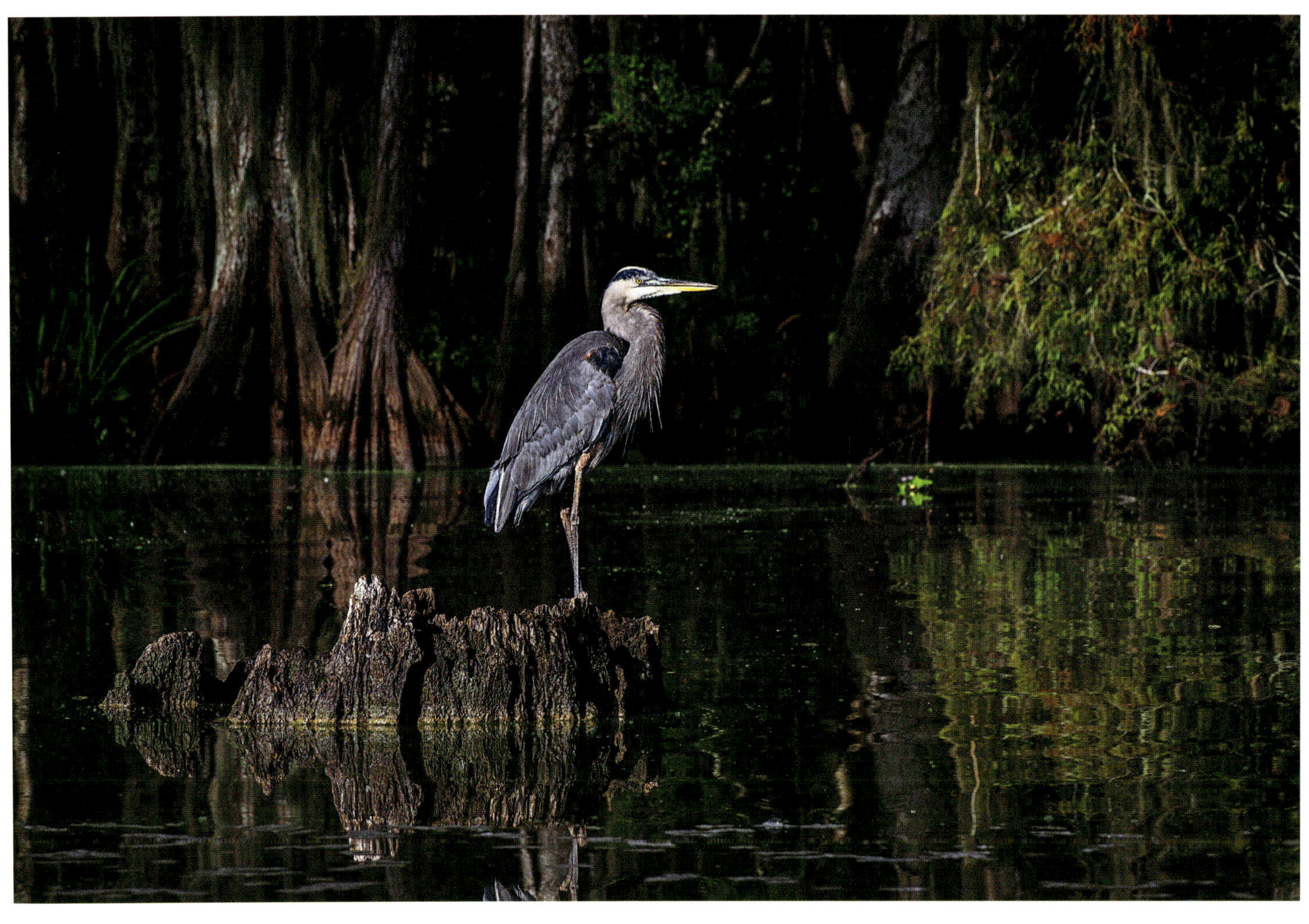

Herons' beautiful plumage really shines when the sun illuminates it. Appearing gray when in shadow, the feathers' true colors come out in the soft morning light.

Opposite page: Edges of bayous are favored hunting grounds for great blue herons. This one was resting in a cypress tree after stalking the shallow waters of Avoca Island Cutoff, which circles the eastern side of Lake Palourde. Note the beautiful fall color in the background.

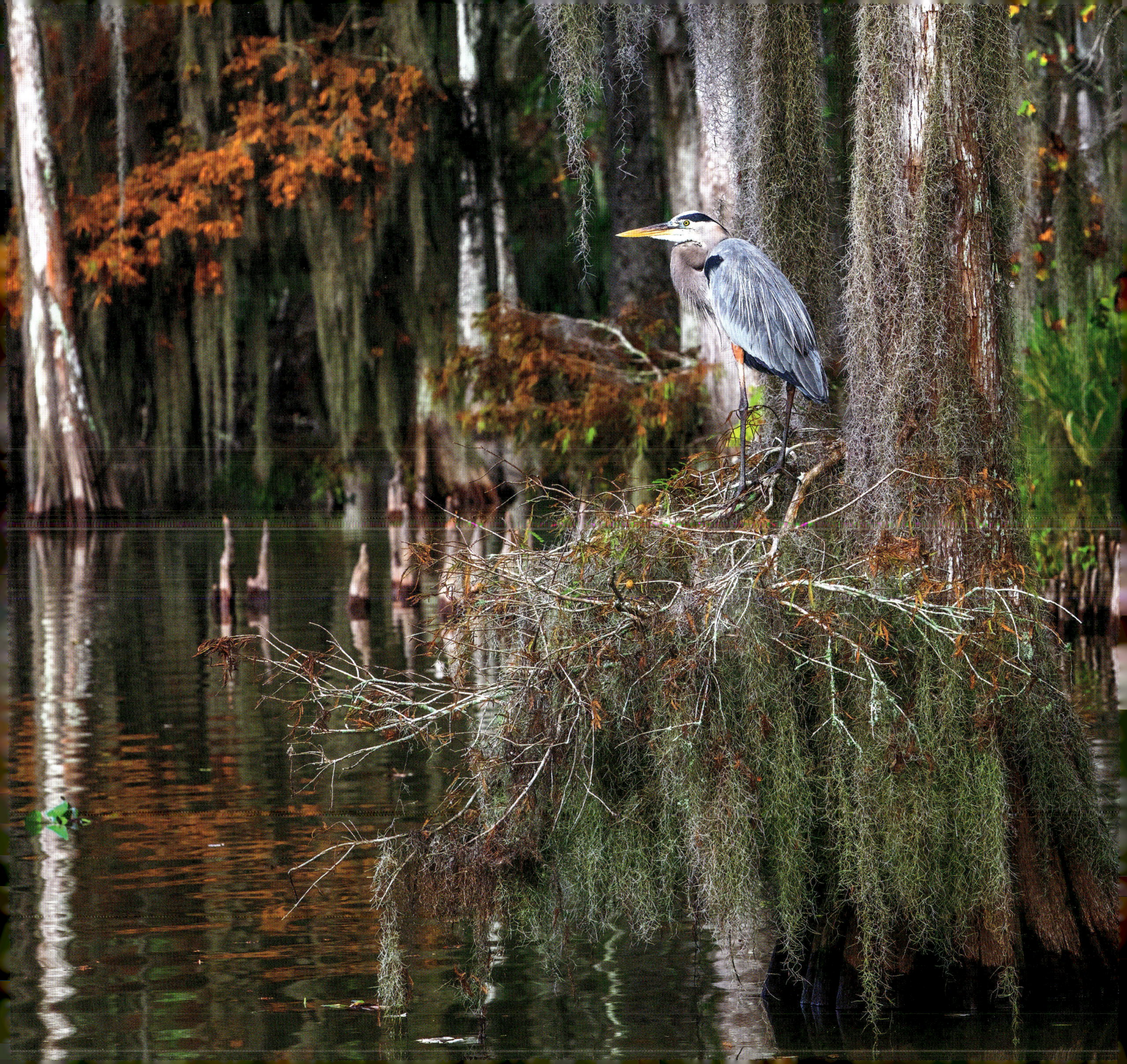

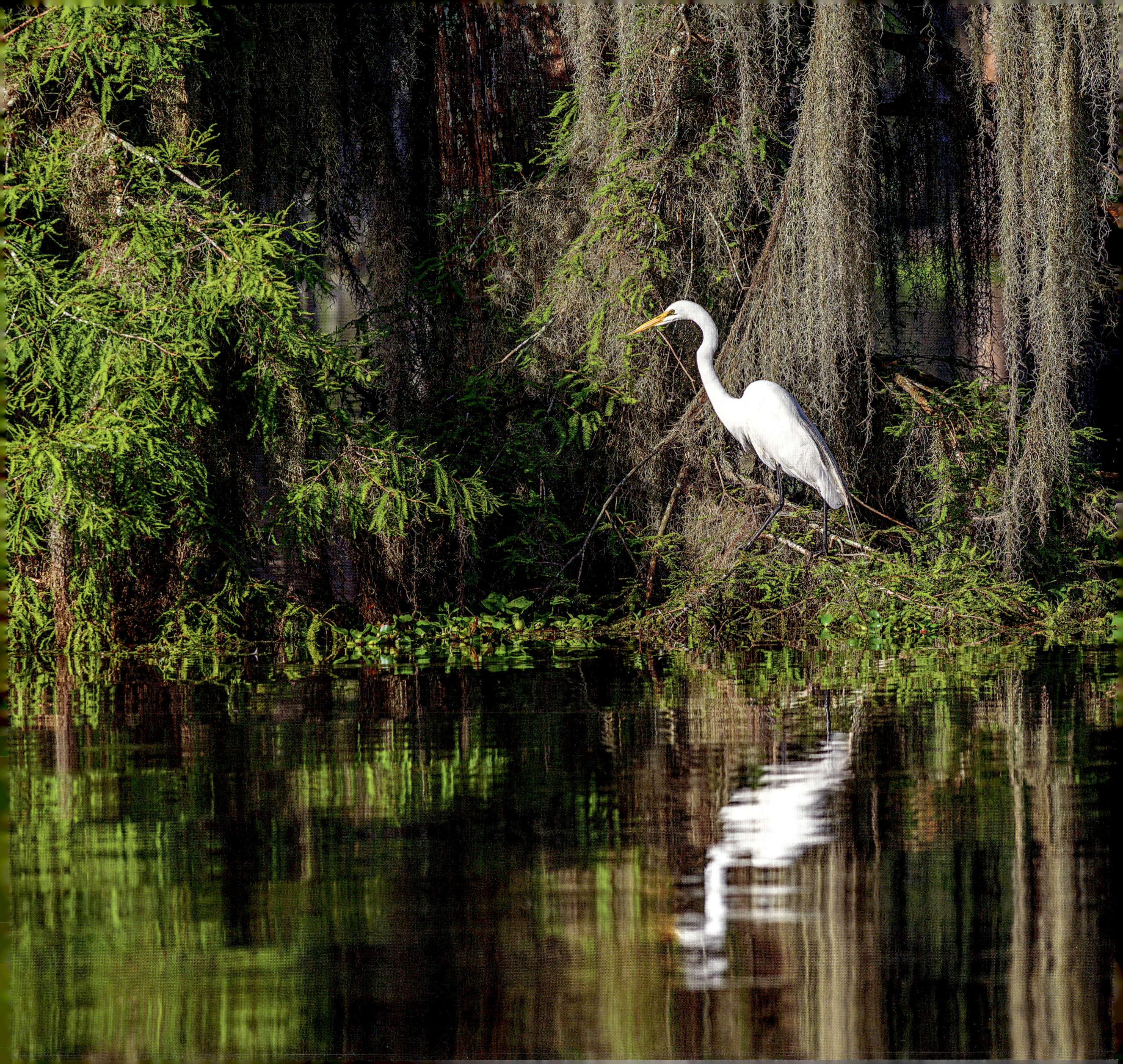

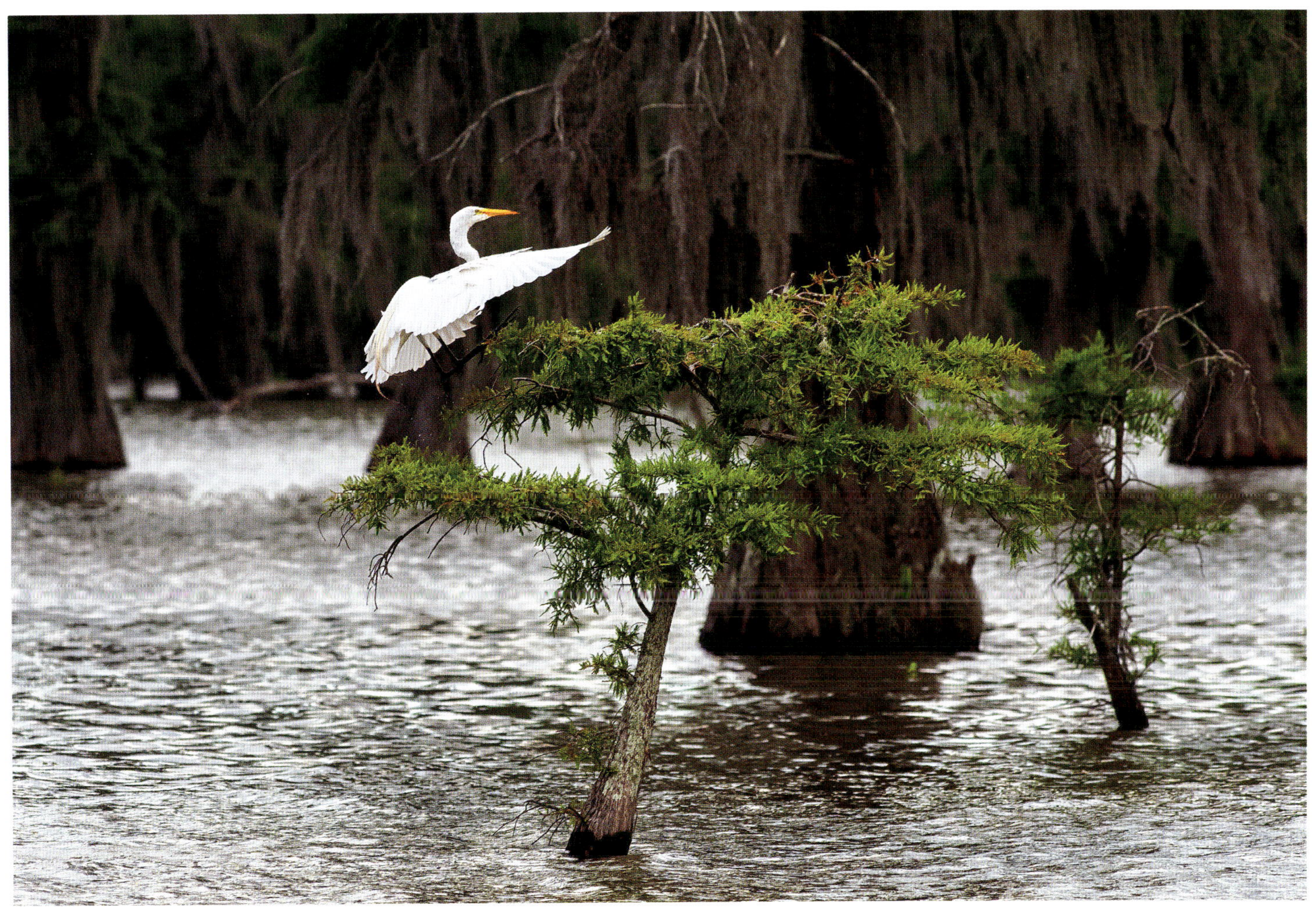

Opposite page: Great egrets round out the large predatory wading birds of the swamp. Like great blue herons, they often line the shores in apparent favored hunting locations to pick off fish, frogs, and insects.

Between feeding periods, great egrets often retreat to cypress trees to rest up. This bird picked a small tree in the beautiful Lake Martin near Lafayette.

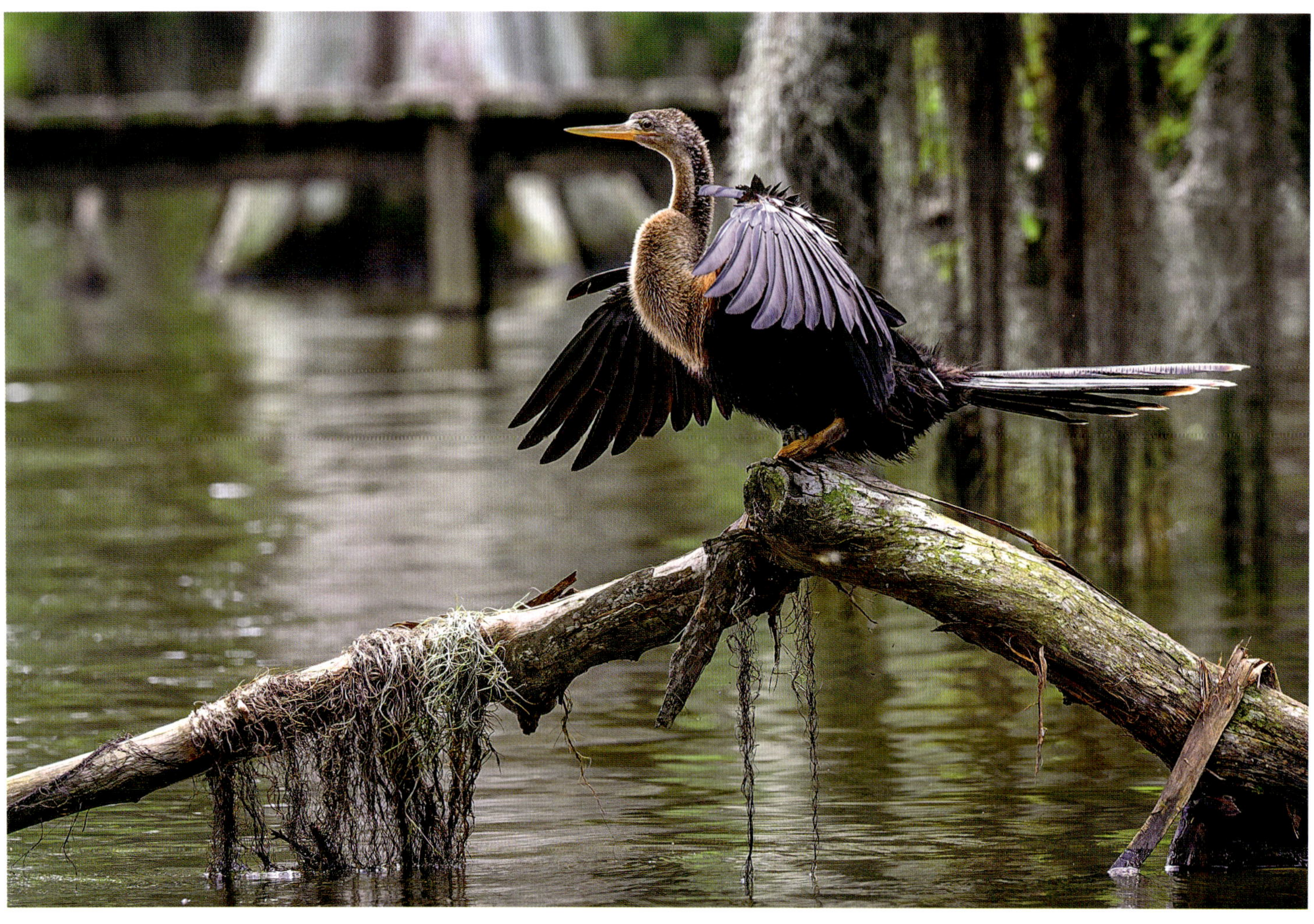

Anhingas are some of the strangest birds in the swamp. They are anything but graceful in the air, usually struggling to launch. However, they are quite at home in the water, often diving to nab fish. They are often seen perched with outspread wings, which allow them to absorb solar heat.

Opposite page: Yellow-crowned night herons are incredibly beautiful, with vivid red eyes and yellow legs contrasting wonderfully with the blueish-gray plumage. Half the size of great blue herons, these night herons stalk the same areas, looking for crawfish, insects, fish, and frogs.

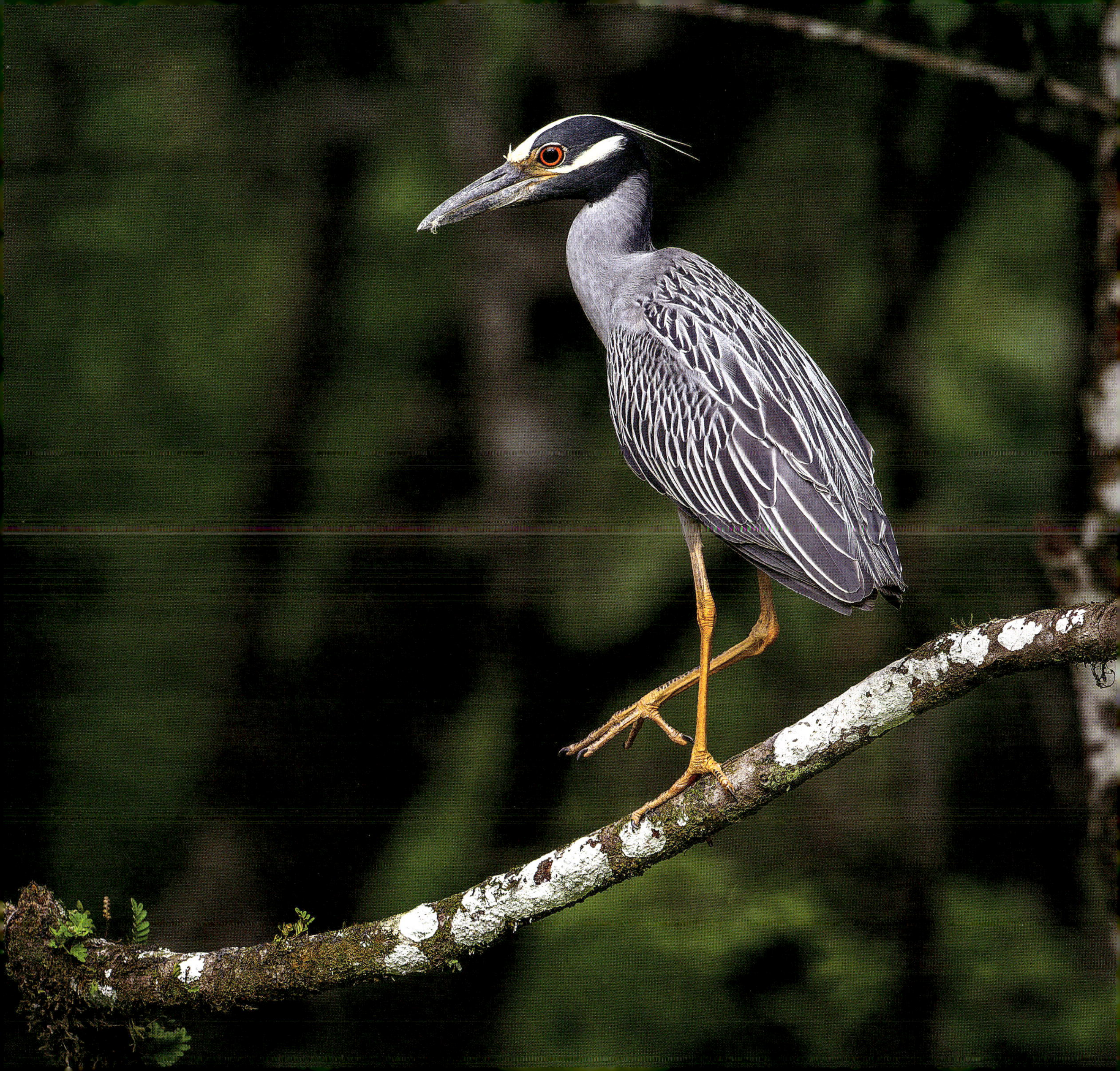

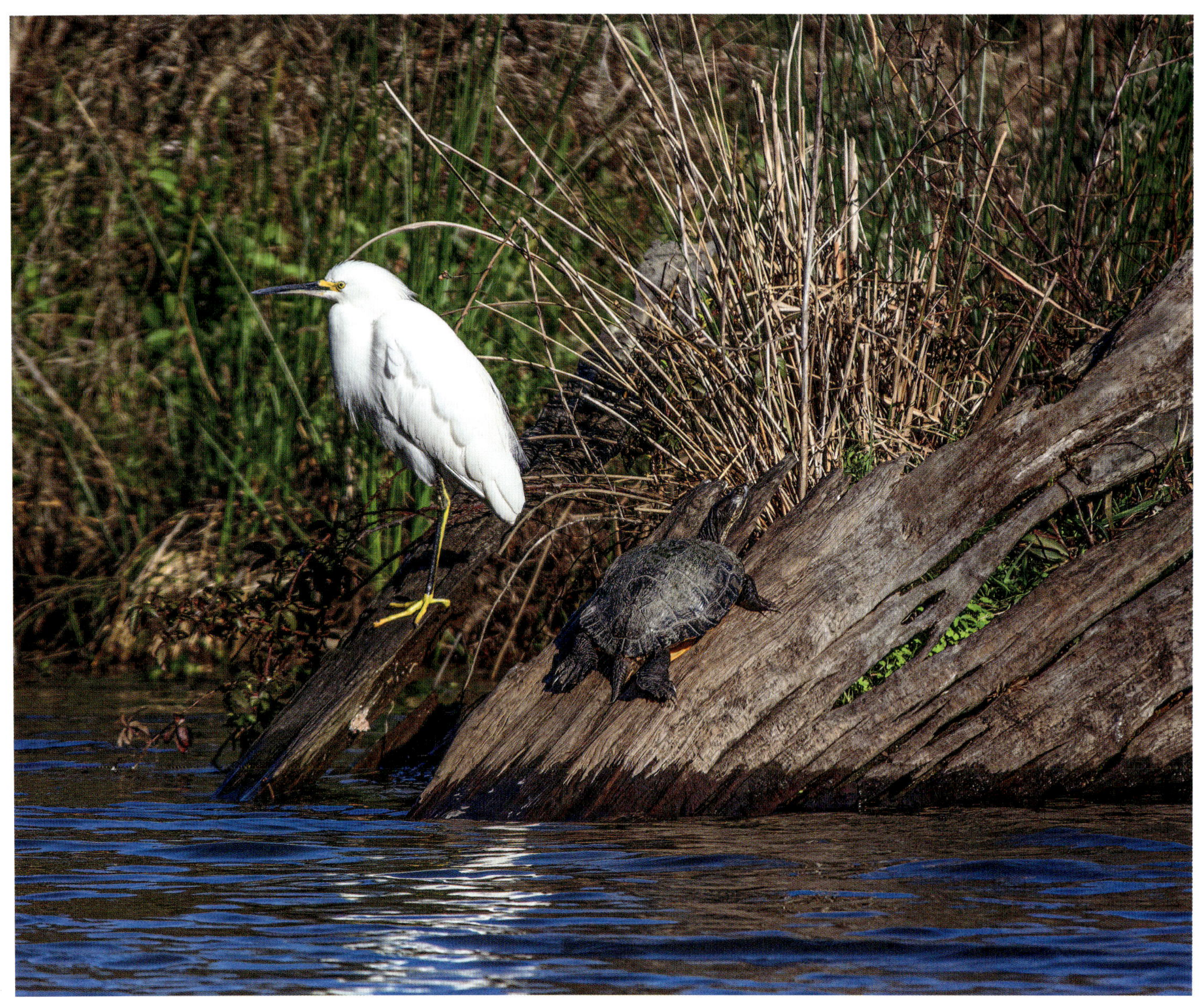

Wading birds and turtles are common throughout Louisiana's swamps and often are found near each other. Here, a snowy egret shares an old log with a pond slider.

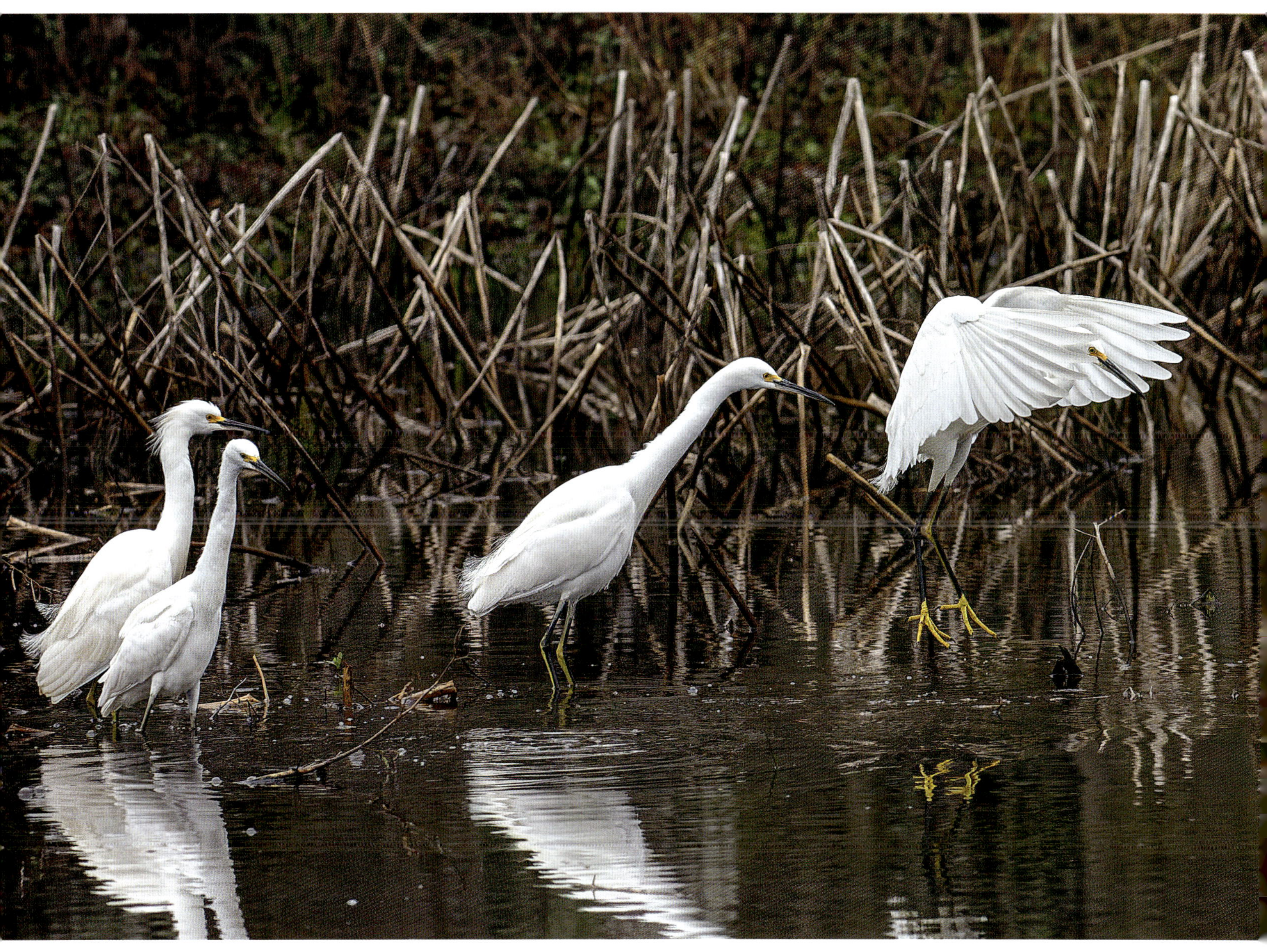

It's not unusual to see a flock of snowy egrets feeding together, stirring up the muddy bottom to find crustaceans and other prey.

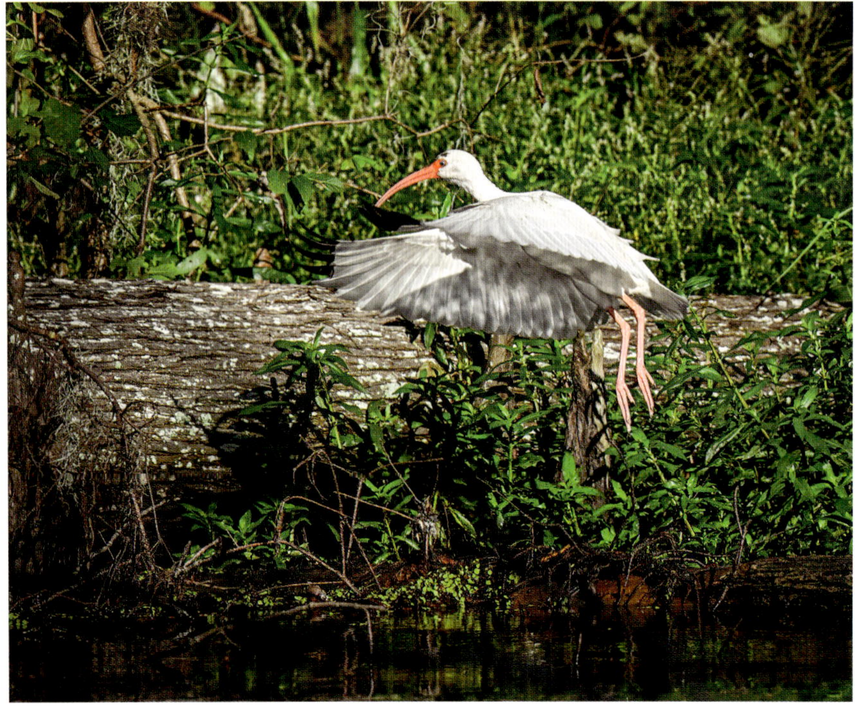

White ibises are constantly on the move when they feed, often flying from one prime location to the next.

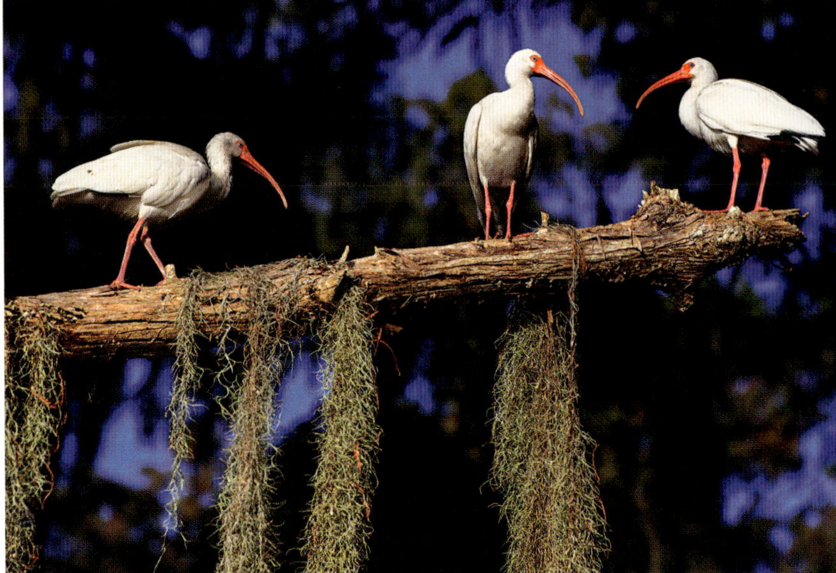

White ibises love the bogs of Louisiana's swamps. They perch in trees between feeding periods. Their striking orange bills and legs stand out wonderfully from the white plumage.

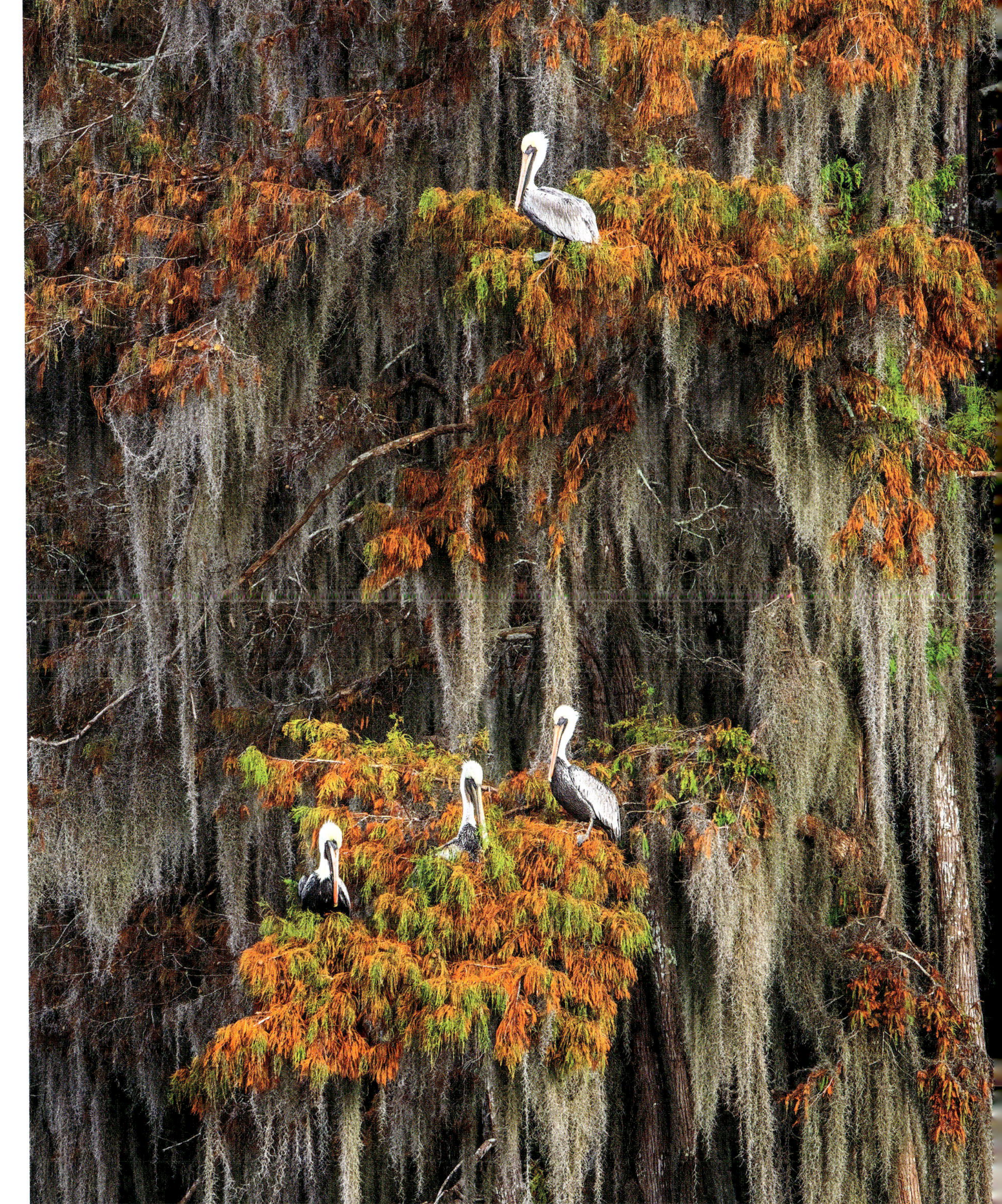

The brown pelican is Louisiana's official state bird, and they are all over the coastal areas. They do frequent the swamps, but I had never seen them roosting in cypress trees until I found this quartet along Avoca Island Cutoff.

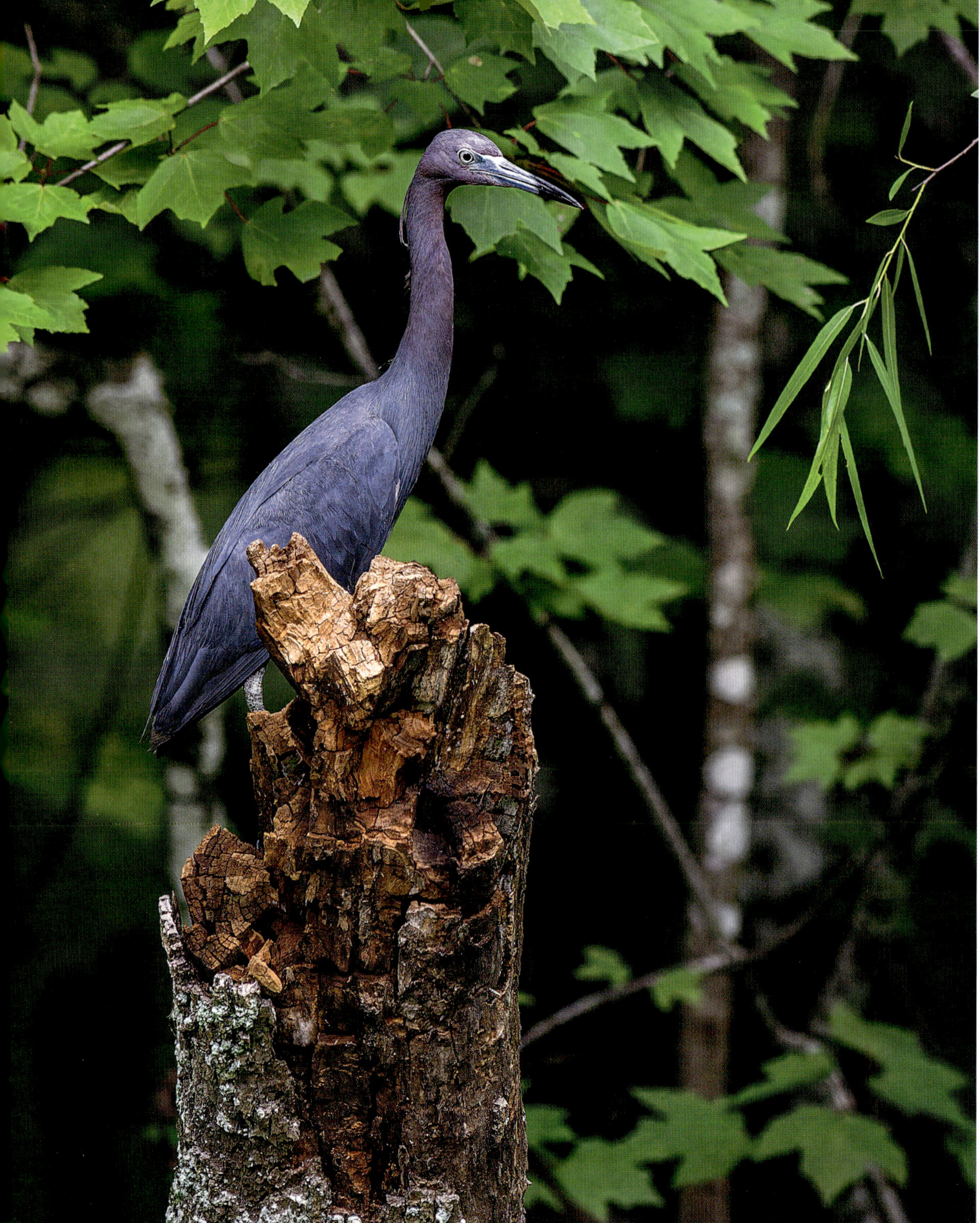

The little blue heron is small in stature, standing less than 2 feet tall. It is wonderfully colored and hunts for insects, small frogs, and other prey near bayous and swamps.

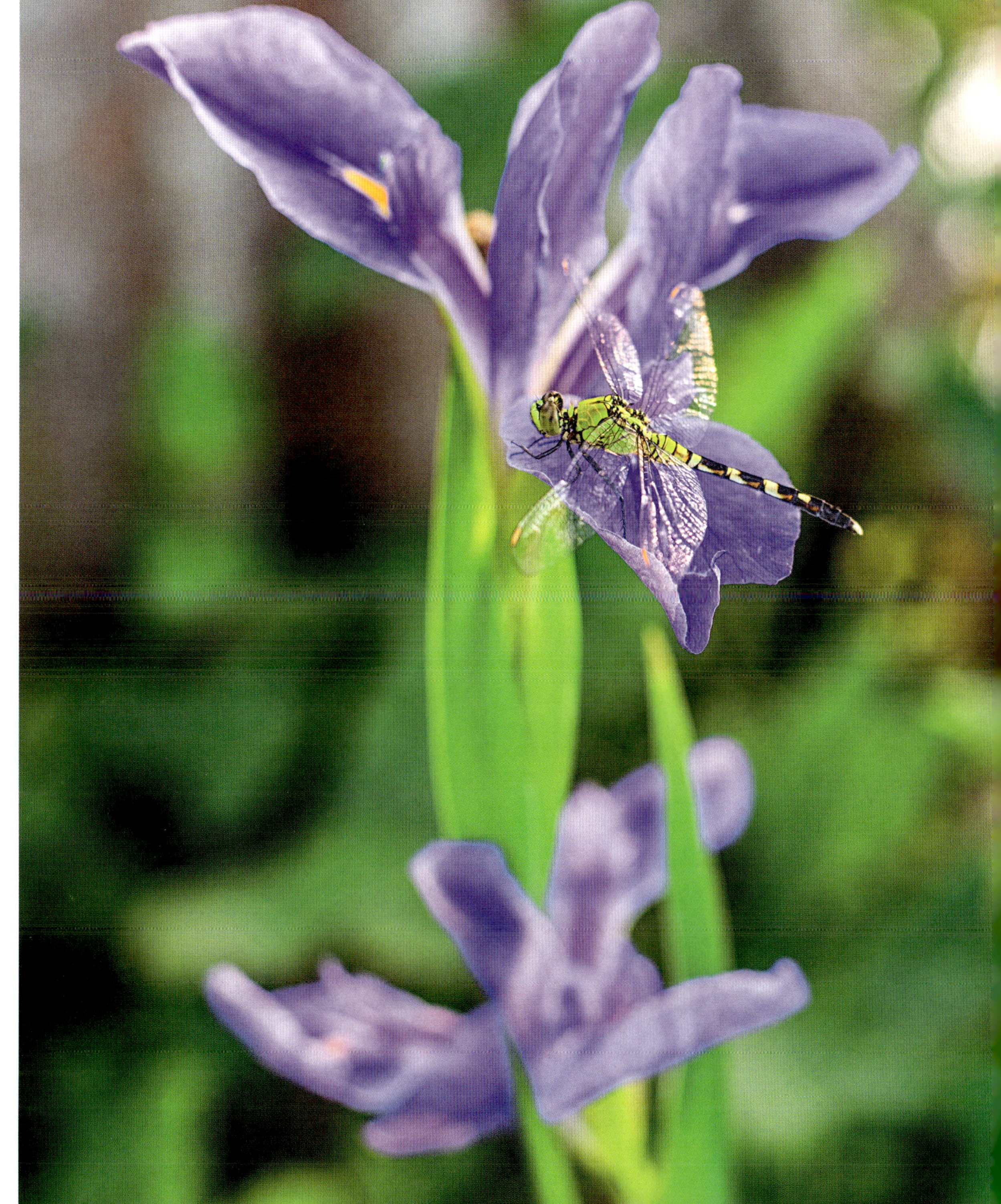

Mosquitoes aren't the only insects calling the humid swamps home. Myriad other species also live there. Here, a dragonfly perches on a purple iris, which grows wild in some areas.

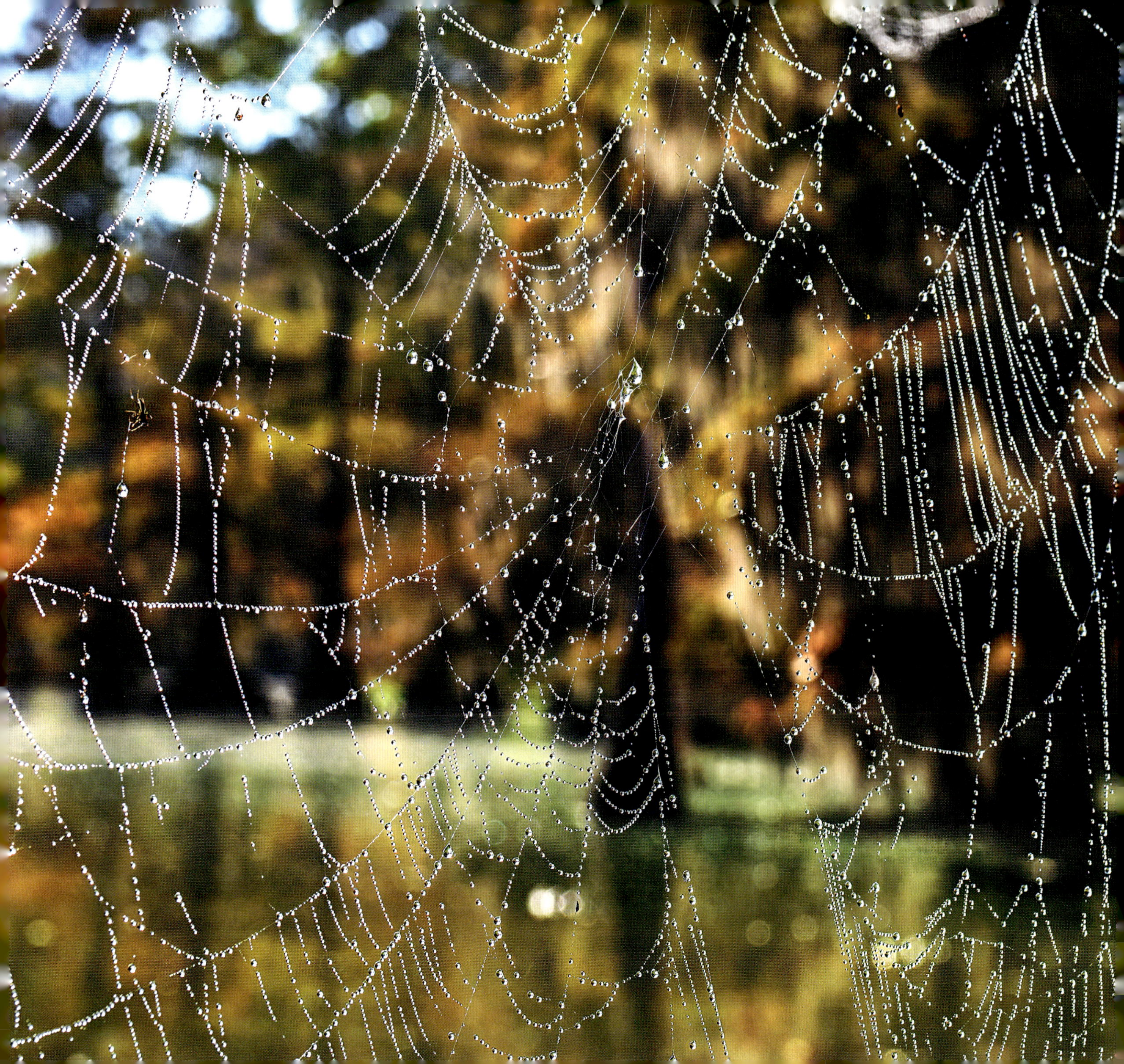

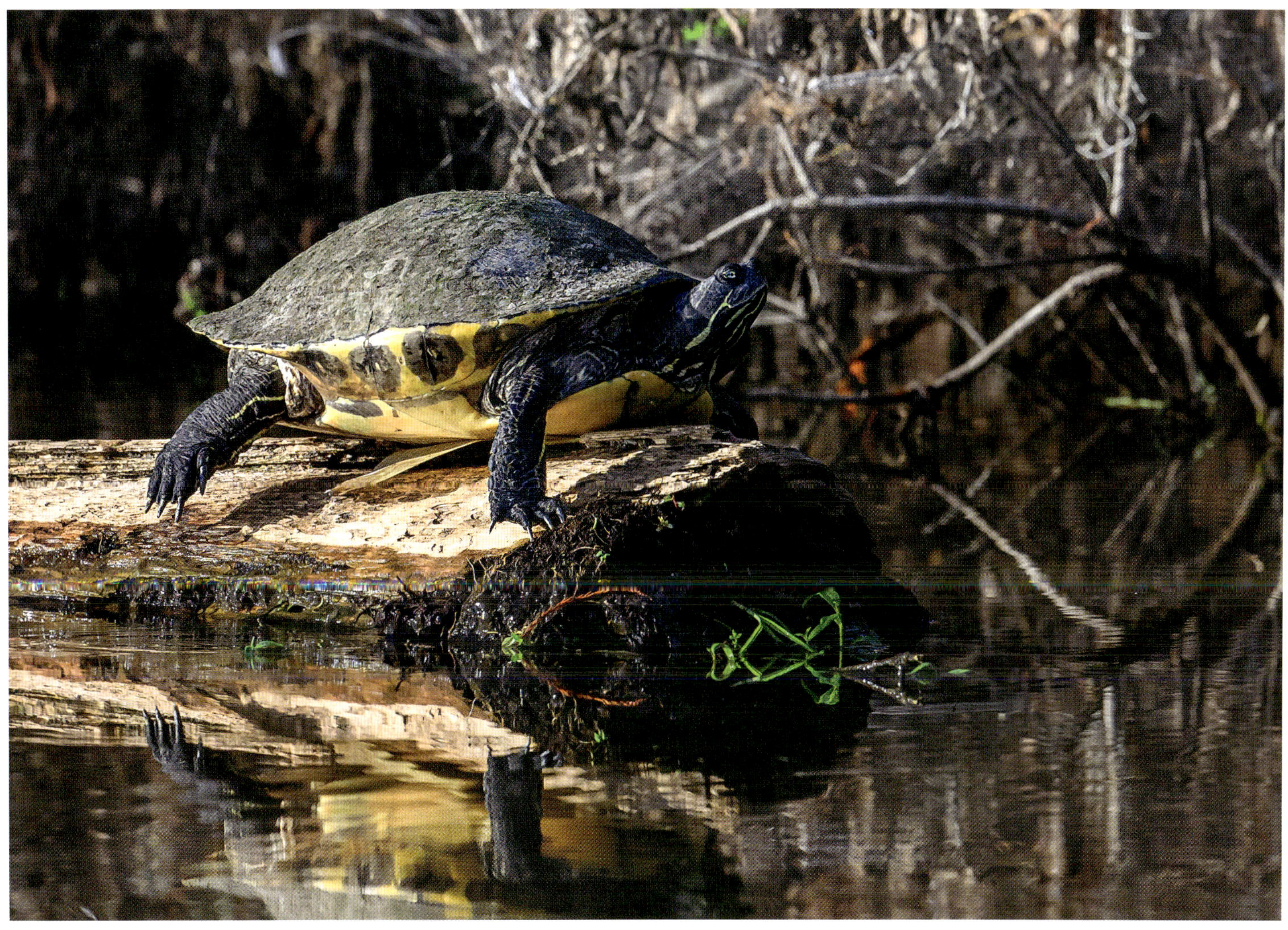

Opposite page: Spiders spin webs between cypress knees and tree branches, targeting flying insects. Their webs are incredibly intricate, perfectly illustrated by morning dew covering the sticky threads.

Turtles love to sun on logs floating in the swamps. Louisiana species include the pond slider (pictured), painted turtles, box turtles, and alligator snapping turtles.

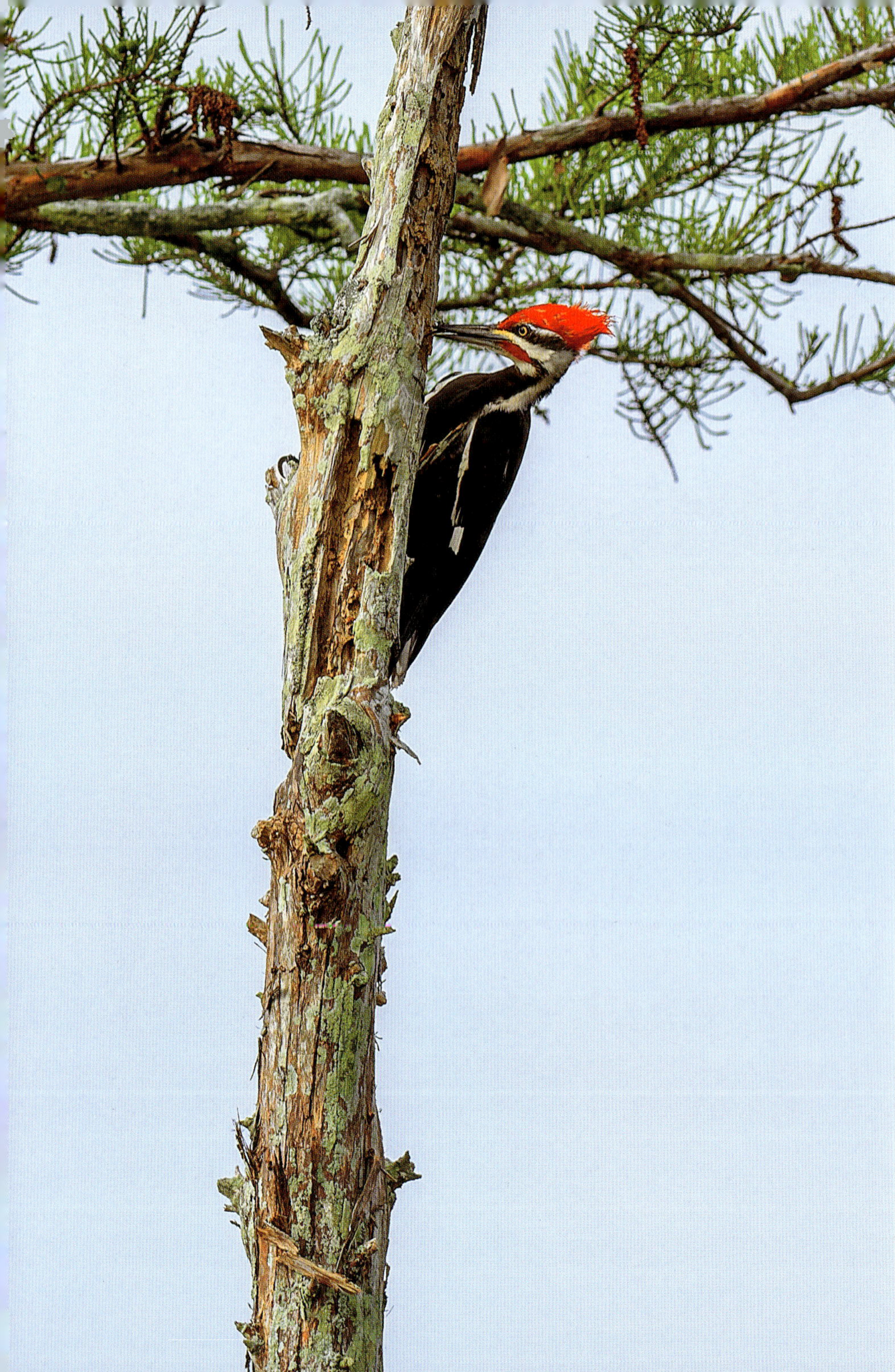

The hammering of woodpeckers often reverberates through the swamps. The pileated woodpecker (shown here) is just one of the species found in this part of the state.

Opposite page: One of the smaller birds that prowls around looking for insects is the sandpiper. They are so much fun to watch, as they do a little dance while walking along old logs.

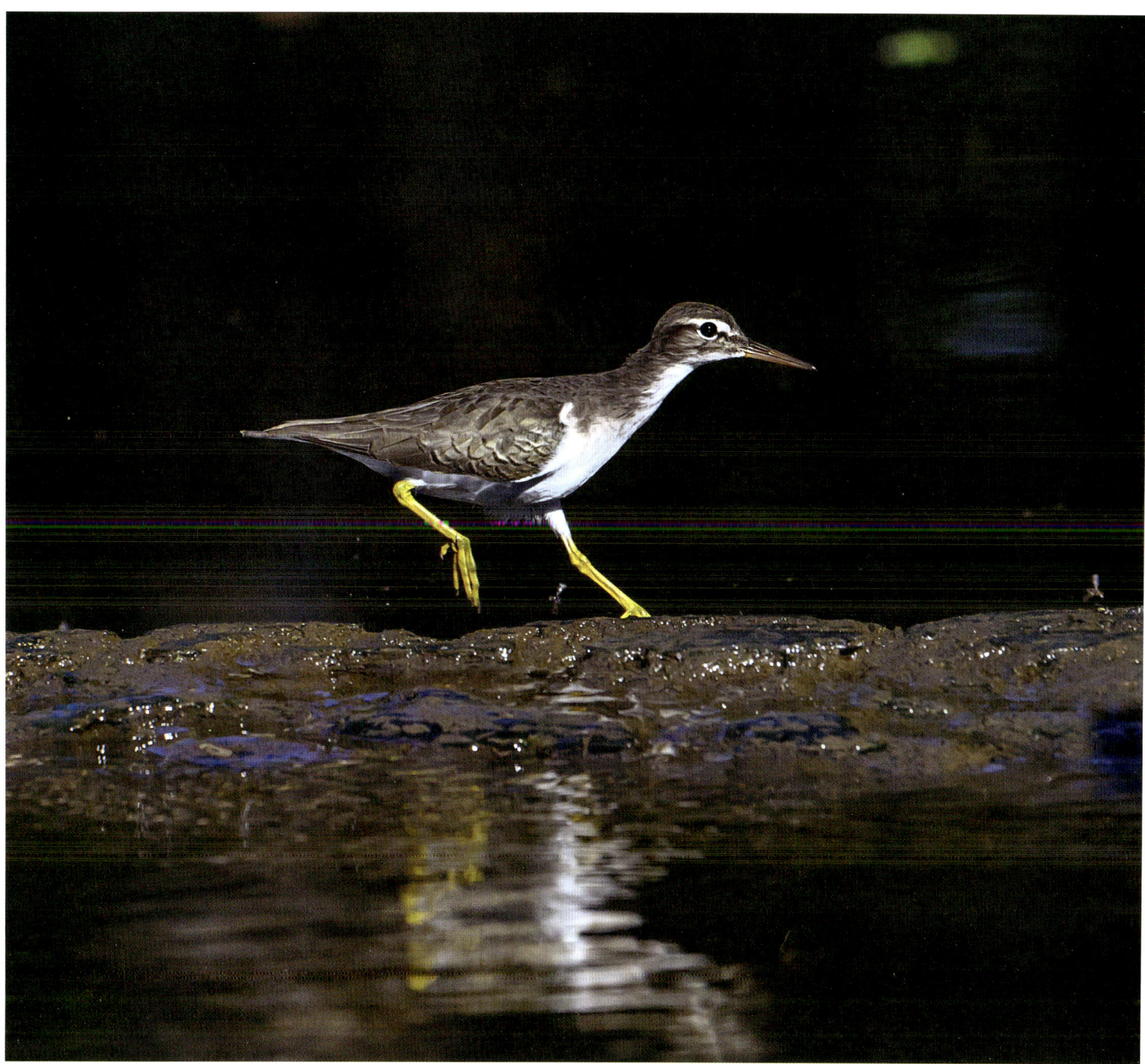

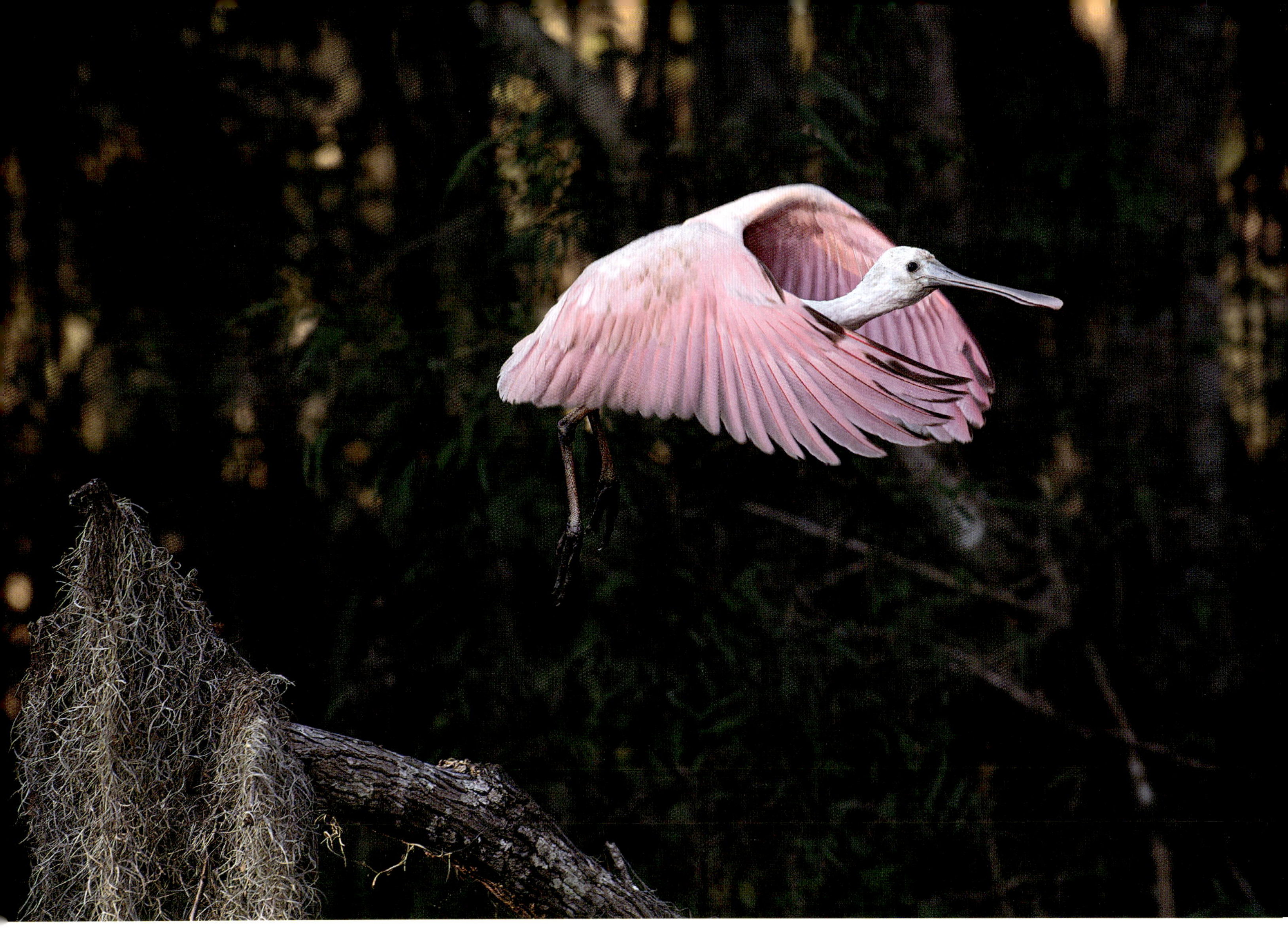

This is one of my favorite roseate spoonbill photos. I just love the way the birds cup their wings when they take off, and this spoonbill's wings perfectly frame the head and neck.

Opposite page: The colorful roseate spoonbill feeds in the shallows of the swamps, using its feet and spoon-shaped bill to stir up bottom muck while searching for crawfish and other small creatures.

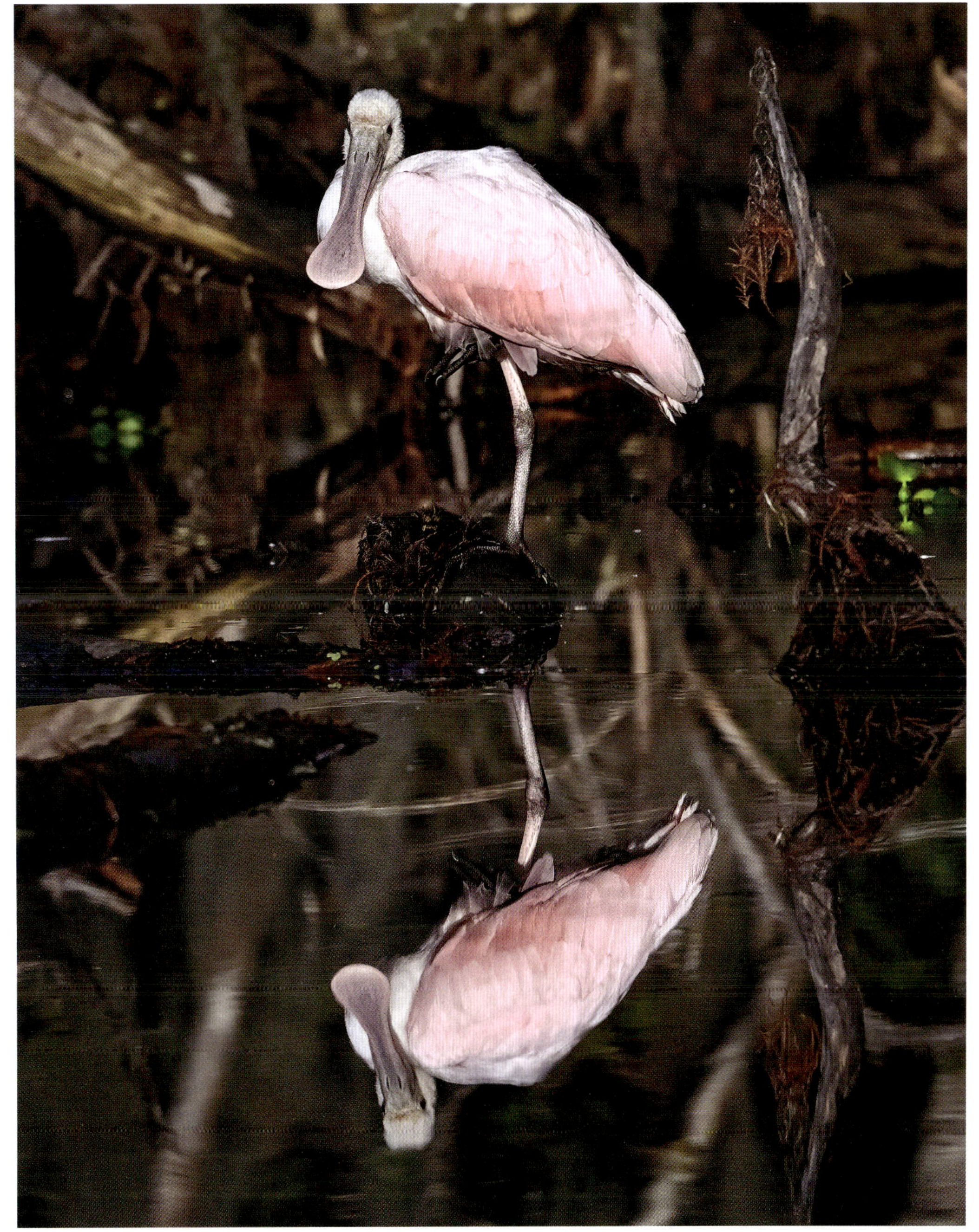

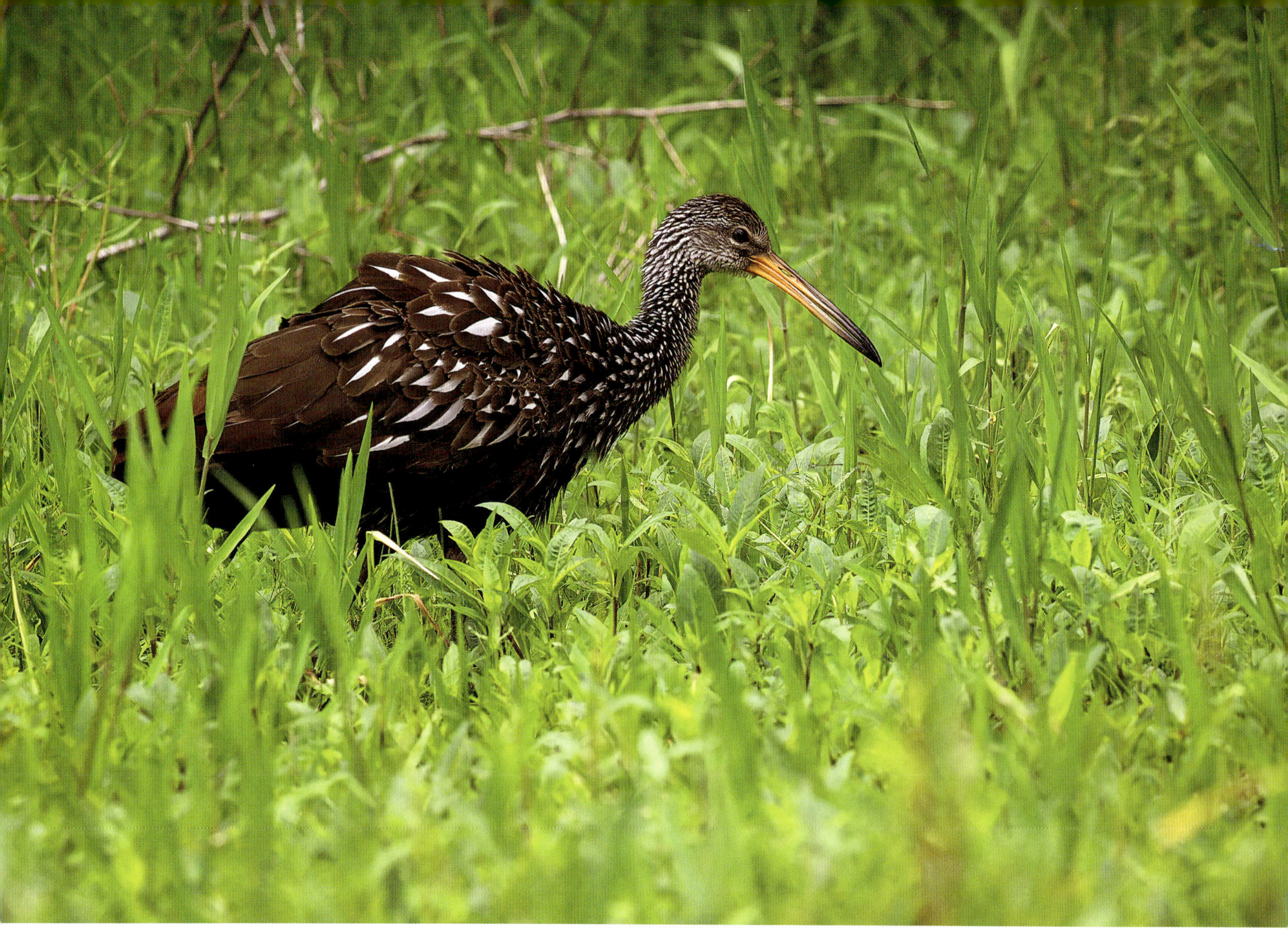

A recent immigrant to coastal Louisiana is the limpkin. These Florida natives have been found in increasing numbers since 2017. While not native to the Louisiana swamps, the upside of limpkins' arrival is that they feed heavily on invasive apple snails, which have become a real problem in Louisiana's marshes and swamps.

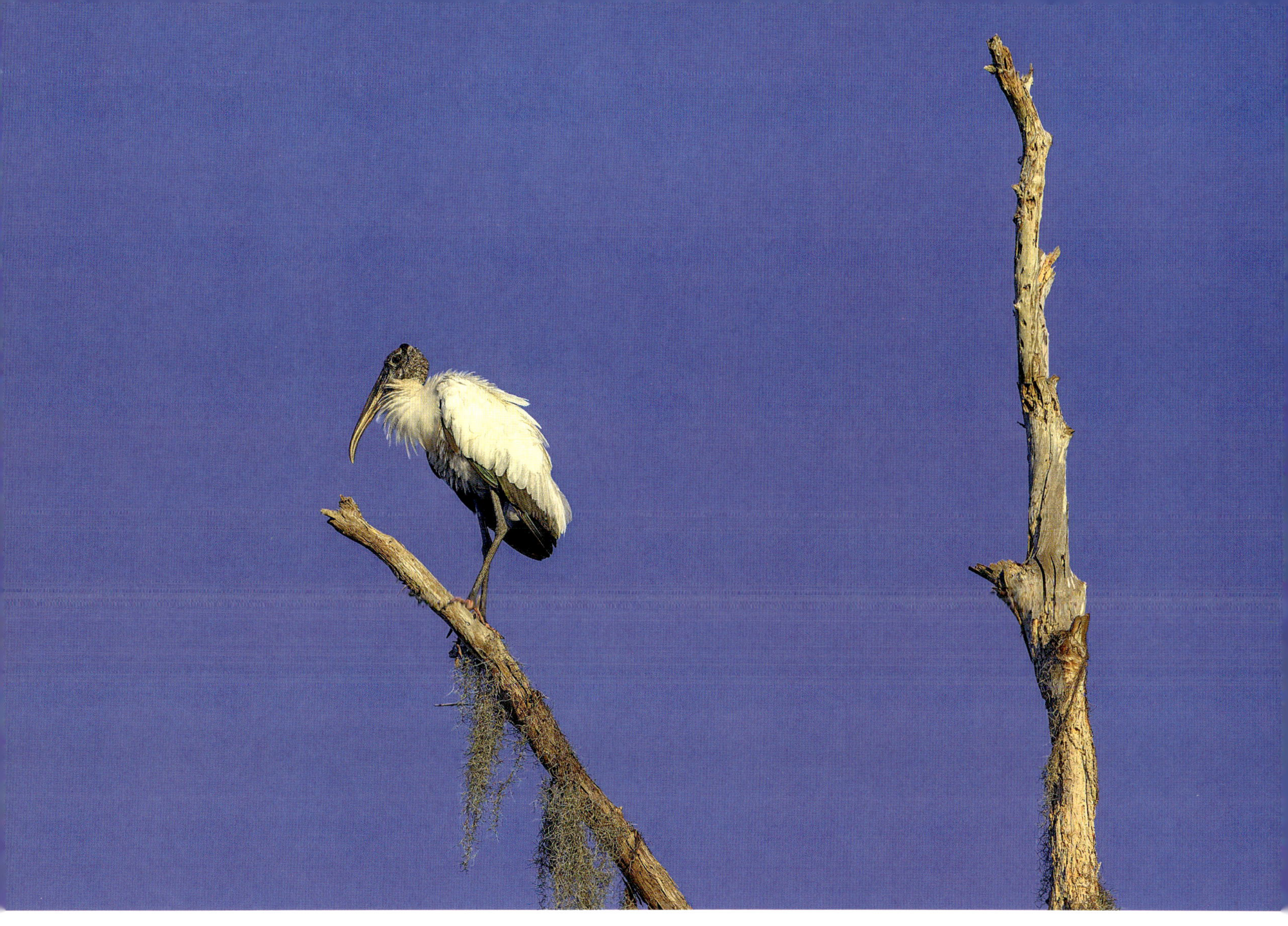

One of the strangest-looking swamp denizens is the wood stork, the only stork species in North America. These prehistoric-looking birds stand upward of 44 inches tall with wingspans that can top 5 feet. They are not all that common. I've only seen two.

CHAPTER FOUR

HUMANS AND THE SWAMP

We South Louisianans live in a world of water, with bayous and swamps everywhere we turn. And those wetlands have become part of our everyday lives. Camps have been scattered throughout these amazing swamps for generations. Even in the Atchafalaya Basin, the nation's largest river swamp at more than 1 million acres, it's common to find hunting and fishing camps dotting the bayous and lakes. Many of these camps are reachable only by boat, providing a break from the workaday world of the twenty-first century.

However, human coexistence with the swampy landscape does have negative aspects. These amazing wetlands were deemed worthless by those who mapped out the area, and then eyed with greed by those who traded in timber during the end of the nineteenth century. Virgin cypress trees fell until they were all but gone.

Invasive species began to appear, and today the impacts of those introductions are seen throughout the sprawling wetlands. From vegetation like hydrilla, water hyacinth, and salvinia that cover miles of swamps to such exotic species as nutria, Asian carp, and apple snails, the swamplands have been assaulted by a host of invaders.

Today, much of the swampland is protected from logging as part of a network of state and federal land. And managers work hard to maintain the health of these swamps. That sometimes means spraying water hyacinths and salvinia to minimize the impact of these fast-growing species. In places like Henderson Swamp, which features a water-control structure to manage water levels, annual drawdowns dry out shallow areas to knock back vegetation that would otherwise completely cover the swamps.

It's a continuous battle, but still the swamps endure.

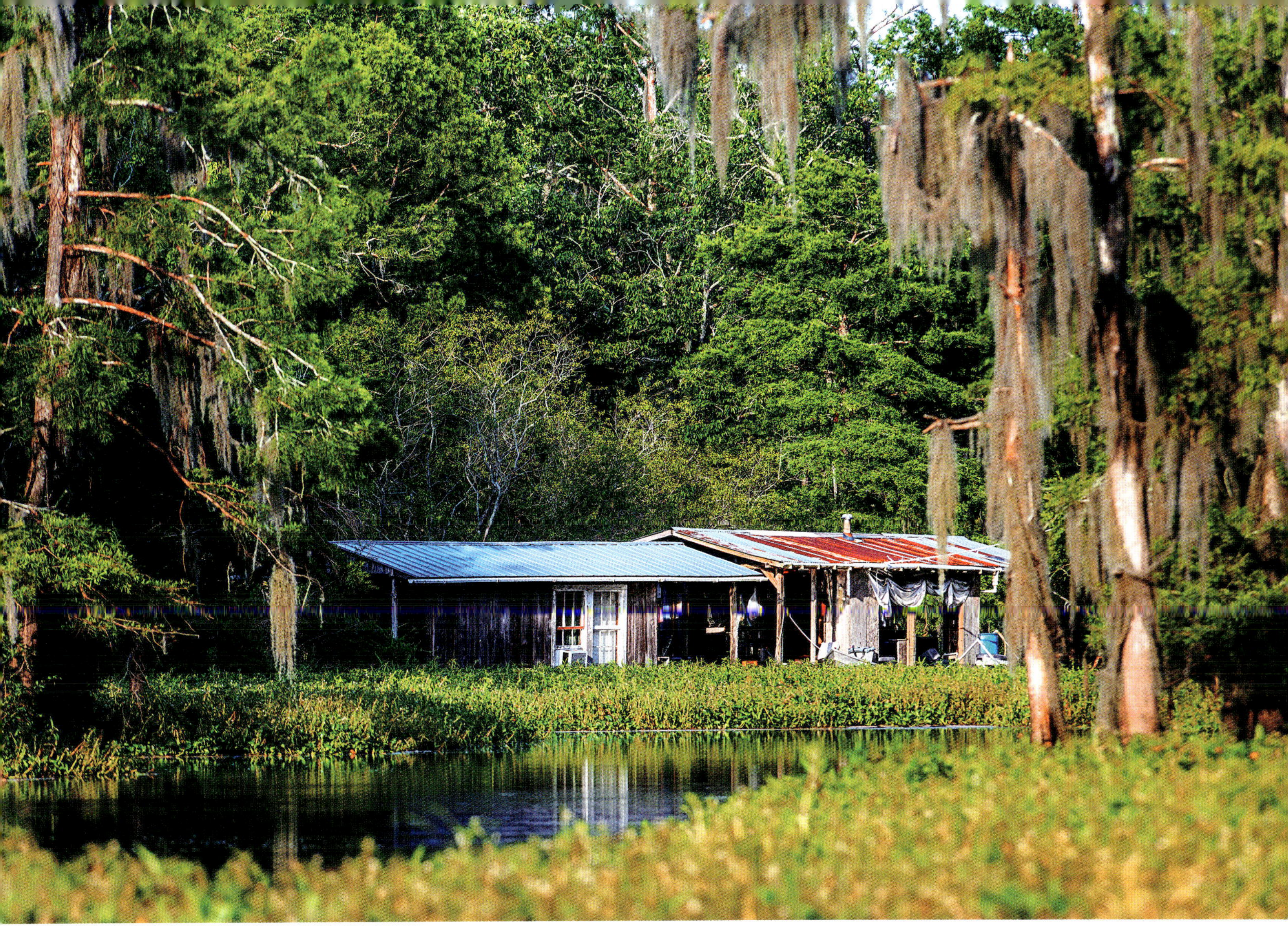

Many camps in the sprawling Atchafalaya Basin are accessible only by boat. This old houseboat camp is tucked into a small cove of Grand Lake in the geographic center of the Basin. Any electricity used at these camps is provided by small generators.

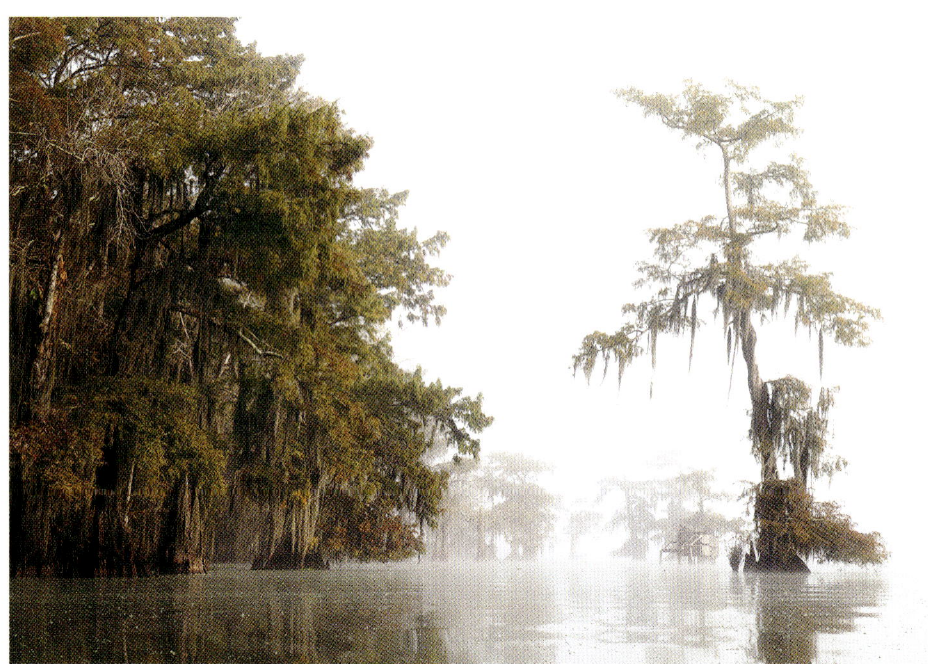

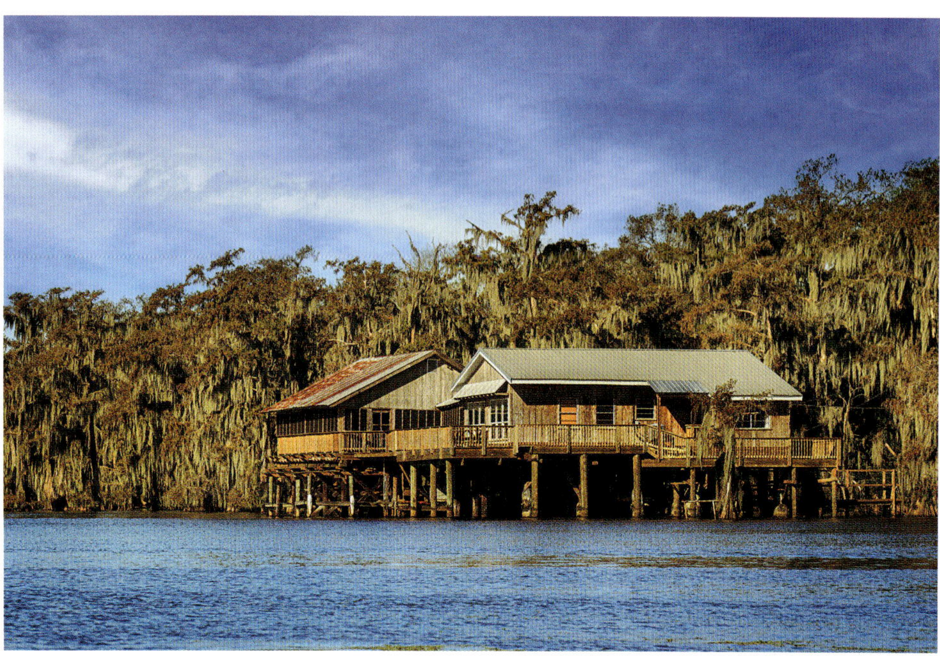

South Louisiana's swamps have been a source of sustenance for humans for thousands of years. Duck blinds dot the swamps even today, testifying to the integral link between these fertile wetlands and local residents.

The families who own these beautiful camps on the edge of the Lake Verret swamp have front-row seats to sunsets over this picturesque lake.

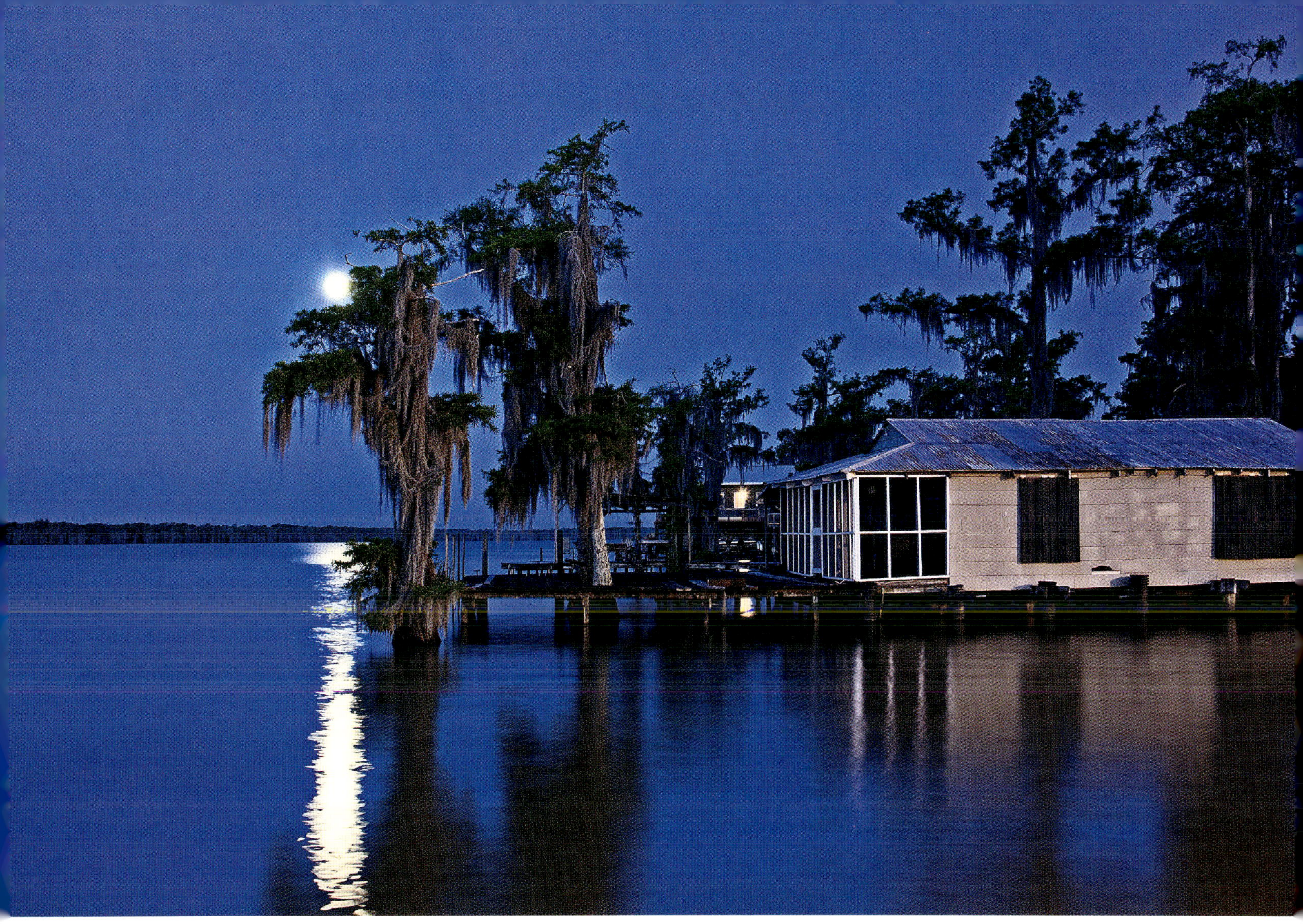

The moon rises over a fishing camp on the edge of Lake Verret. These wonderful camps, which keep Louisianans tied to the natural beauty of the state, dot the swamps and are often passed from one generation to the next.

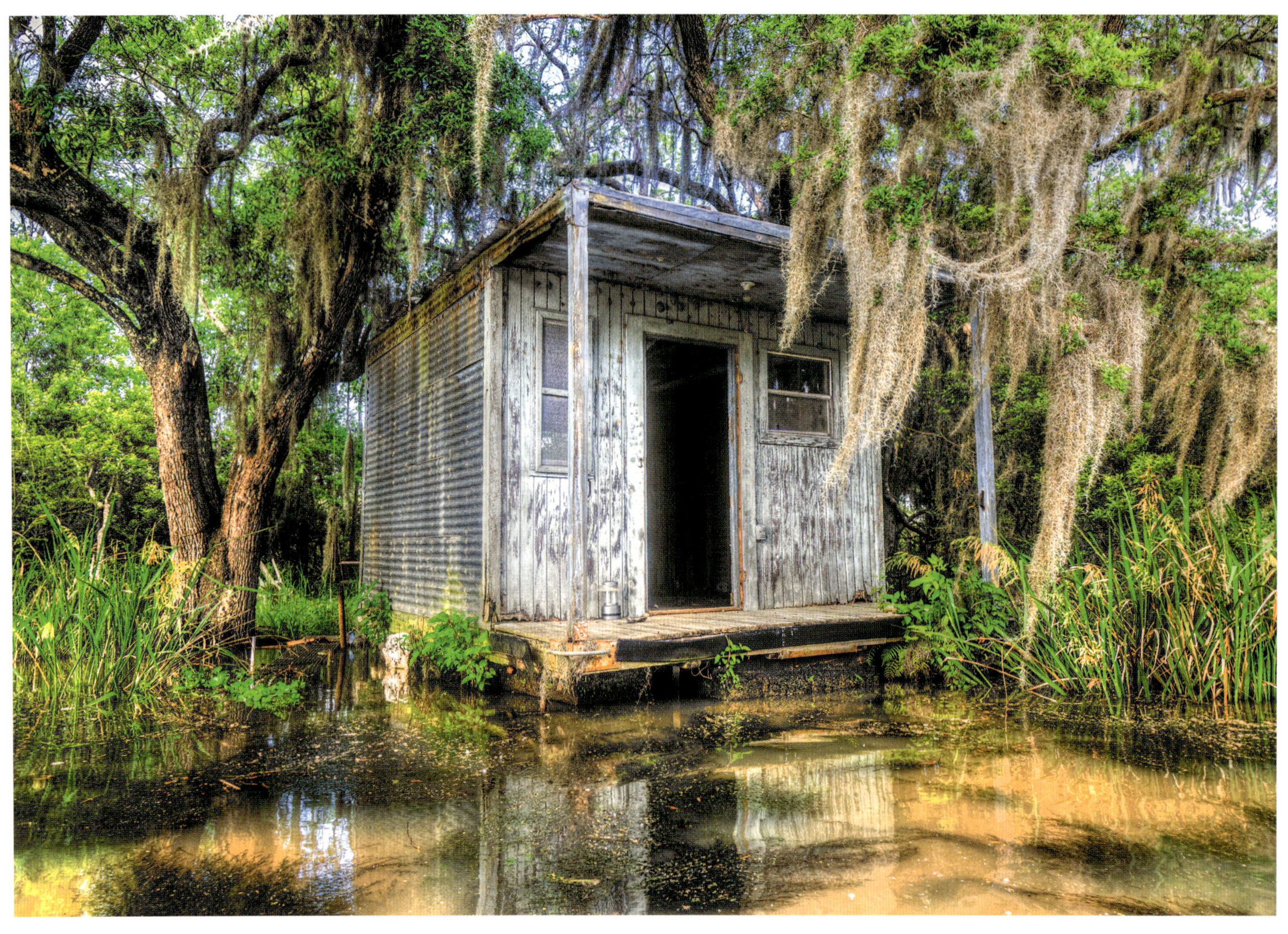

Not all camps are grand affairs. This small shack built on pontoons, located along an oak chenier in the swamps near New Iberia, is just large enough to provide a place to sleep between fishing and hunting trips.

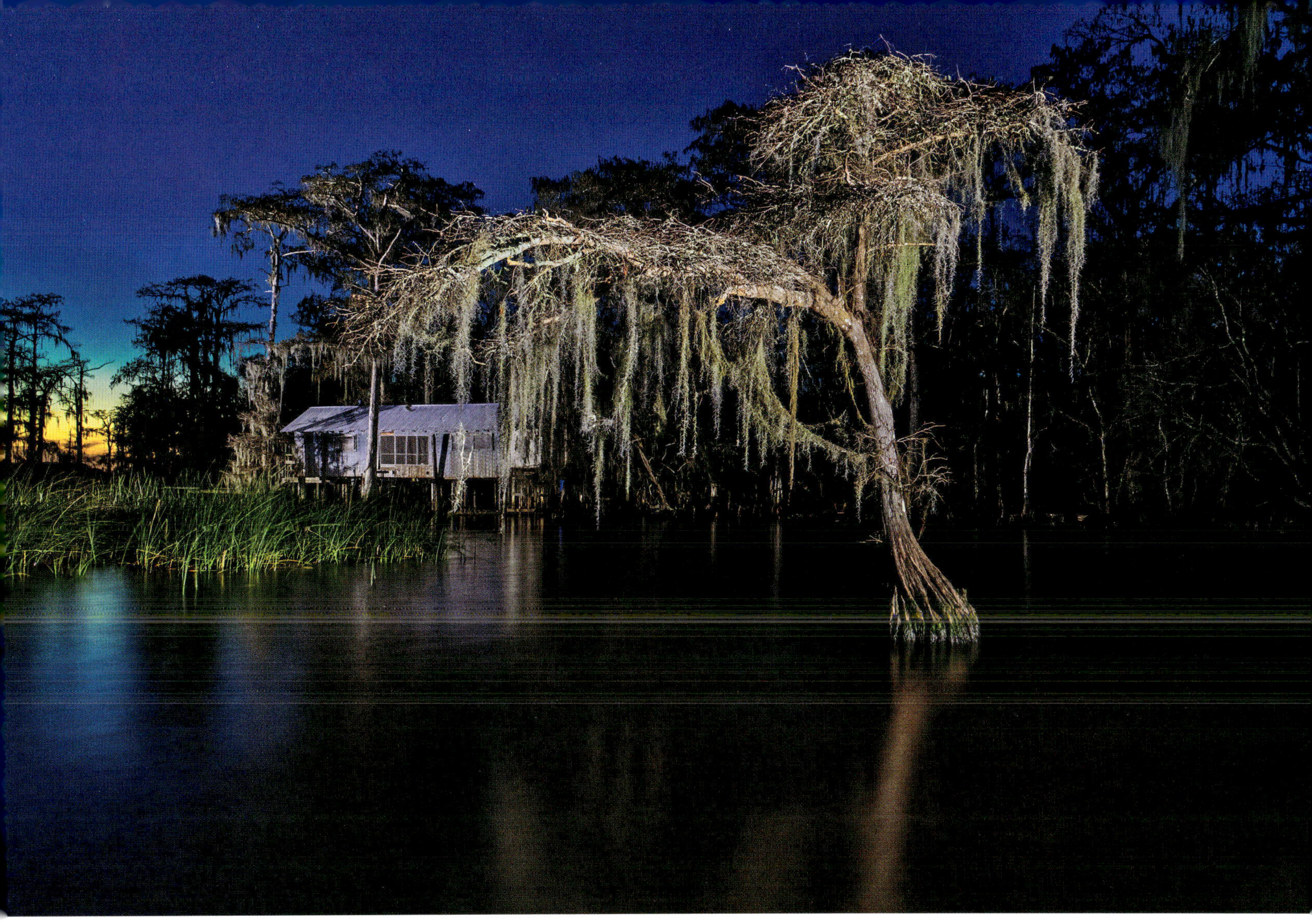

Some camps have served generations. This camp was built on the banks of Lake Maurepas in 1965 after Hurricane Betsy destroyed the original structure. This version was wiped out by Hurricane Ida when the eye of the storm swept right over the lake in 2021.

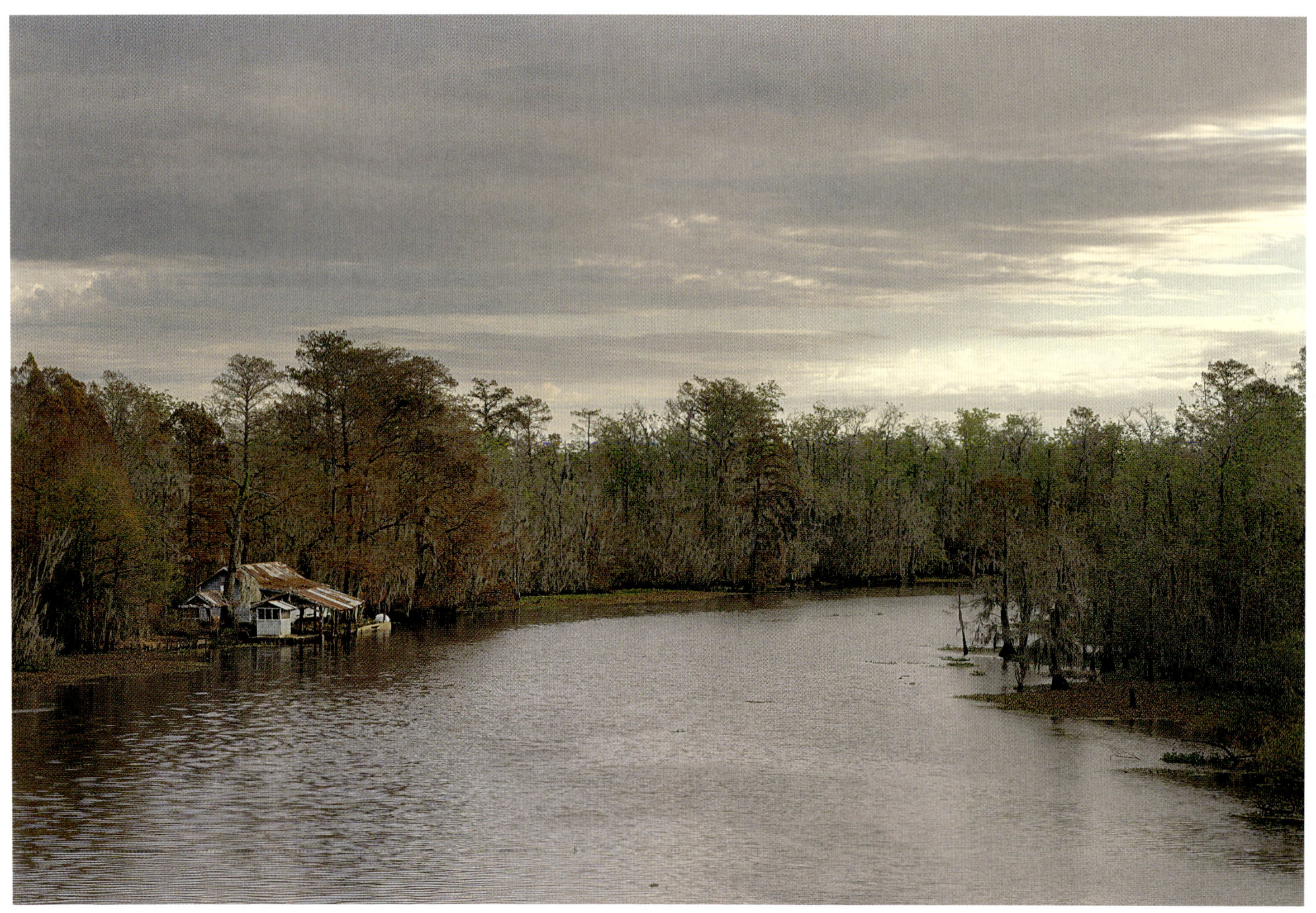

This tin-covered camp has been a fixture on Blind River between Baton Rouge and New Orleans for decades, and it's survived several tropical storms. It is now surrounded by the vast Maurepas Swamp Wildlife Management Area, which stretches from Sorrento to Interstate 55 just west of New Orleans.

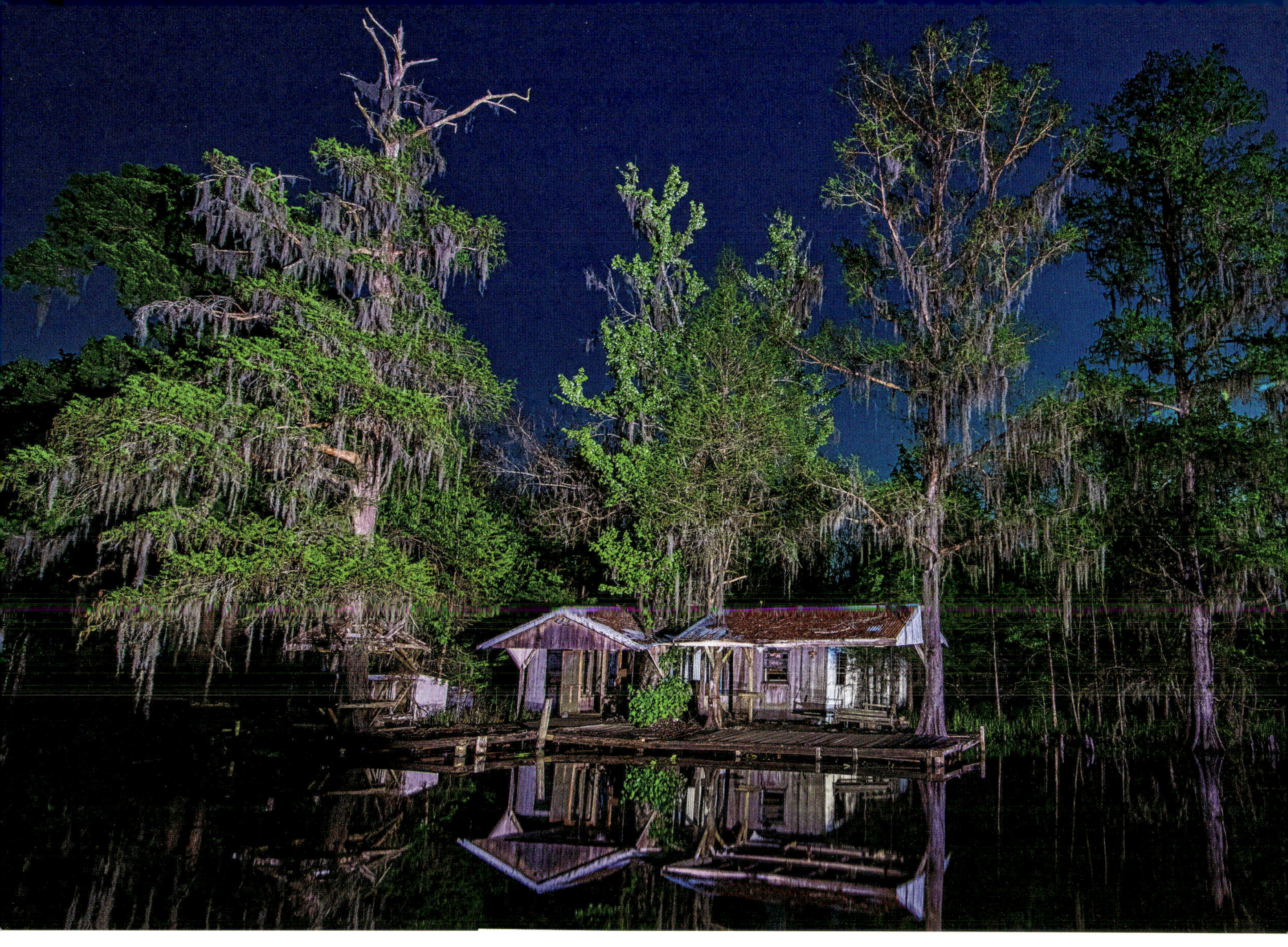

Some hunting camps are no longer in use. This old camp, built decades ago, was abandoned when the surrounding swamps became part of the state-owned Maurepas Swamp Wildlife Management Area.

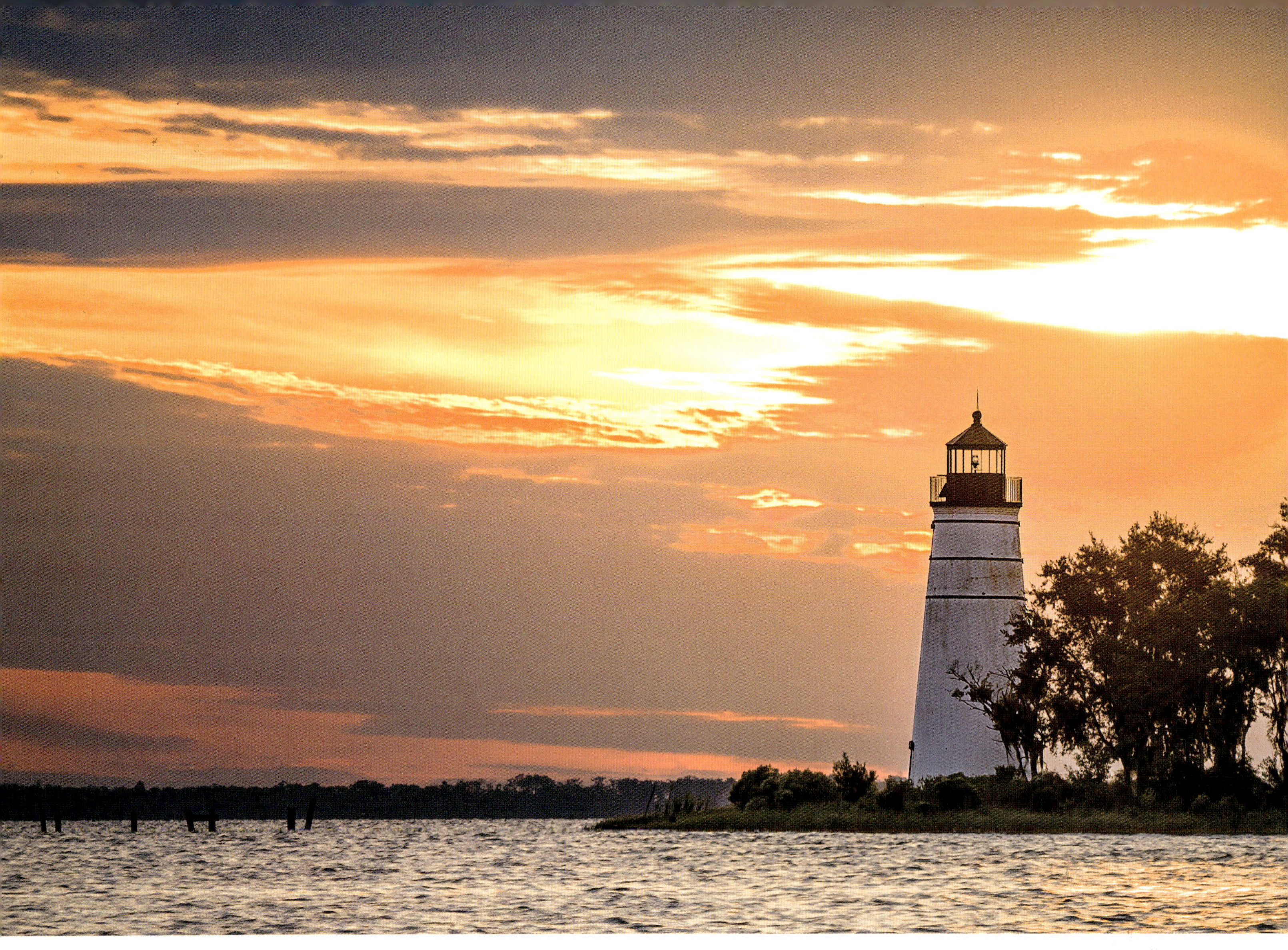

The old Tchefuncte River Lighthouse near Madisonville was rebuilt in 1868 following the Civil War. Although no longer lit, the lighthouse remains a marker for the mouth of the river that snakes through the cypress swamps on the north shore of Lake Pontchartrain.

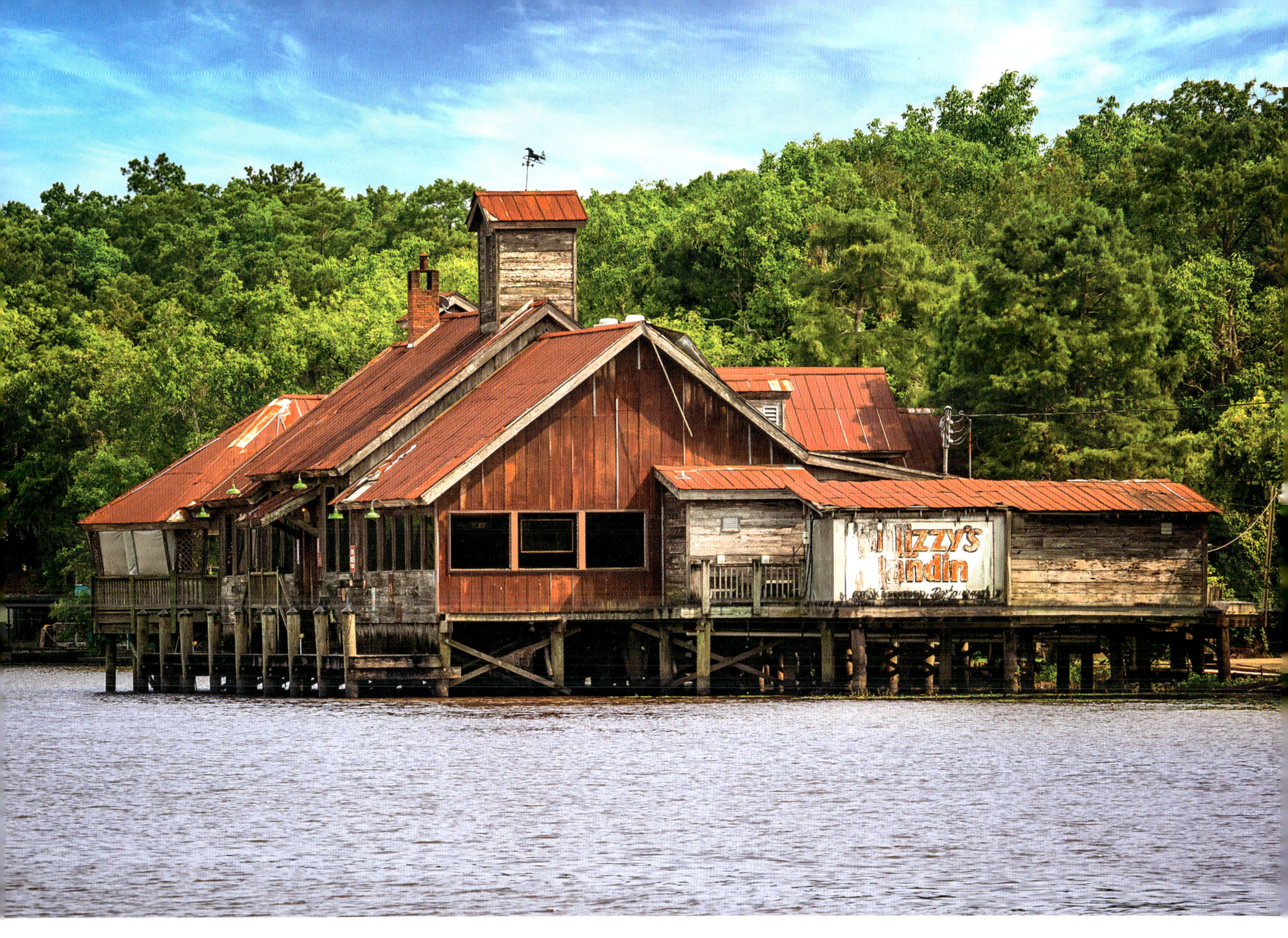

It's also not uncommon to find eateries and bars perched on the edges of the swamps. The beautiful Tin Lizzy's Landin' once was a popular waterfront restaurant and bar along the swamp-lined Tickfaw River. At this writing, it is closed.

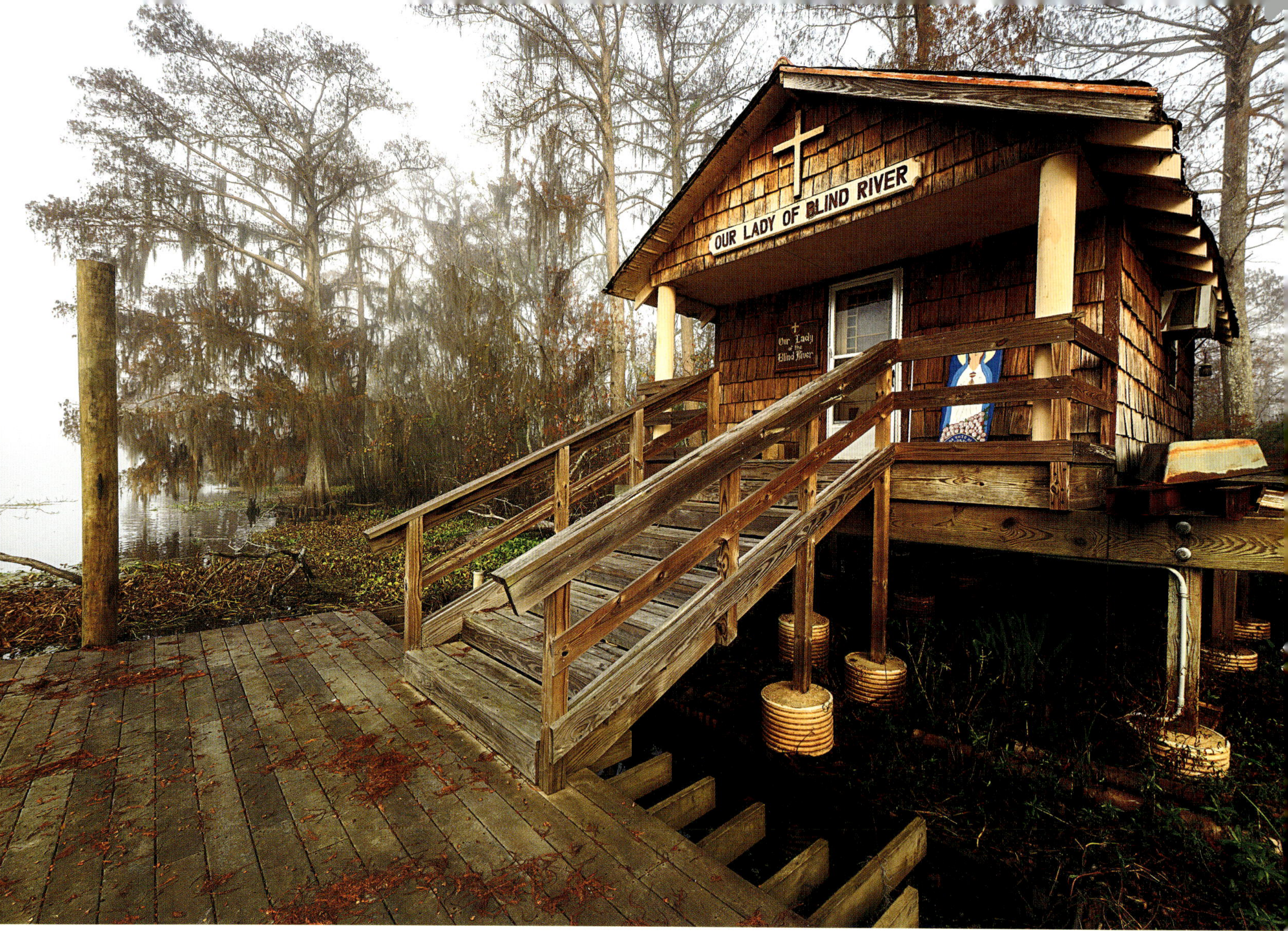

The area's religion even infiltrates the swamps. The wonderful Our Lady of Blind River chapel was built decades ago along Blind River as a place of reflection for camp owners.

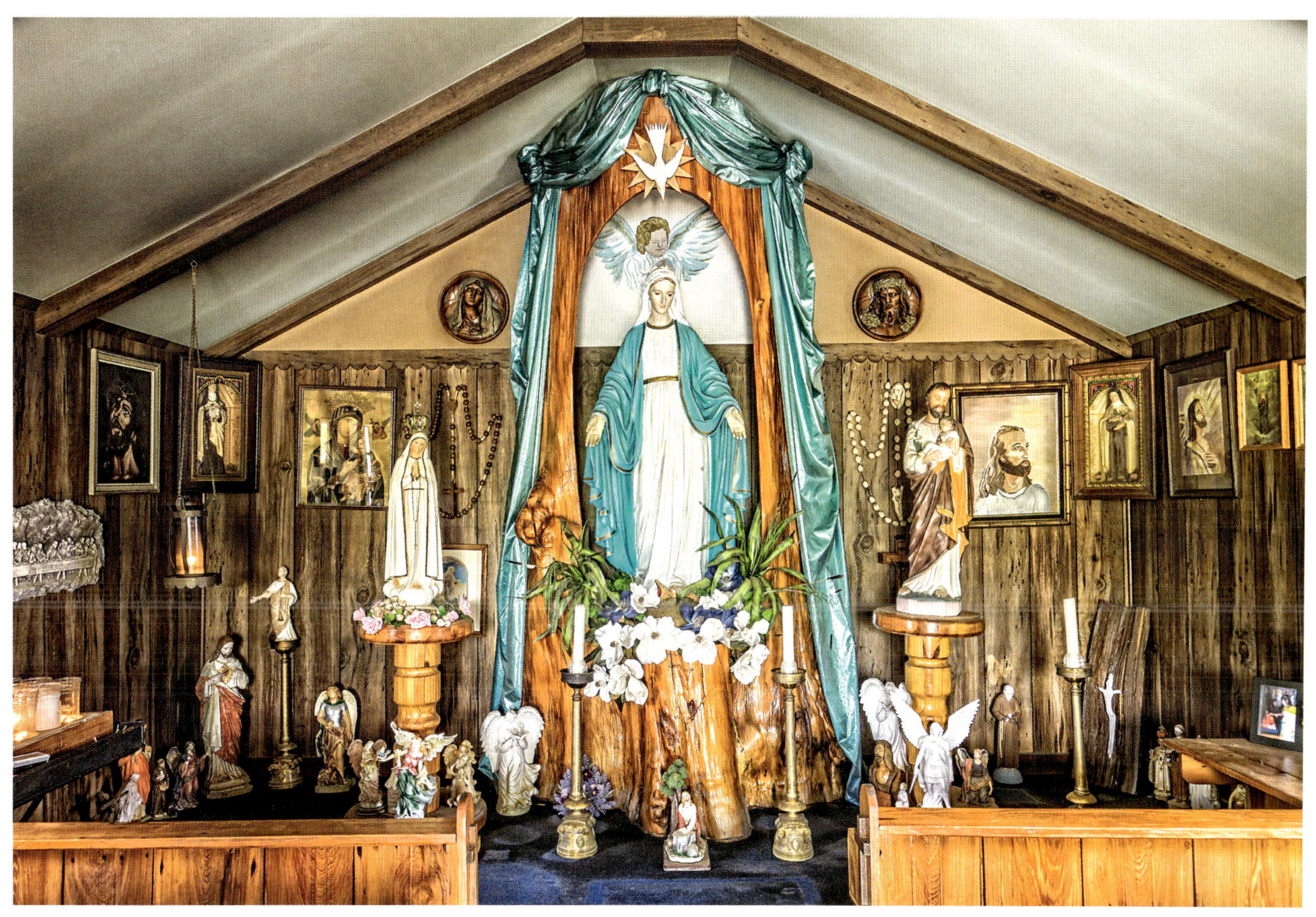

The altar of Our Lady of Blind River is carved right into a cypress stump protruding through the small chapel's floor. It's a wonderful place to spend time in quiet prayer and meditation.

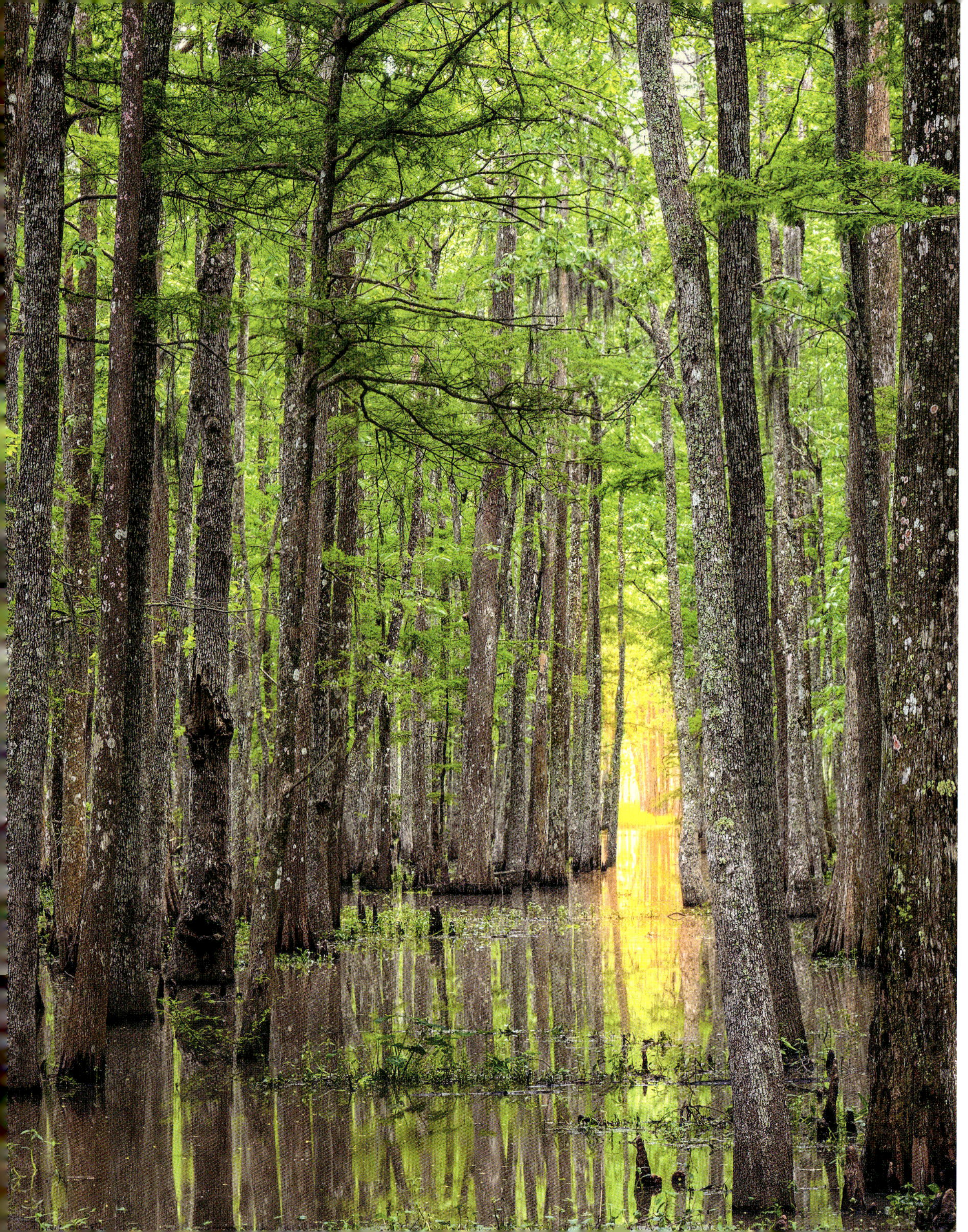

Some impacts to the swamp, however, are less positive. Timbering boomed in the swamps from the late 1800s through the 1920s, and many of the virgin forests were felled. Scars of that work remain. This trenasse or ditch through this stand of cypress trees in the Bayou Teche National Wildlife Refuge marks where logs were dragged from the swamps.

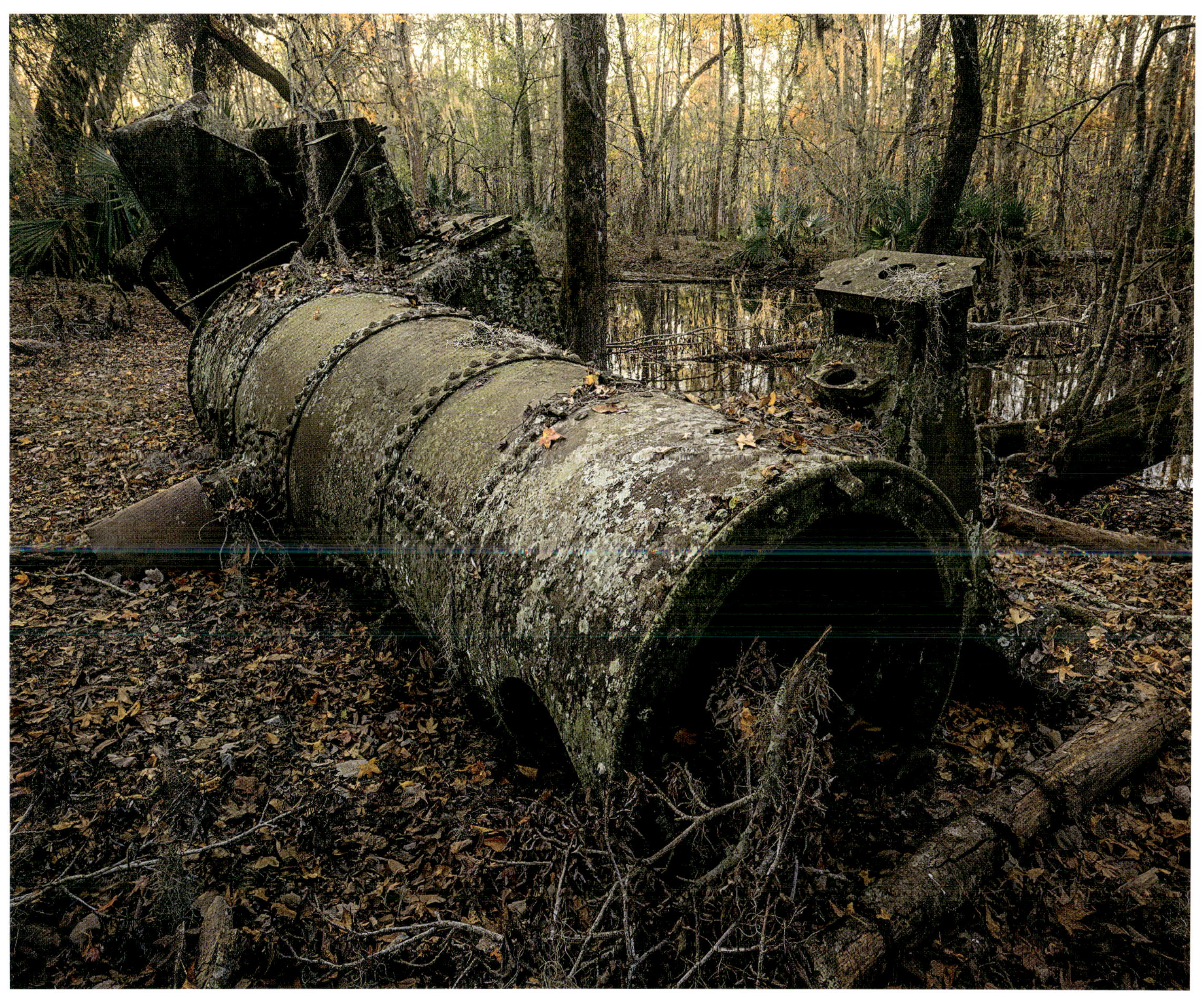

This old locomotive boiler lies on the edge of Lake Verret, evidence of the years when railroads were built into the cypress forests to efficiently transport cypress trees to mills.

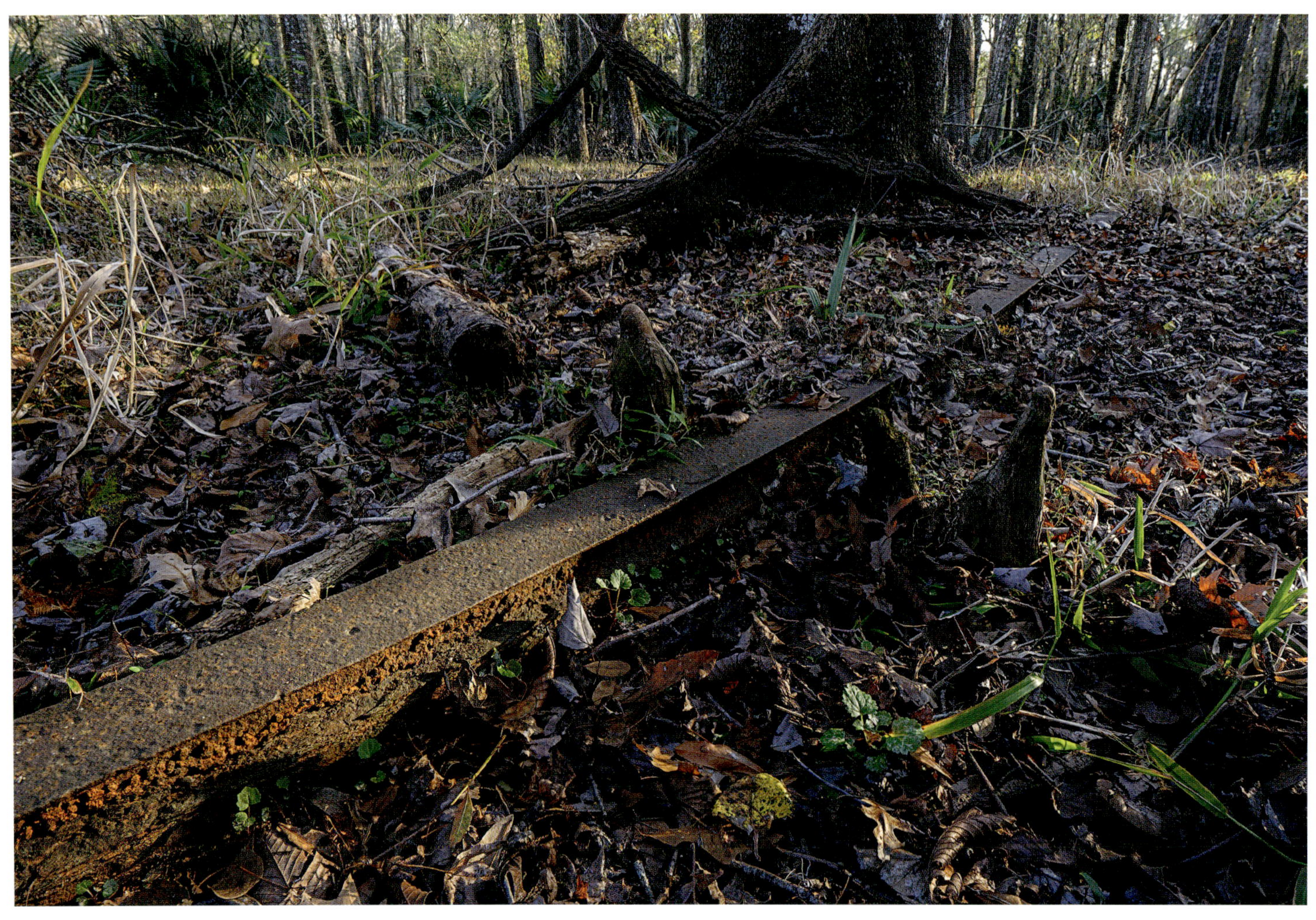

There are even rails remaining as evidence of the old days, when the rot- and insect-resistant cypress trees were cut to fuel the building boom of the early 1900s.

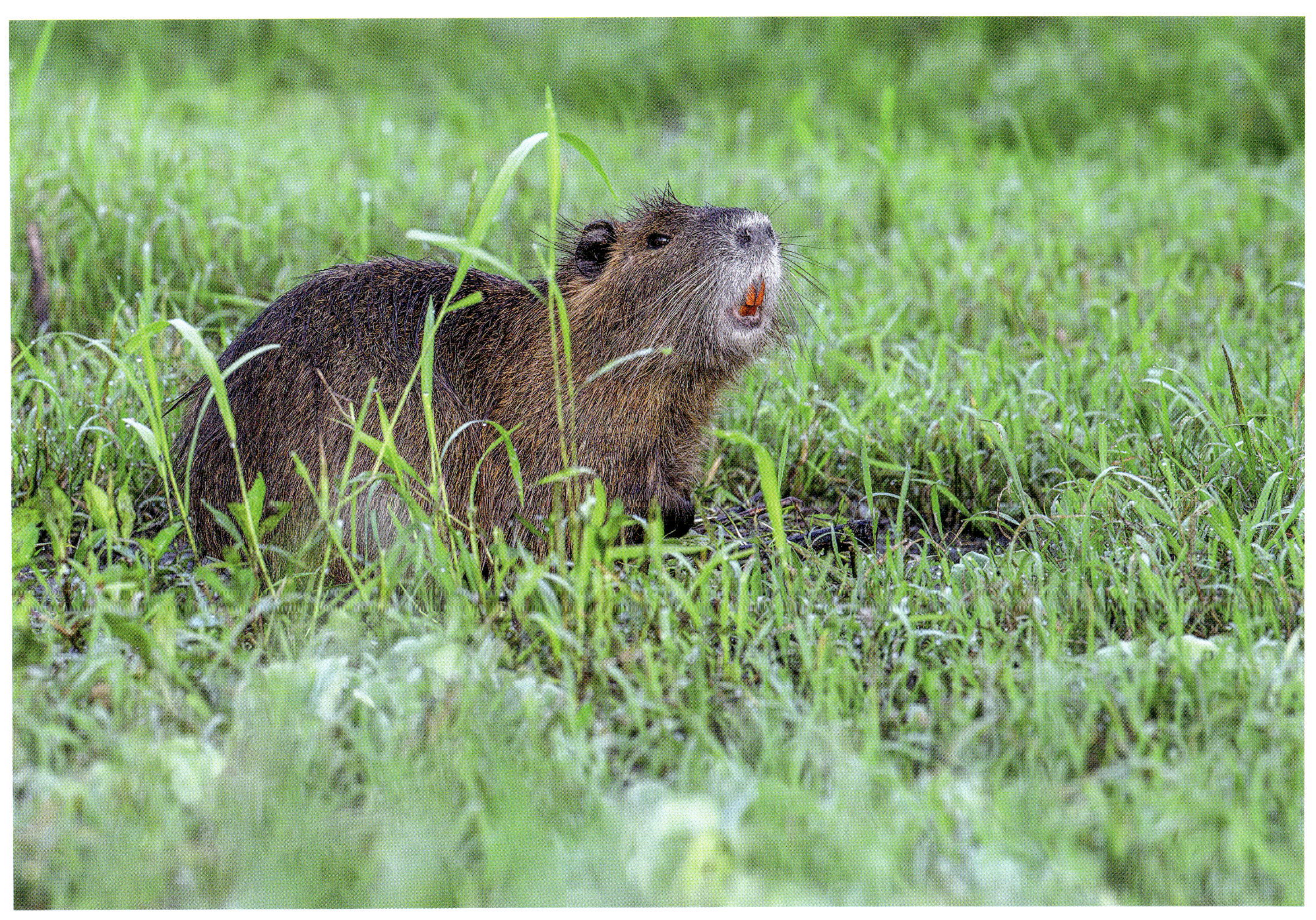

Animal introductions have been a plague. Nutria, imported into Louisiana in 1937 to begin a fur-farming operation on Avery Island, eventually escaped and adapted to the wetlands of Louisiana. Populations boomed and have caused great damage as they compete with native wildlife.

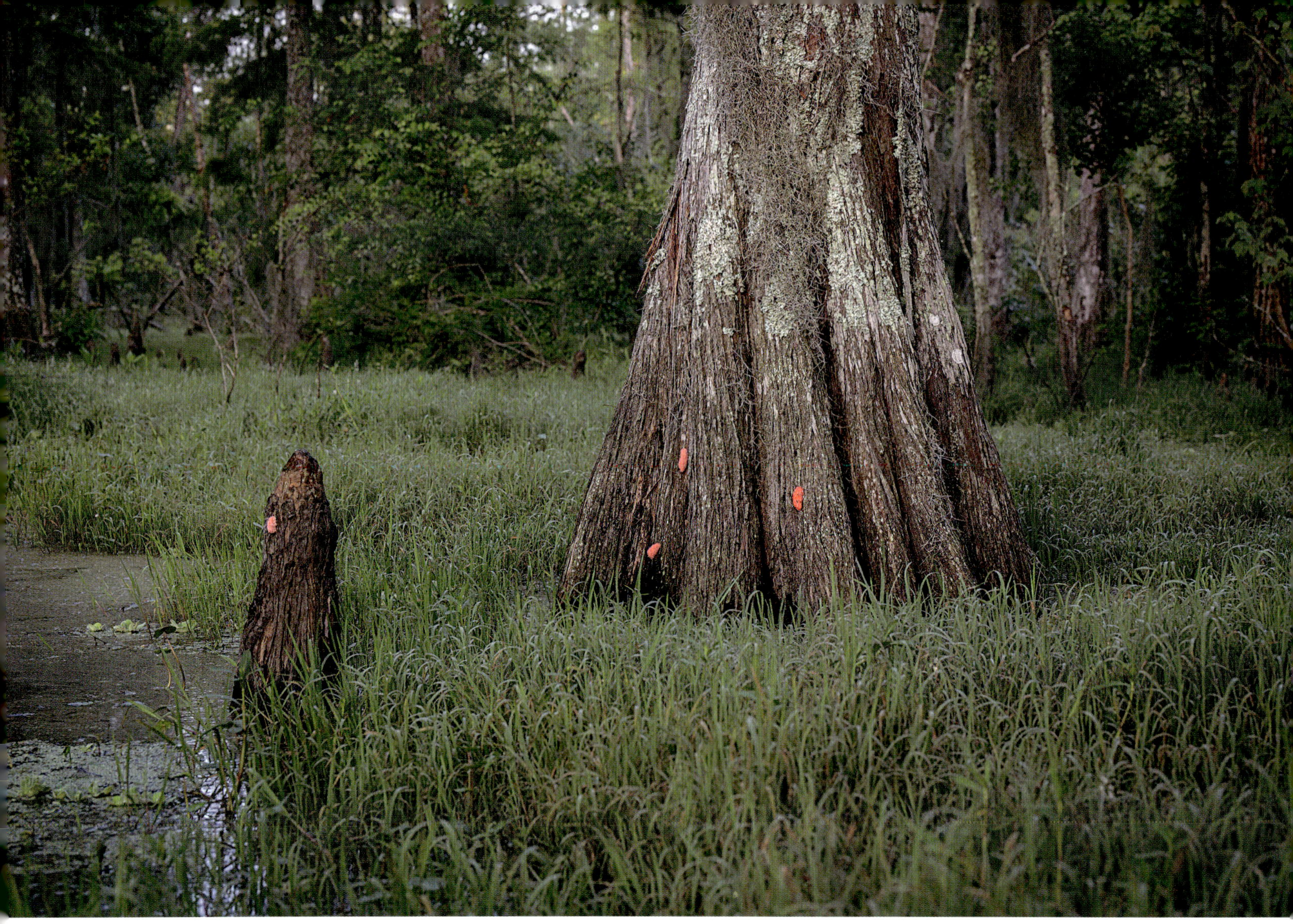

A more recent invader is the apple snail, introduced into Louisiana waters in 2006. Their bright-pink egg sacks can be seen throughout South Louisiana. The snail has spread quickly thanks to its prolific reproduction. Raccoons, limpkins, otters, and alligators are known to feed on them but lack the population needed to greatly reduce the snail's numbers.

Opposite page: Each apple snail egg sack contains up to 700 individual eggs, making control of the species very difficult. The lack of natural predators early in its introduction, along with the toxic nature of the eggs, allowed snail populations to explode.

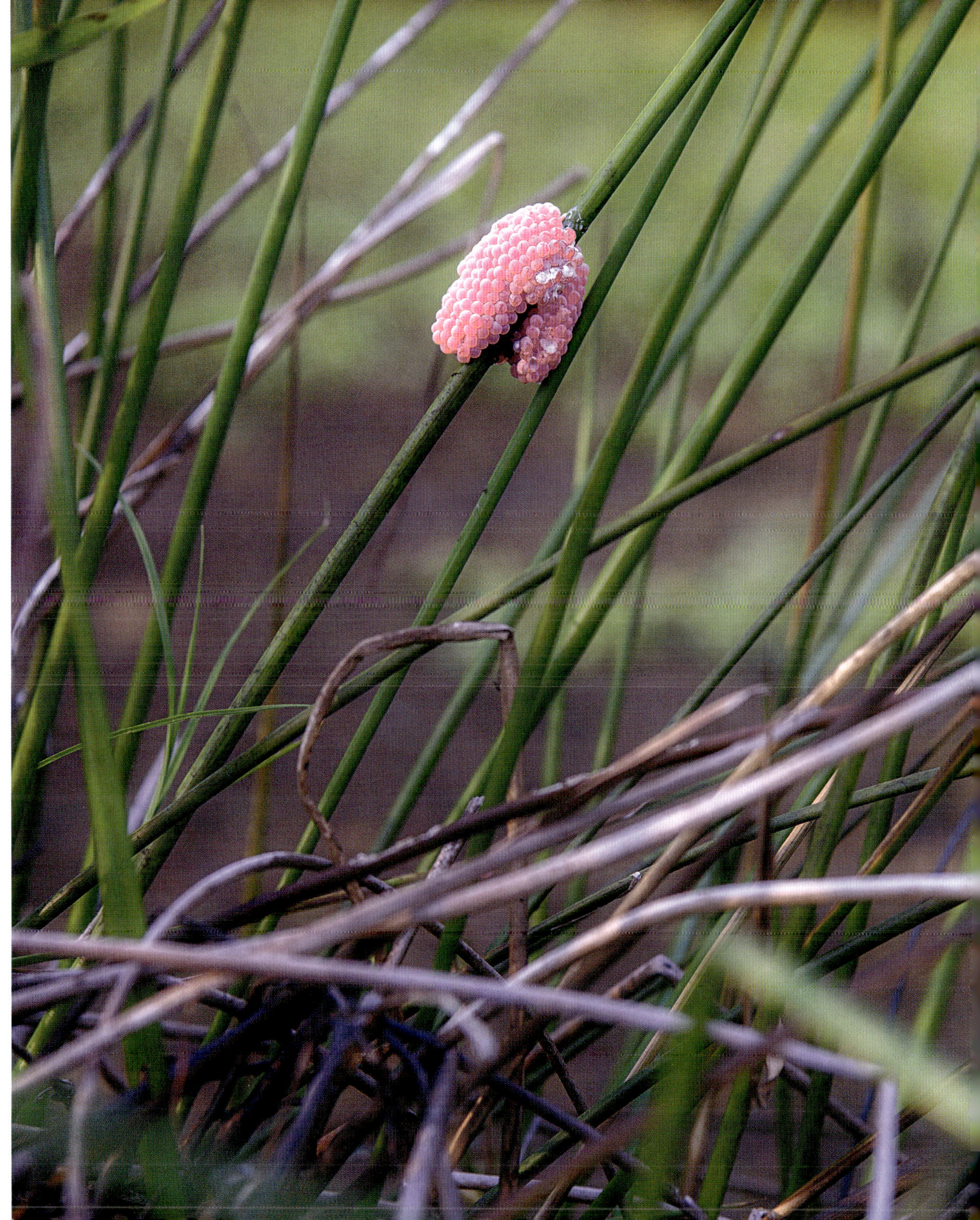

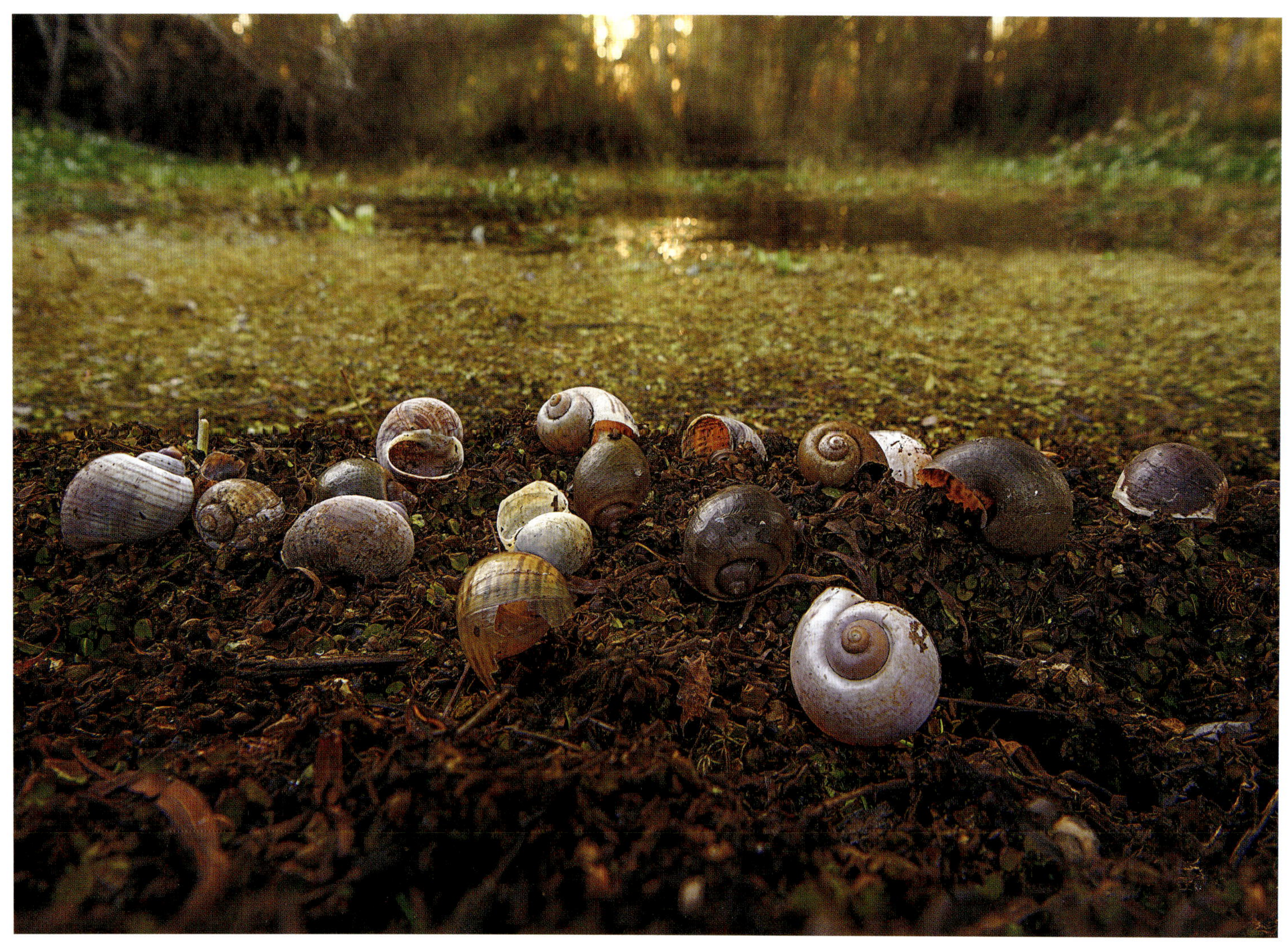

Animals do feed on apple snails, and the banks of many Louisiana bayous and lakes are littered with empty shells. The problem is that the snails reproduce so fast that predation can't control the invasive species. One upside is the arrival of limpkins from Florida, which have a voracious appetite for these large snails.

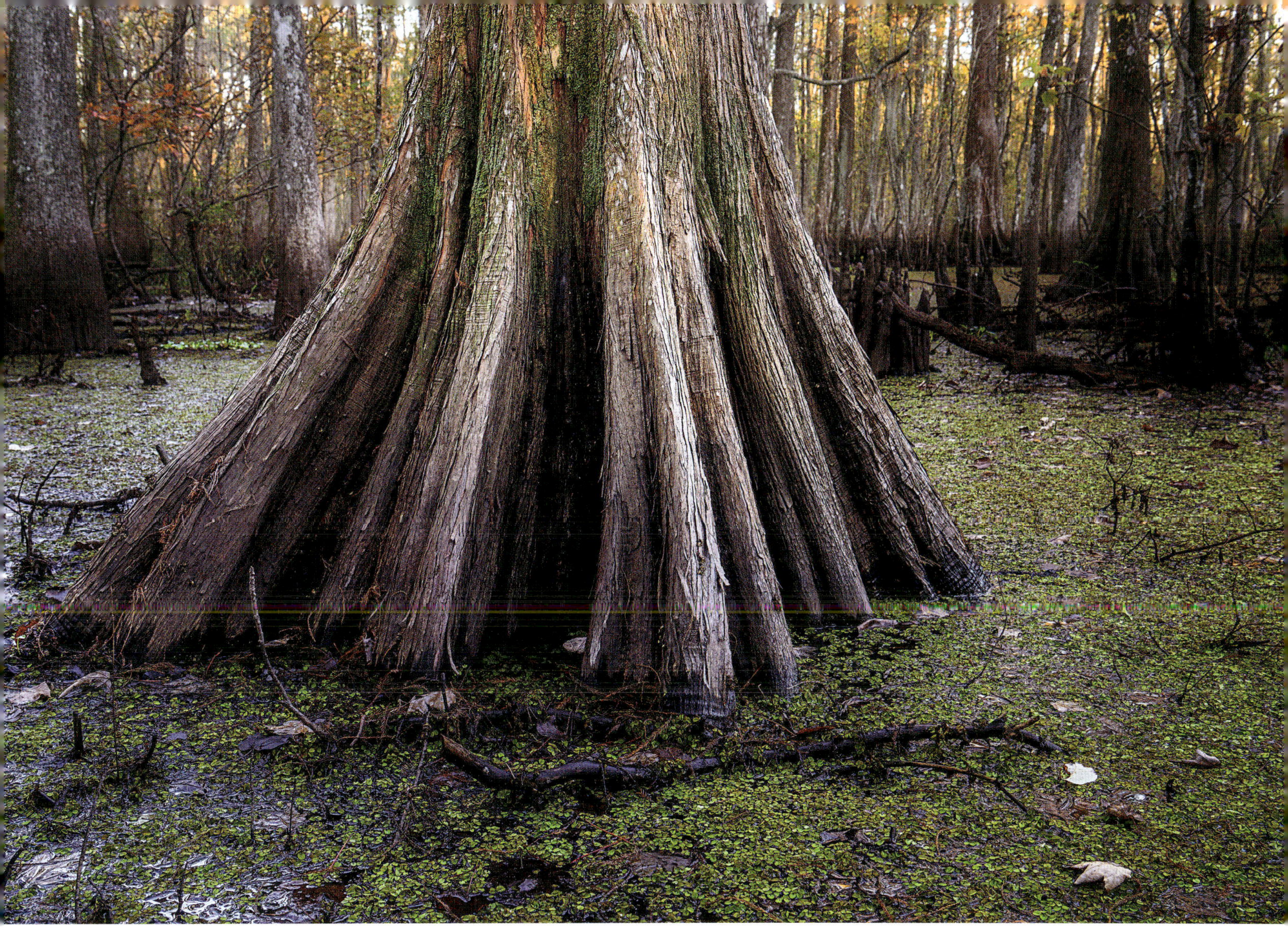

Giant salvinia is another relatively recent invasive species. The fast-growing fern first appeared in Louisiana in the mid-1990s but has since spread throughout the state.

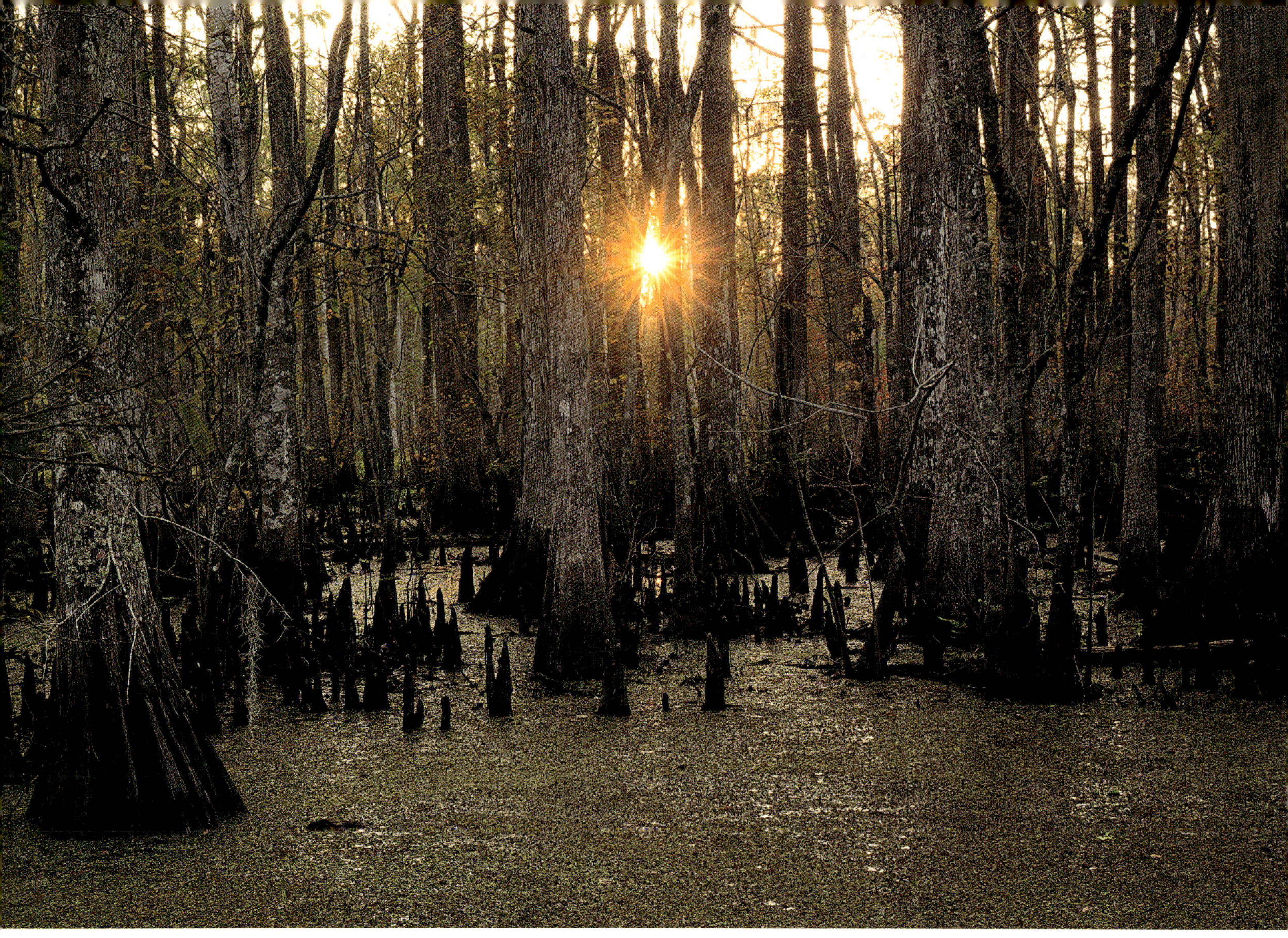

Giant salvinia, native to Brazil, blankets the waters throughout Louisiana's swamps. Mats can double in size every seven to ten days, according to the US Department of Agriculture. These mats reduce access to the swamps and shade out native vegetation.

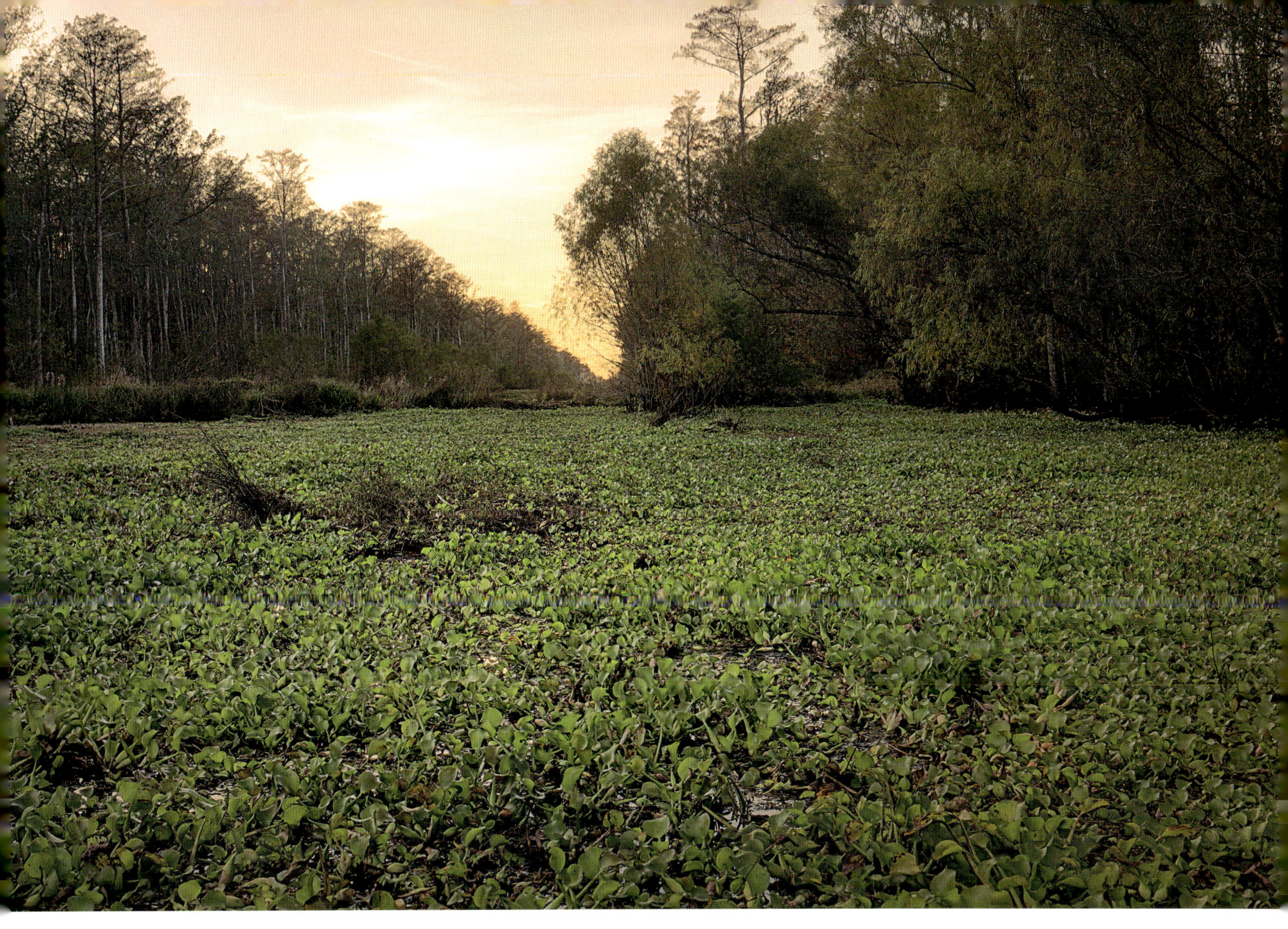

Water hyacinth is another incredibly prolific invasive plant that has caused problems throughout Louisiana. The floating plant, introduced from South America, forms dense mats that can block access to large areas.

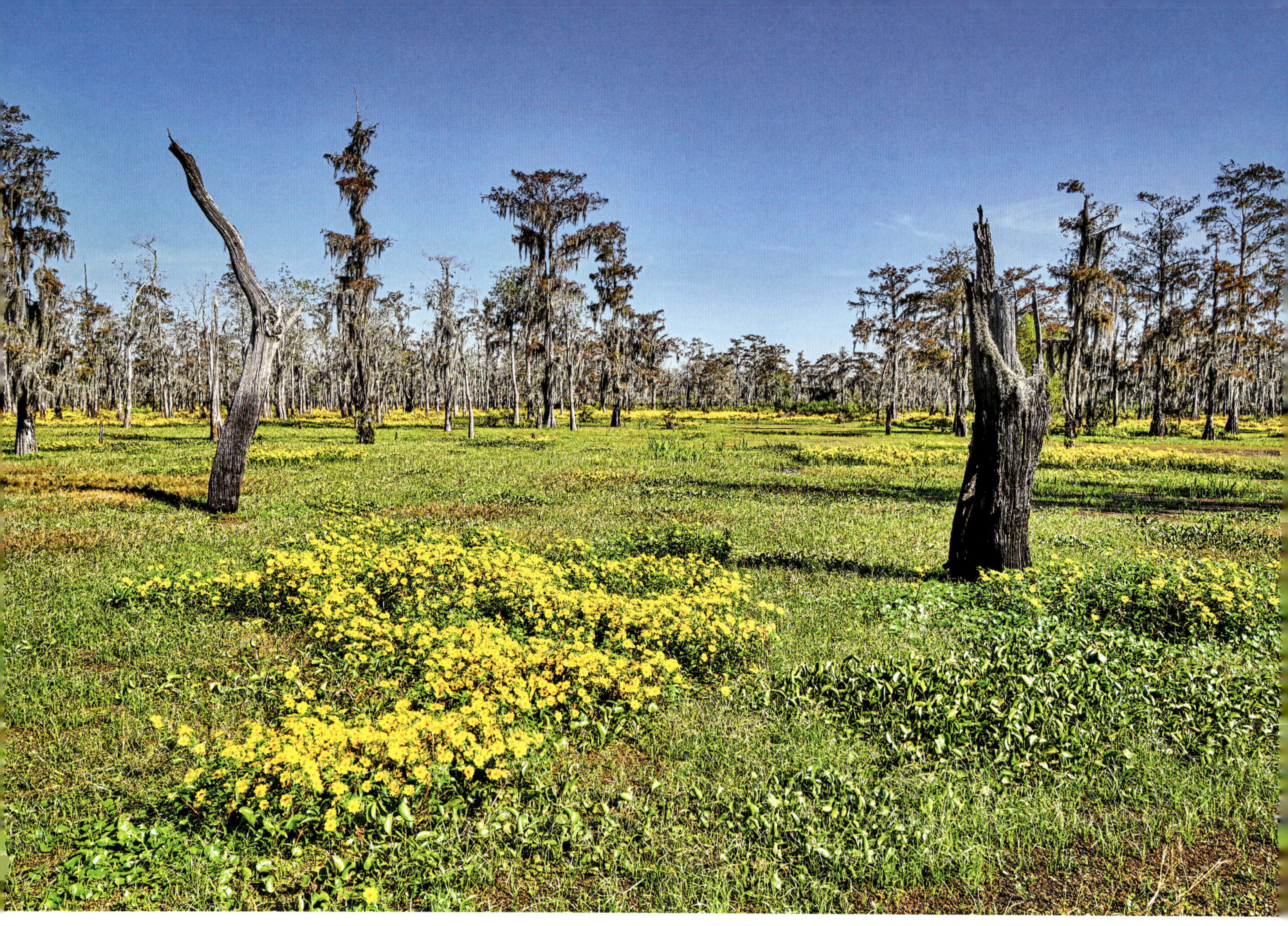

Here, native water primrose (with yellow flowers) grows with water hyacinths, giant salvinia, and alligator weed to cover a large area in the Atchafalaya Basin. The vegetation completely blocks access to this swamp and shades out submerged plants.

The gorgeous Henderson Swamp is one area that has in the past been taken over by invasive vegetation such as hydrilla and giant salvinia. The good news is that this swamp's water levels can be manipulated by water control structures, so managers now conduct annual drawdowns to control the spread of invasive species, helping to revitalize the food chain.

Drawdowns reveal what normally lies below feet of water, illustrating the dynamic nature of swamps. Trees grow, die, and fall to create spawning habitats for fish. These downed trees provide cover and nursery areas for fish and other aquatic species once water levels return to normal. Walking those dried-out flats during the drawdown provides a unique view of the swamp.

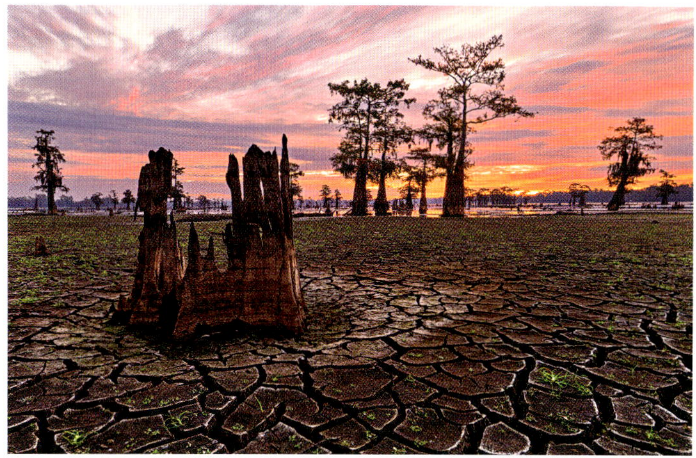

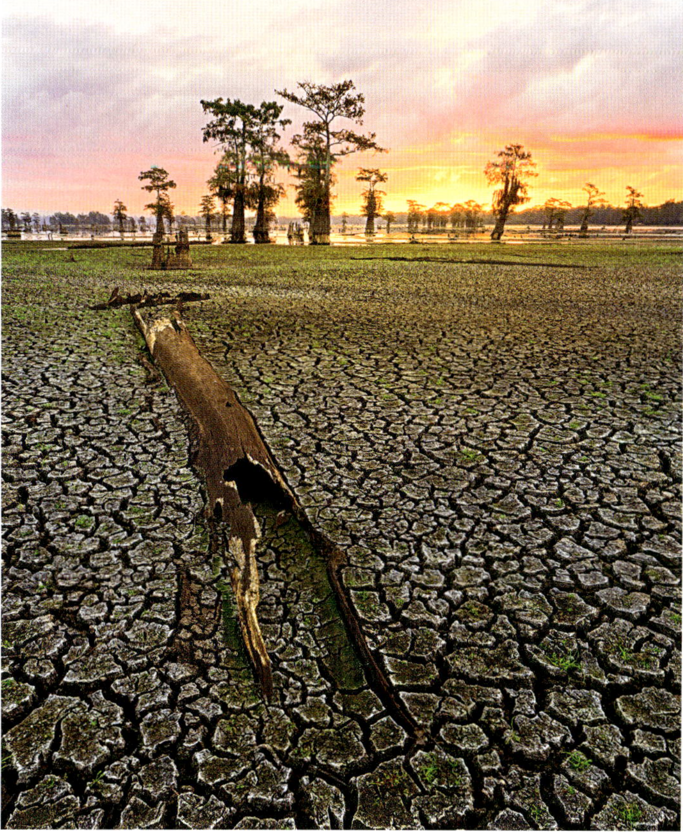

CHAPTER FIVE

AUTUMN

South Louisiana isn't known for having real seasons. Not as most parts of the country know them. After all, we live right on the Gulf Coast and are most likely to wear shorts for Christmas. Sure, there are cold fronts that dip the temperatures, but the heat and humidity in this tropical region are never really defeated.

That doesn't mean we don't enjoy some of the most spectacular late-year colors in the South, however. You just have to launch a boat and head into the swamps for the Deep South's most surprising cypress fashion show.

The late fall is my favorite season to be in the swamps. Usually by the end of October, the lush greens of the cypress trees begin fading, and touches of rust begin to appear here and there as Halloween comes and goes.

By Thanksgiving, the color change picks up speed. There remains a lot of greenery, however, and much of the autumn color is a bit muted.

And then some switch flips and, as December ushers in winter, the swamp explodes in vivid colors. Cypress trees blaze, as foliage turns gorgeous tones ranging from bright rust to orange to deep gold to flashy red. Those wonderful colors contrast with the veils of gray Spanish moss hanging in curlicued masses.

Temperatures moderate and morning fog frequently throws its thick blanket across these watery environs, adding drama and mood to the colorful scenes. It's a time of incredible beauty and amazing contrasts.

By mid-December it's all over. Once-gorgeous leaves turn brown and begin dropping, the swamps settle in for what we call winter, and the trees slumber until spring.

But the autumn memories are glorious.

Opposite page: I was paddling through the Lake Verret swamps one November when the reddish tint of this cypress foliage pushing through the thick veil of moss caught my attention. The contrast was just wonderful.

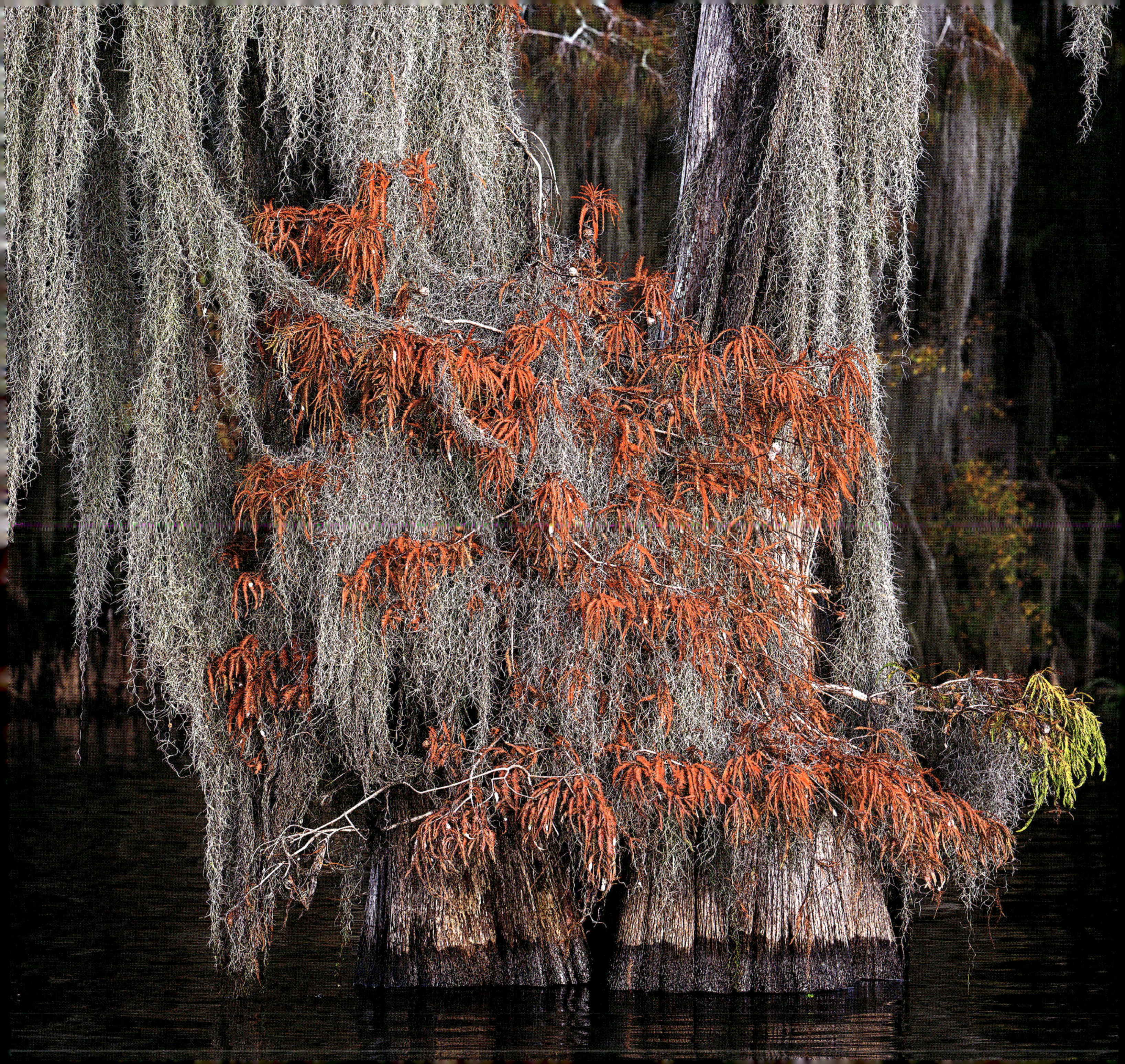

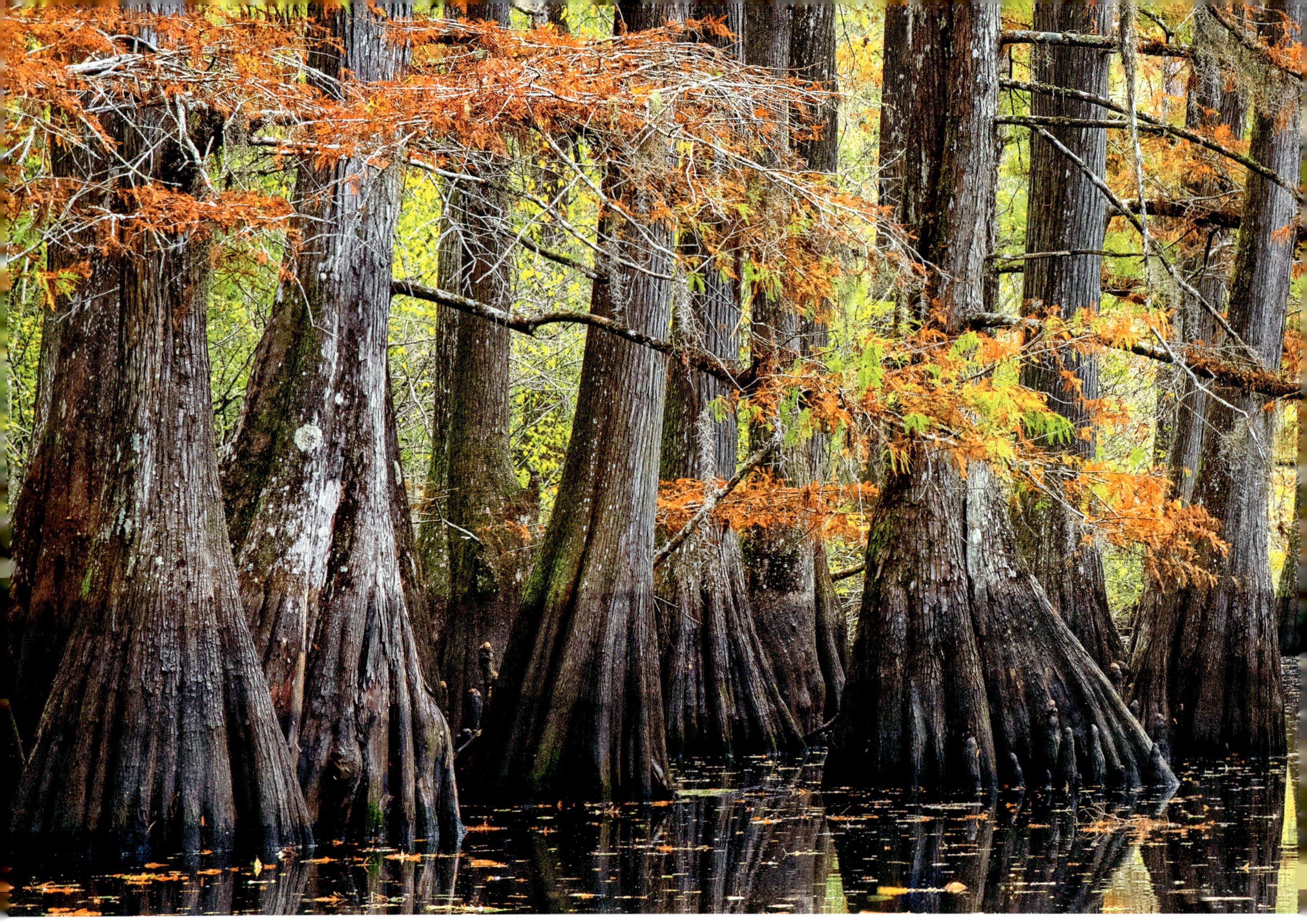

South Louisiana's swamps provide surprising color in late autumn, with cypress trees taking on amazing hues of orange and gold weeks after the color change in the rest of the country remains but a memory.

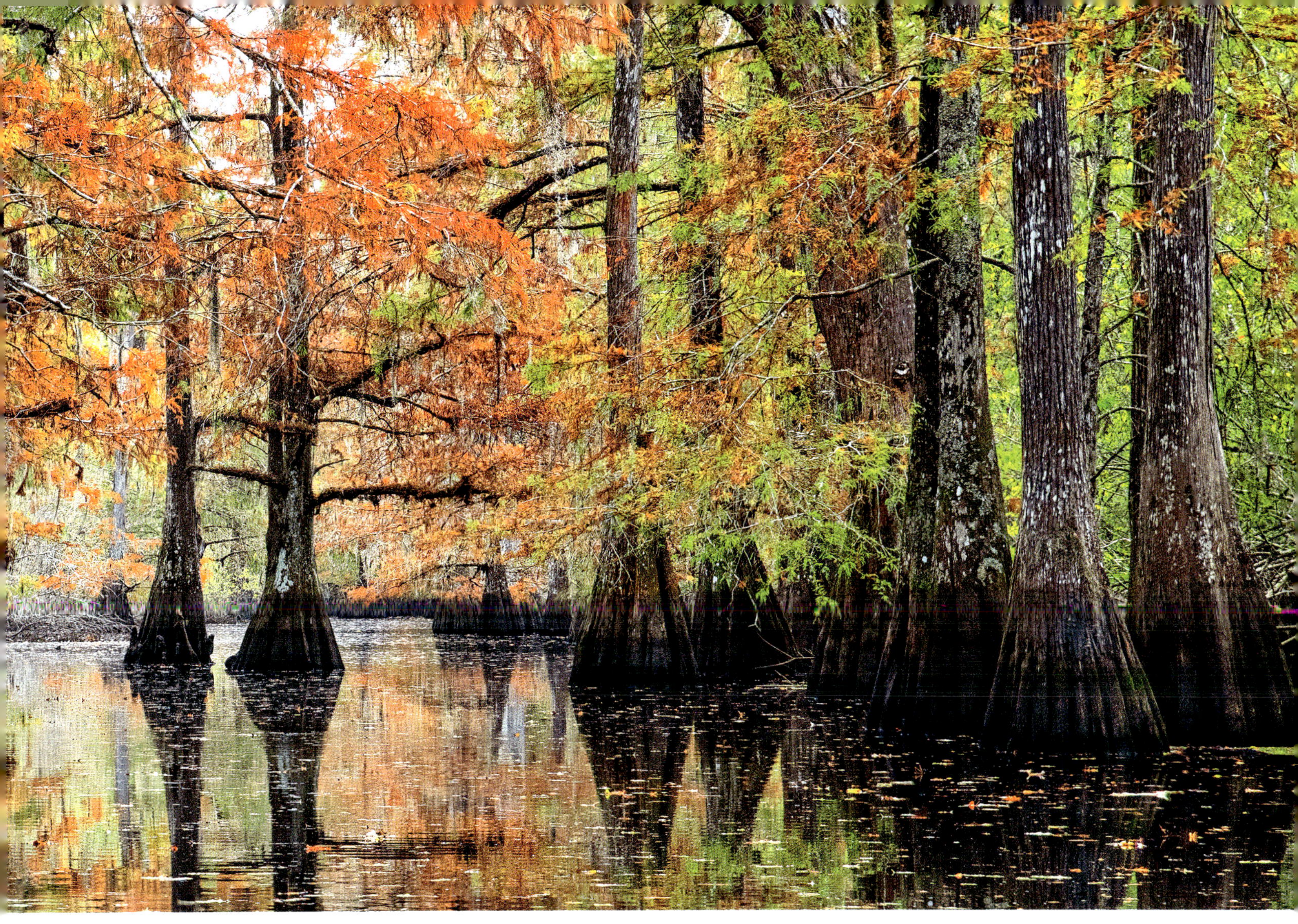

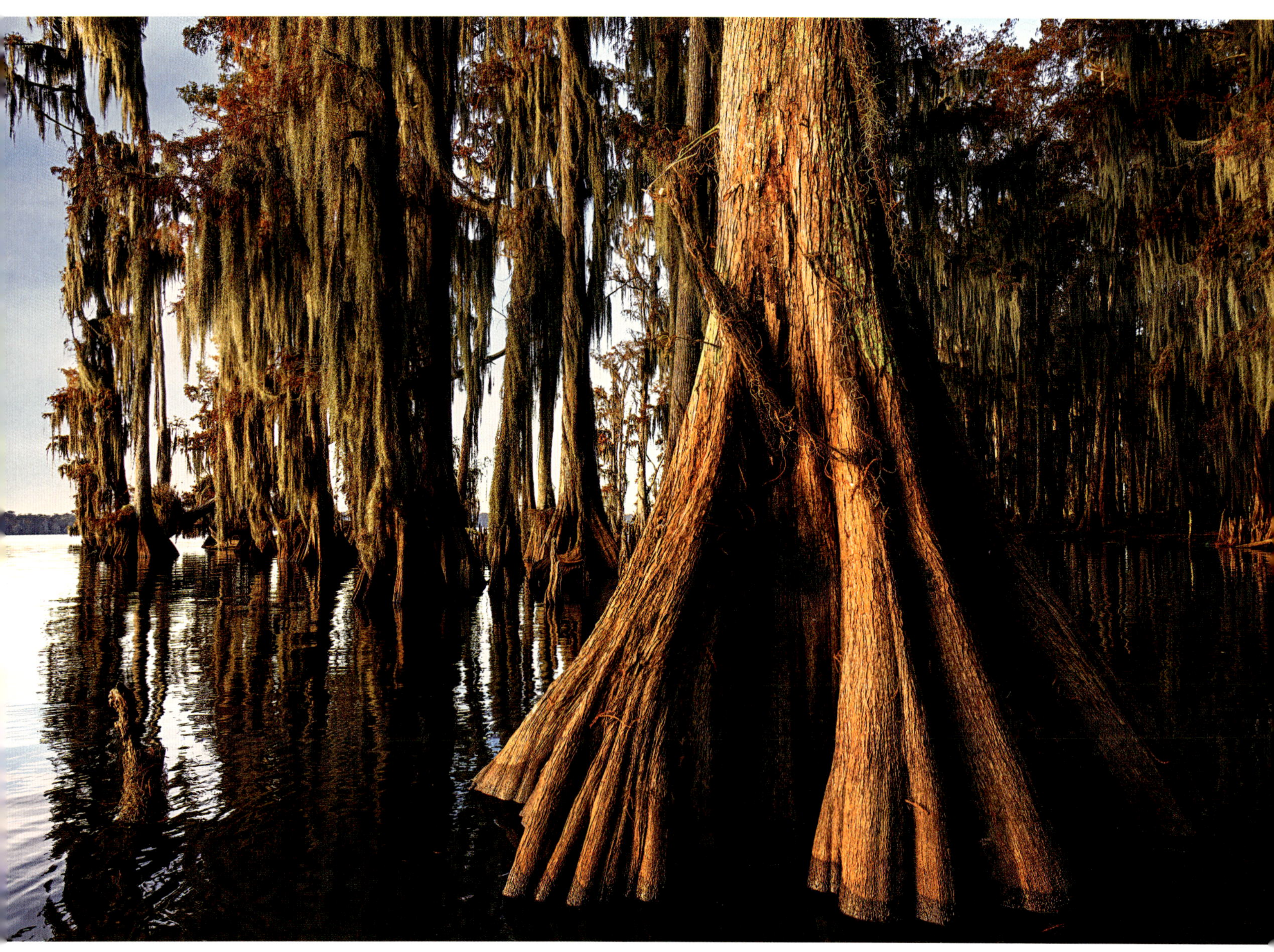

Morning's first light is one of the best times to enjoy the colors of fall, when the rust-colored leaves glow and complement the colors of the cypress trees.

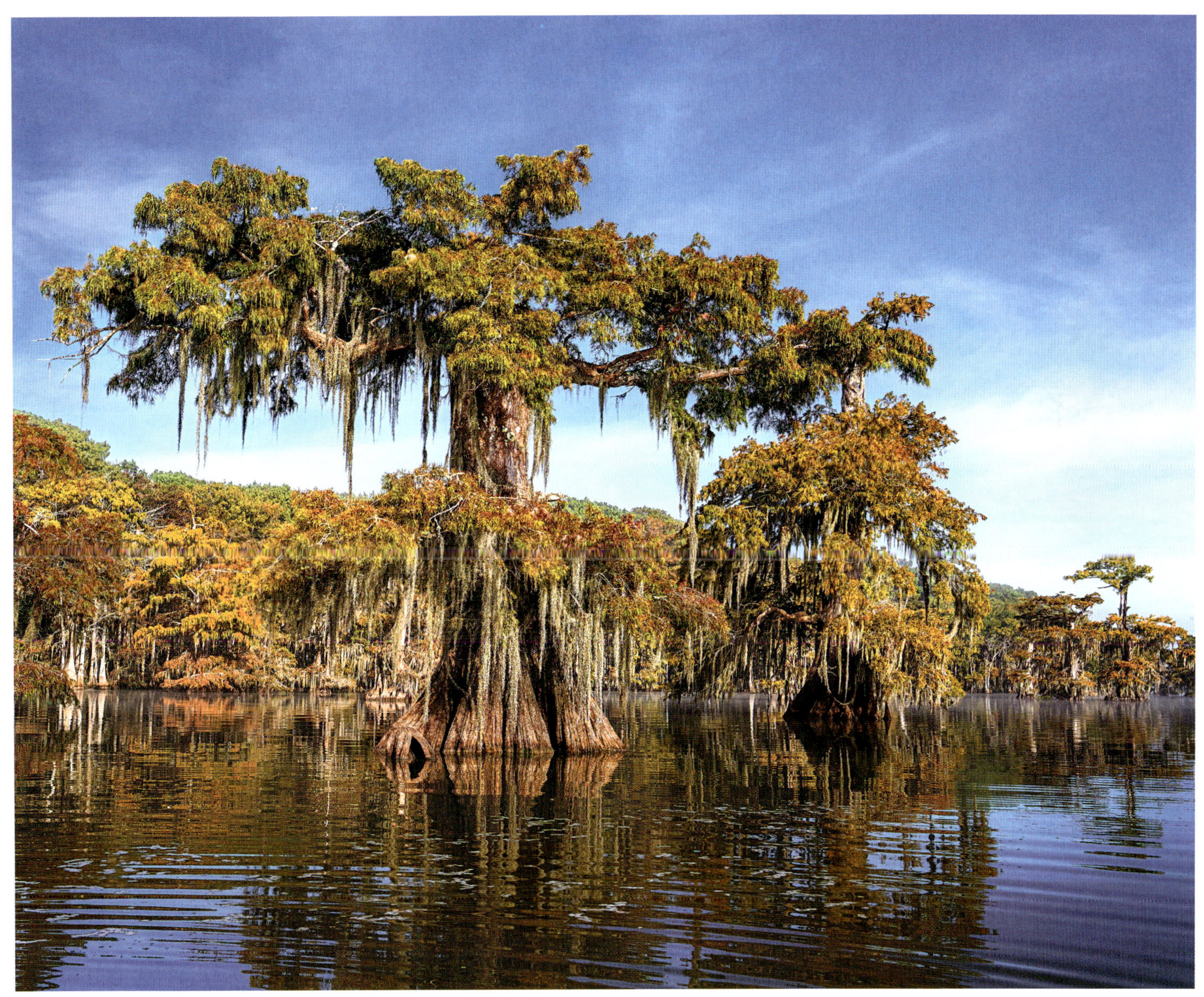

The autumn show is just getting started in the South Louisiana swamps when fall colors are fading in the other parts of the United States. By late October, touches of color begin showing up in places like the amazing Lake Dauterive, but that's just a hint that the real show is on its way.

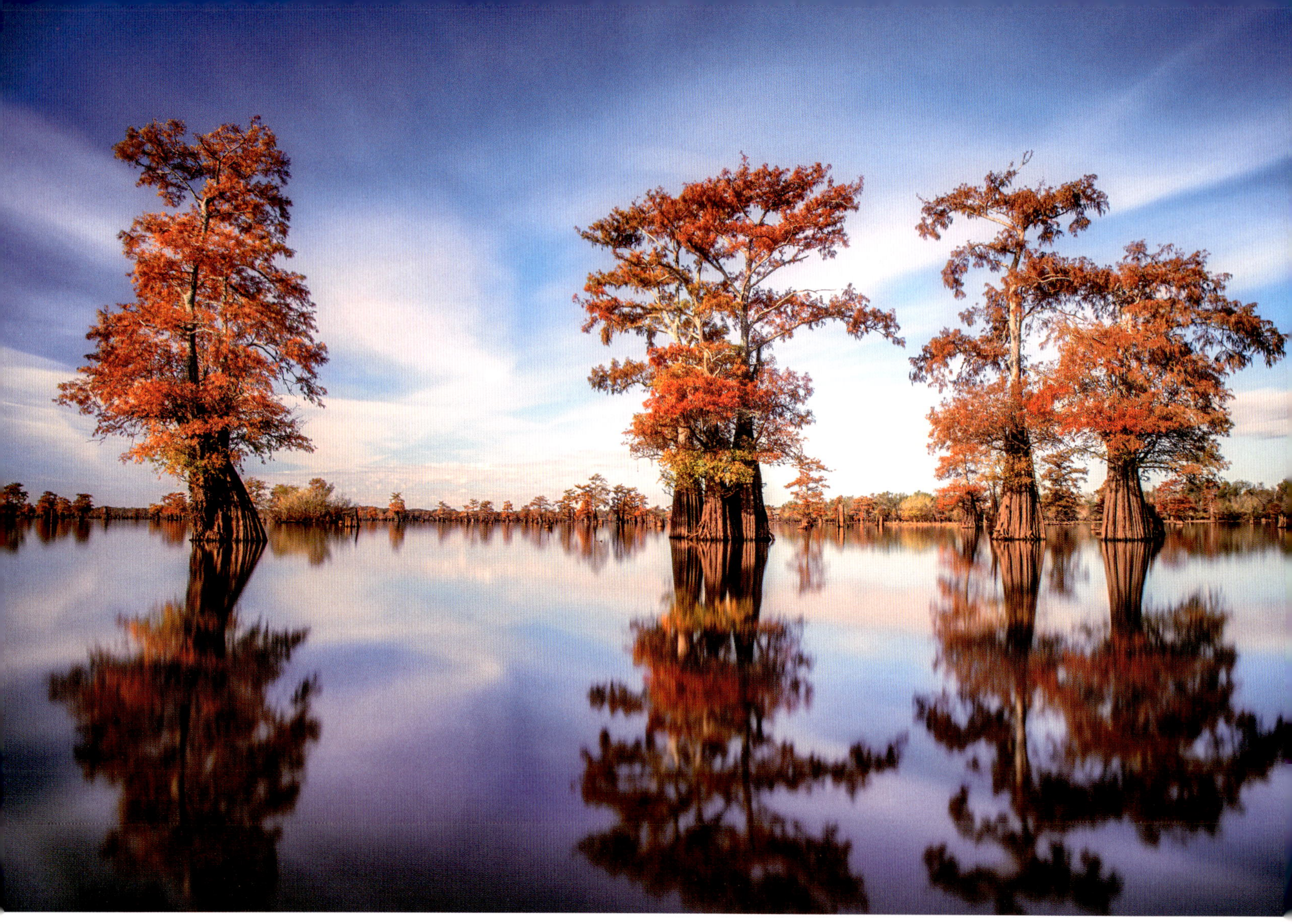

This was another wonderfully calm day during the fall, when I slowed my shutter speed with a neutral-density filter to flatten the water and allow the moving clouds above to create wonderful visual lines that seem to draw the eye into the reddish line of cypress trees.

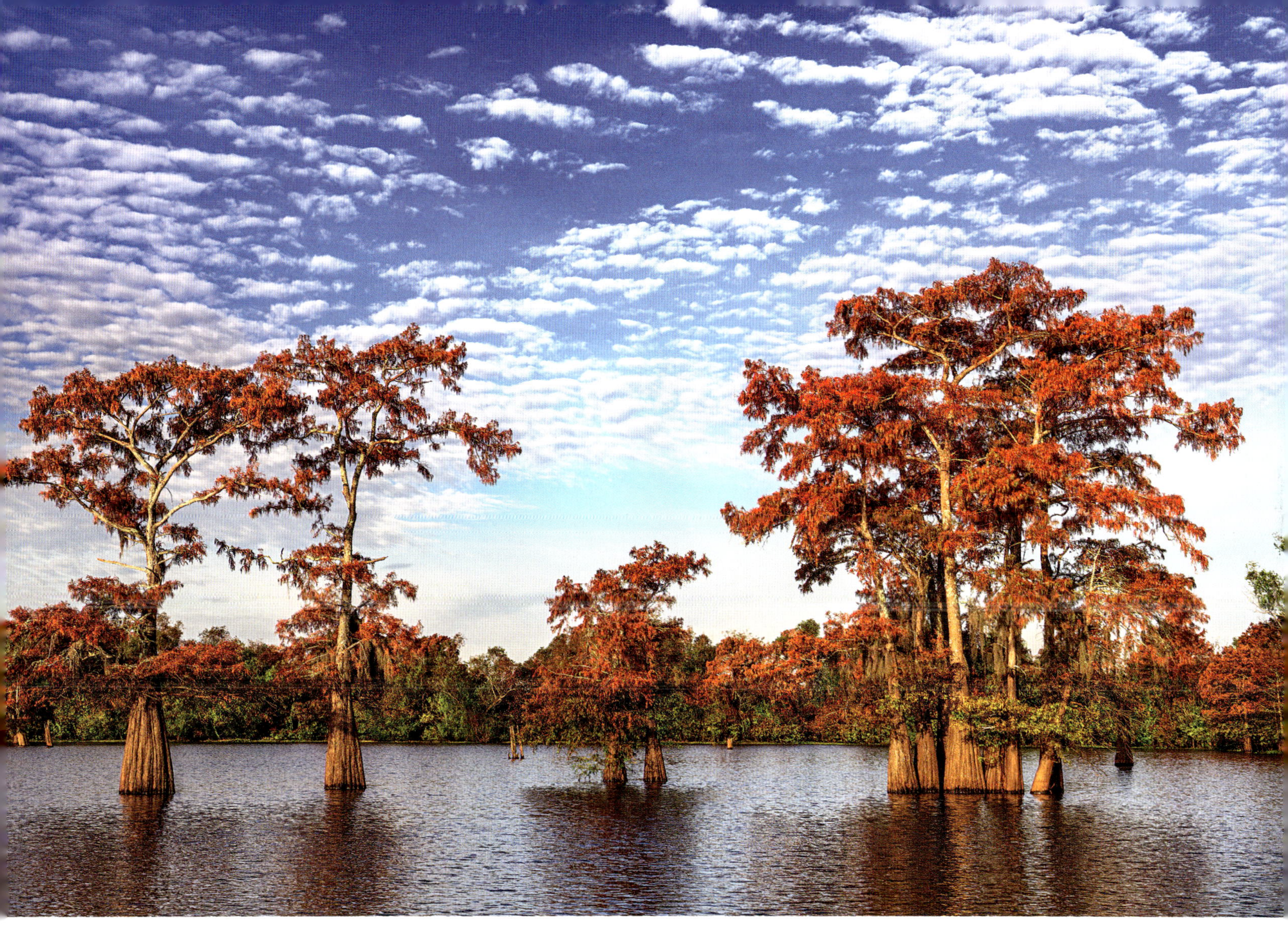

Blue skies are such a complement to the rusty colors of cypress trees during South Louisiana's late fall / early winter color change. Add some nice, white clouds and the swamps really pop.

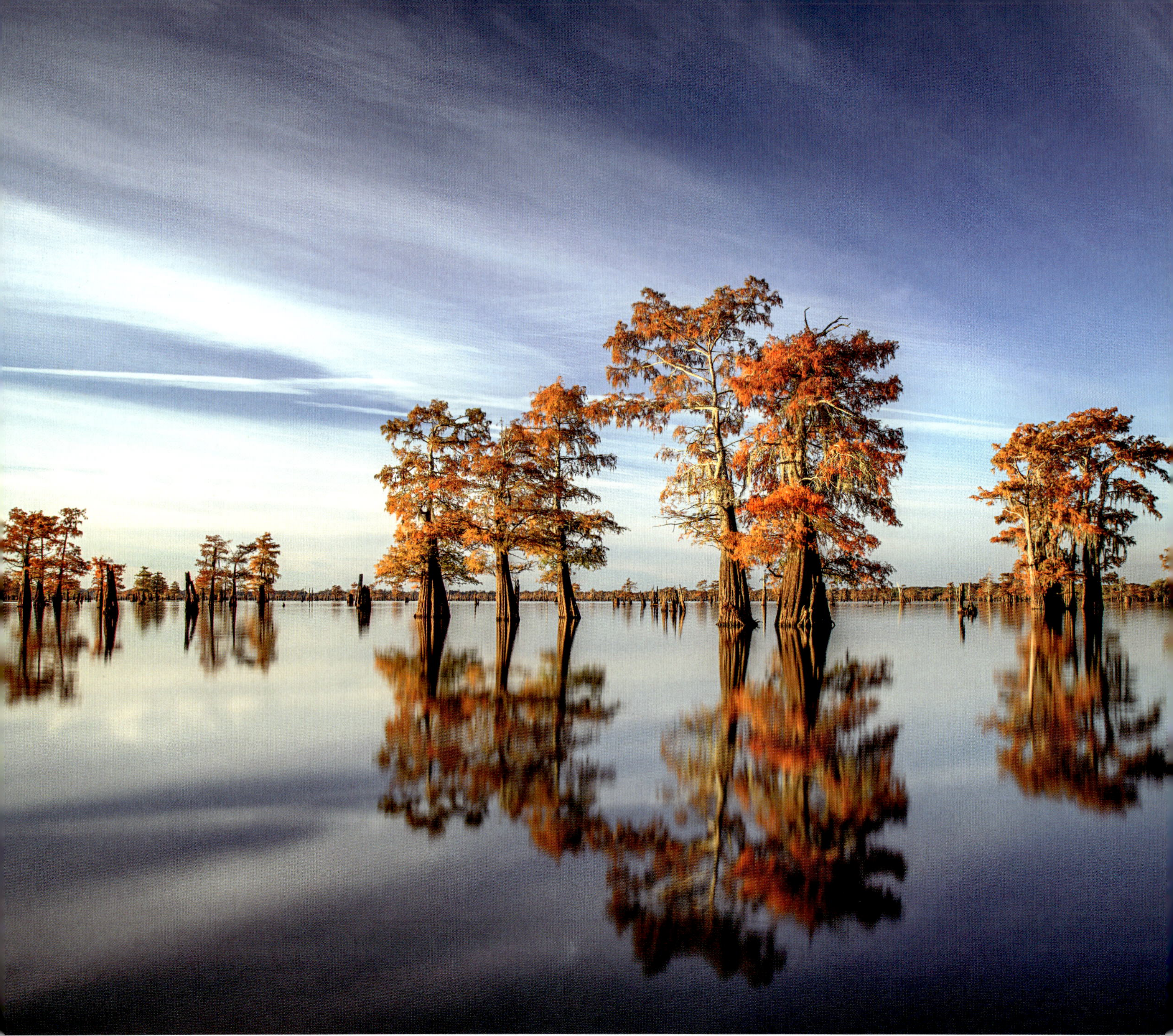

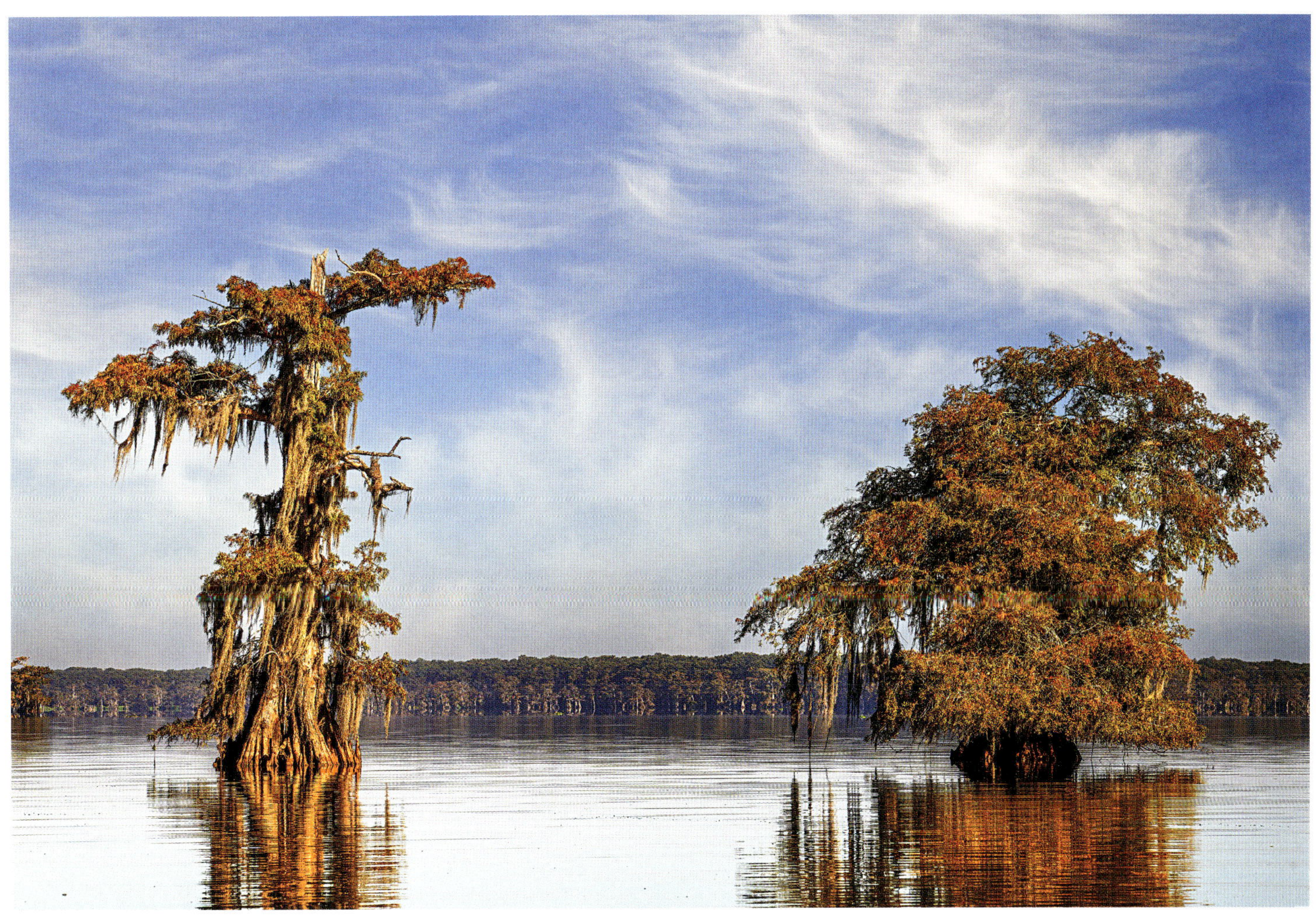

Opposite page: This day still sits in my memory because there wasn't a breath of wind blowing. It allowed me to slow my shutter speed by using a neutral-density filter to enhance the reflective beauty of the dark Henderson Swamp waters. The technique also produced the impression of movement in the clouds above.

These two trees on the edge of Lake Dauterive show signs of the coming color change, sporting both the faded greens of early fall and the first oranges of November.

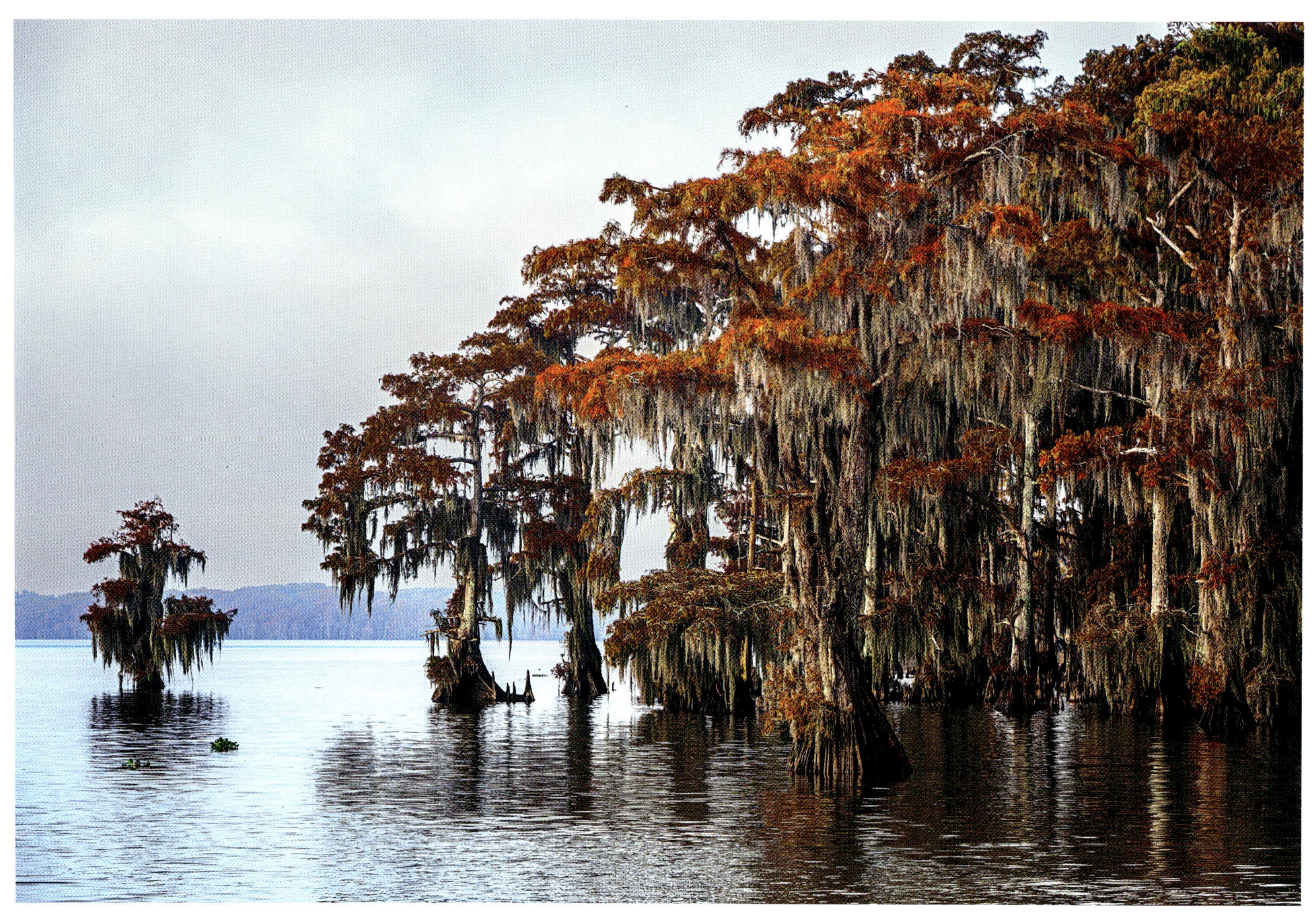

Sunlight breaks through clouds to brighten the oranges and reds of one of the cypress trees standing near a point on Lake Palourde.

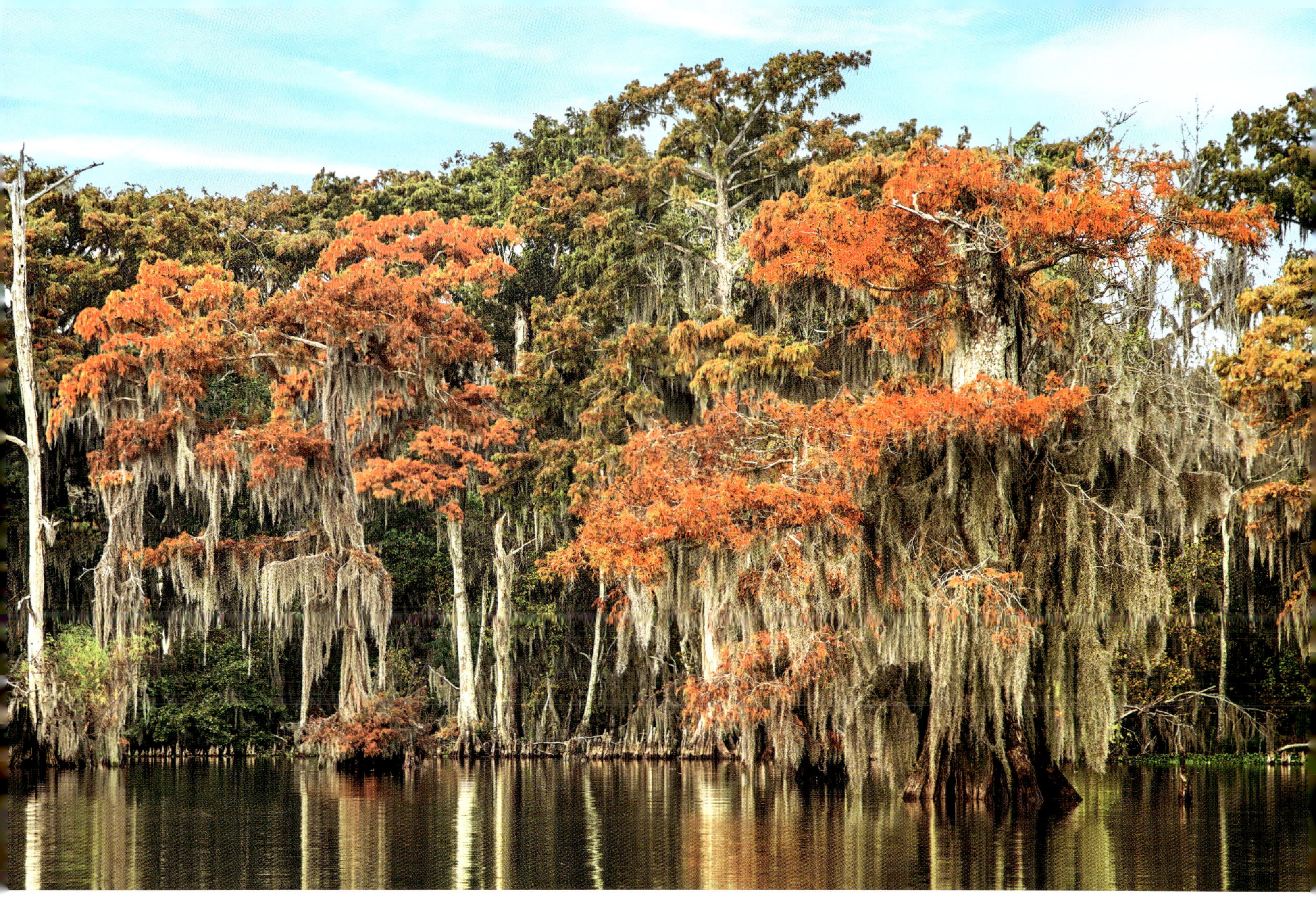

Not all the trees turn at the same time. Seeing those beautiful oranges against the green of trees in the background heightens the beauty of the season.

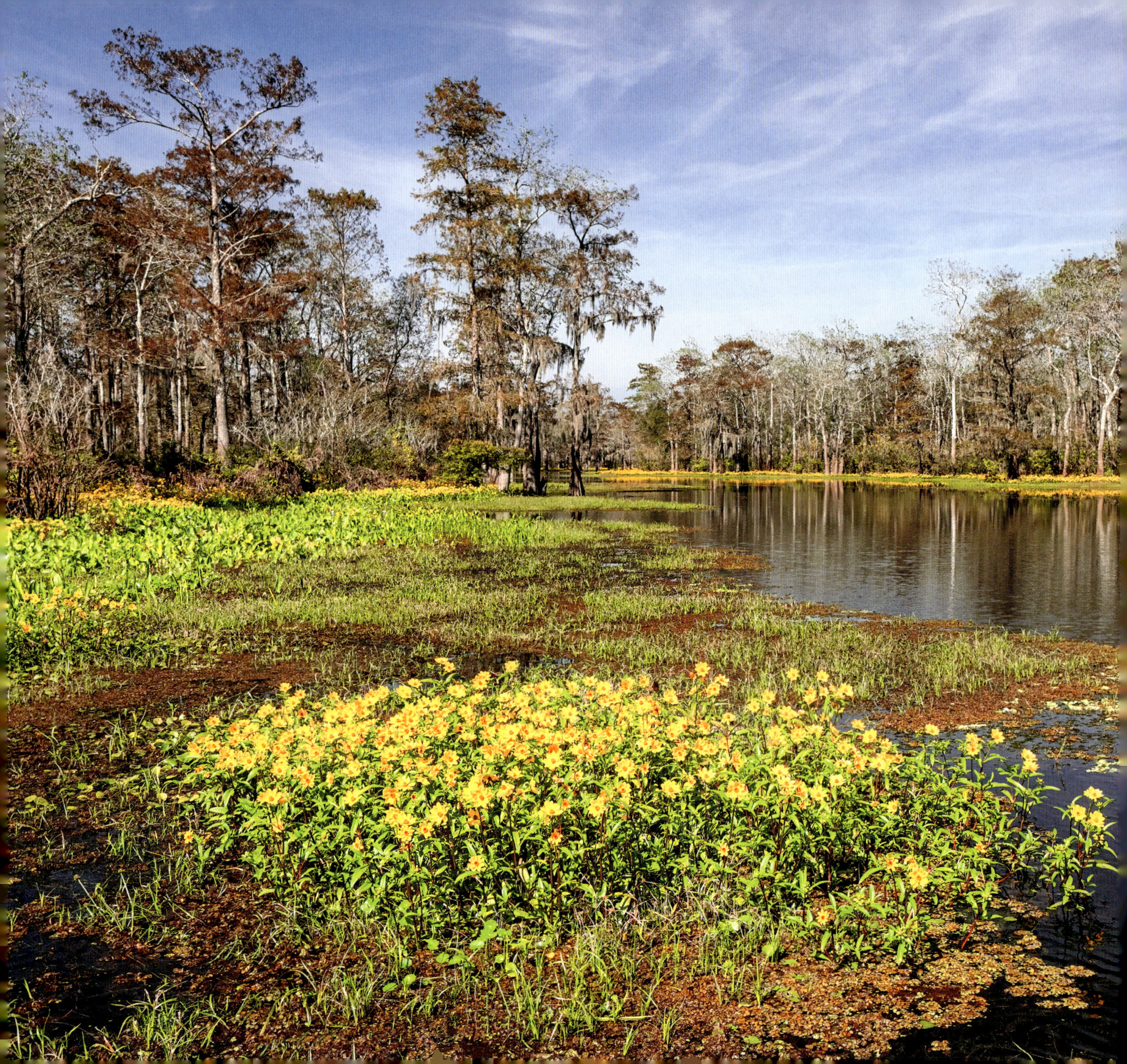

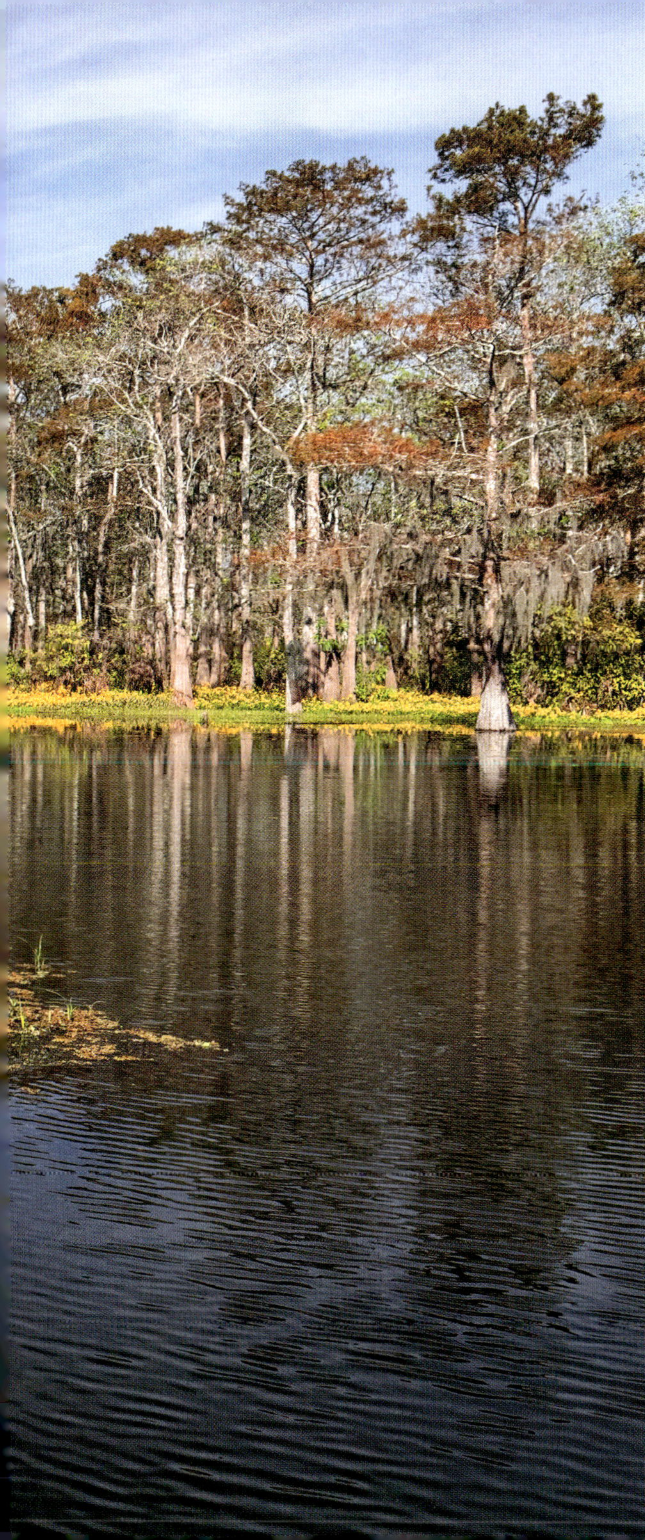

Fall in South Louisiana is all about contrasts, with plenty of lush green attesting to the moderate temperatures of the region. This bayou is lined with green water hyacinths and blooming water primrose, while cypress trees sport the rust-colored leaves of autumn.

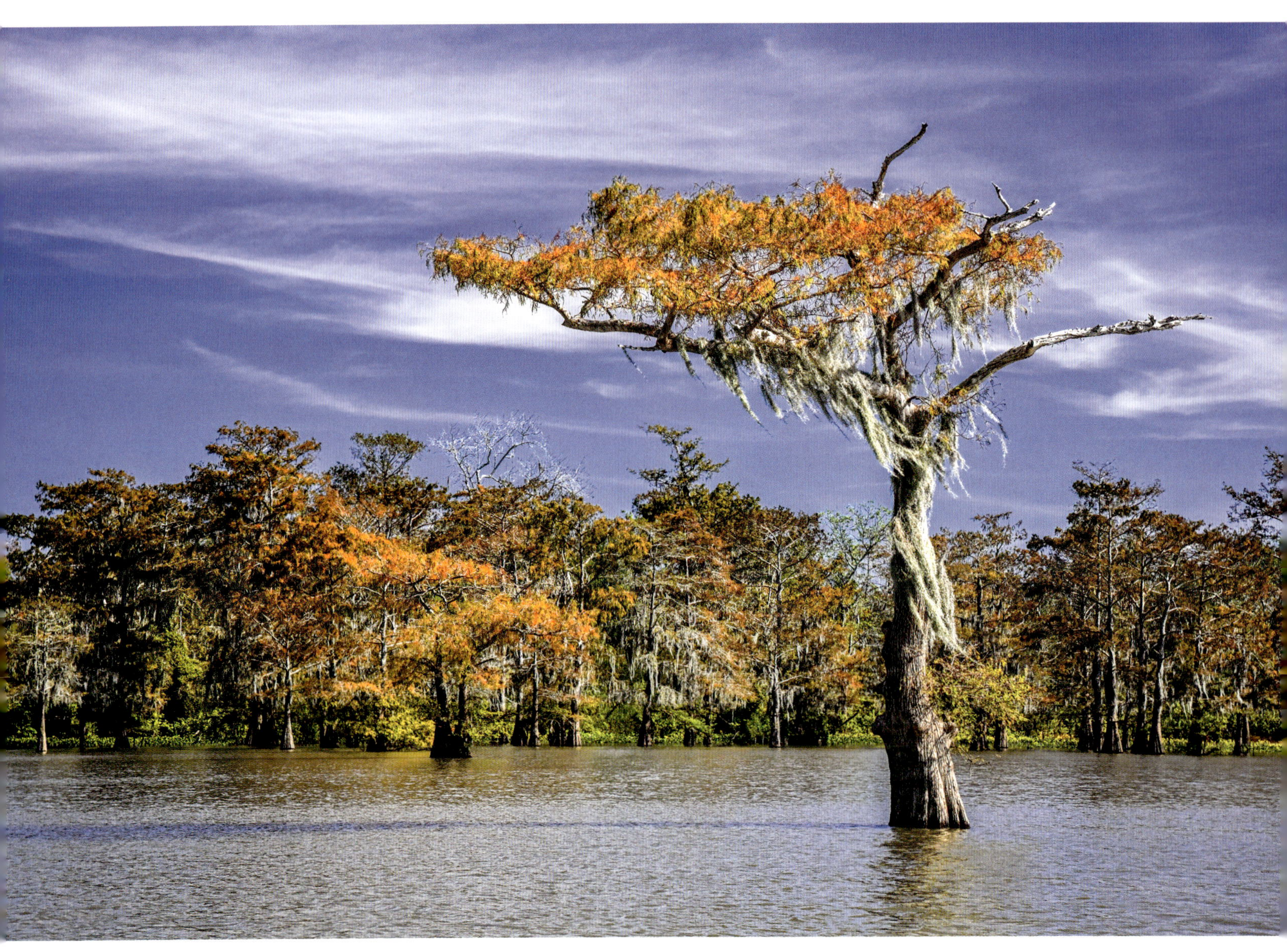

This amazing cypress stands in Grand Lake, which sits pretty much in the geographic center of the massive Atchafalaya Basin. Its autumn-colored limbs seem to frame the main flooded swamp in the background as a stiff breeze pushes through the stands of moss.

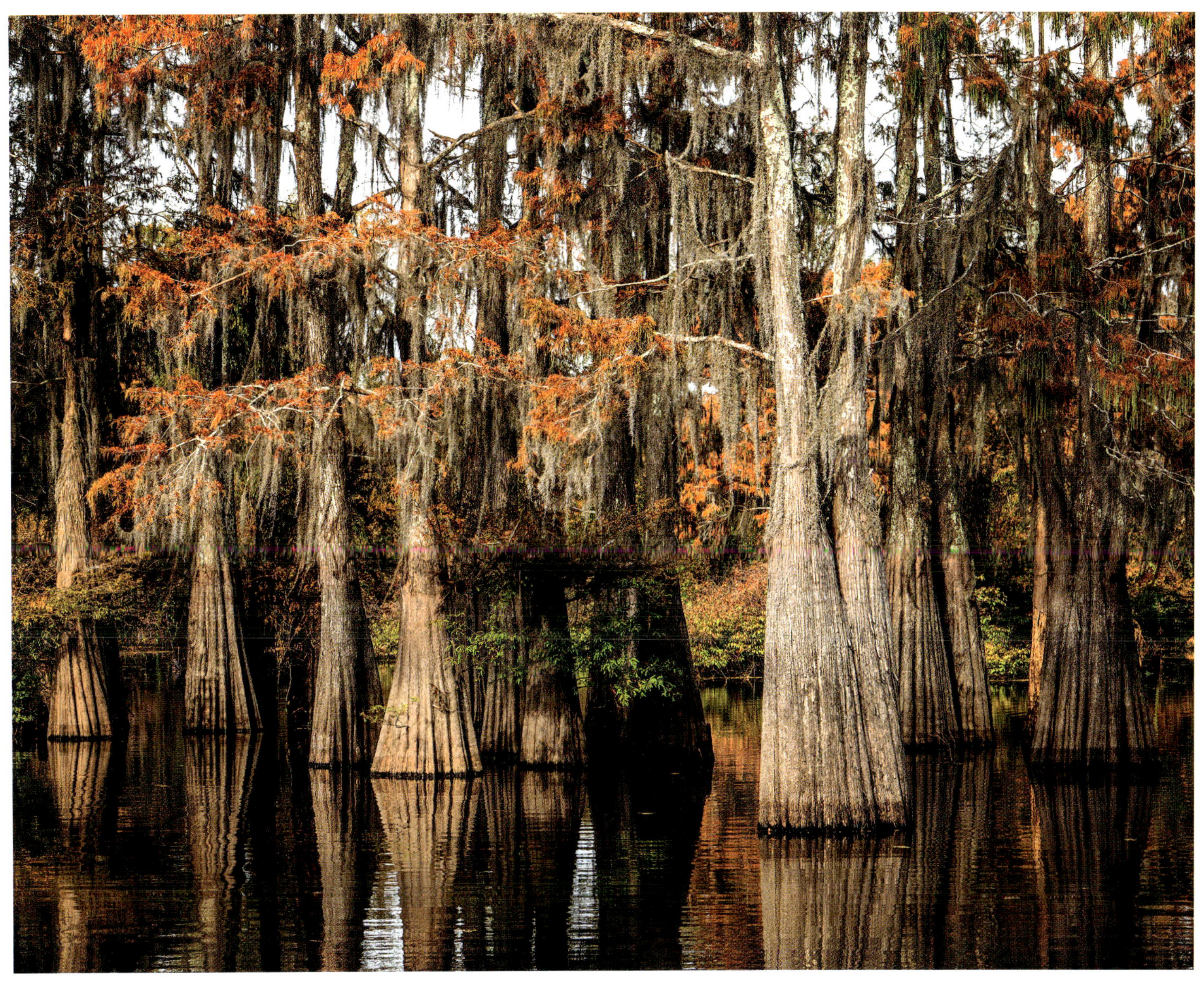

The interplay of orange-colored foliage against a thick stand of brown and gray tree trunks turns a drab scene into one of colorful artistry.

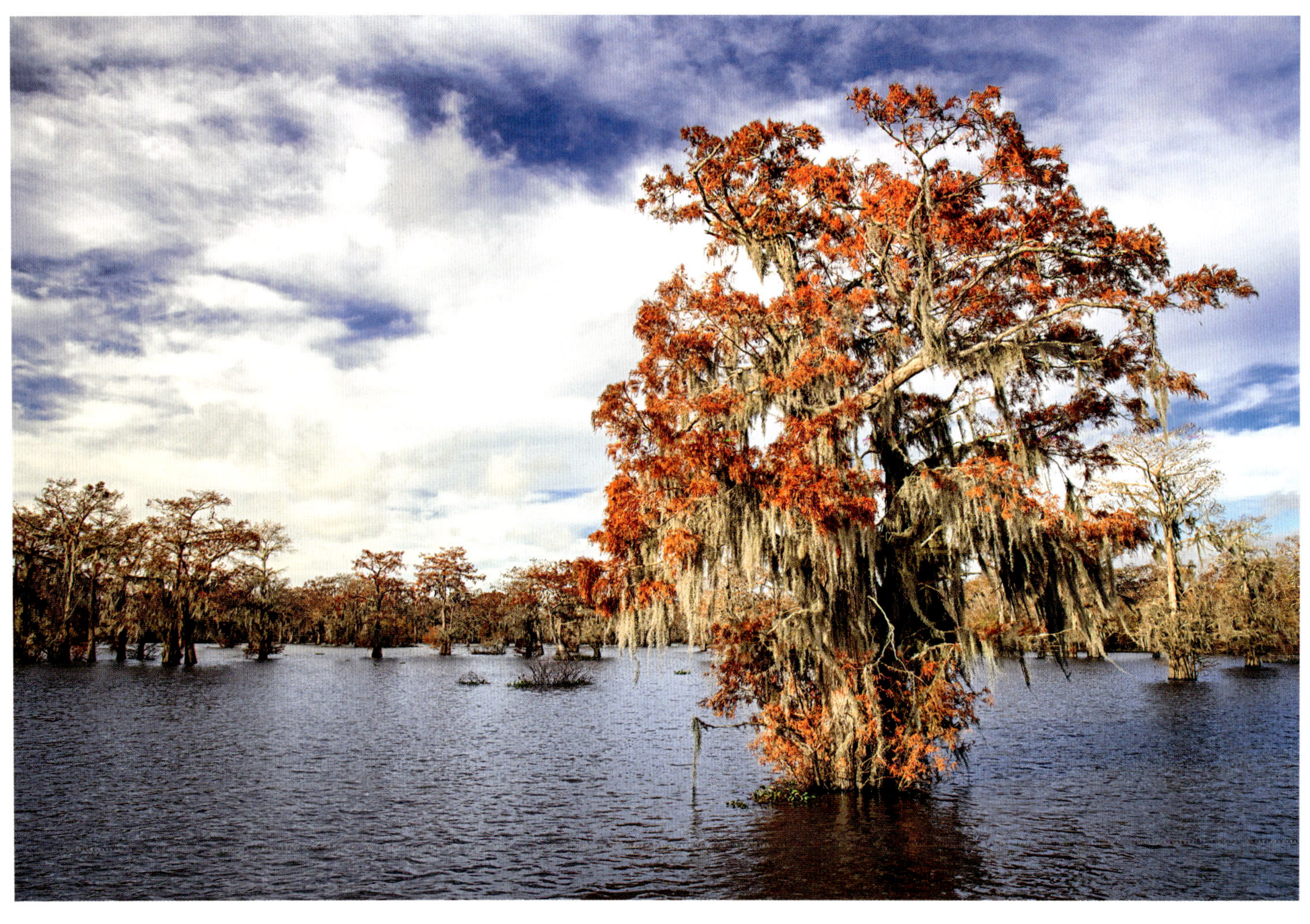

This Henderson Swamp cypress blazes with thick reddish leaves. The color variations can be incredible, and many locals don't realize how beautiful the swamps are this time of year.

Opposite page: Rust-colored leaves stair-step up a tall cypress tree growing in deeper water on Lake Verret. I love to see these autumn-decorated trees illuminated by soft, early morning light.

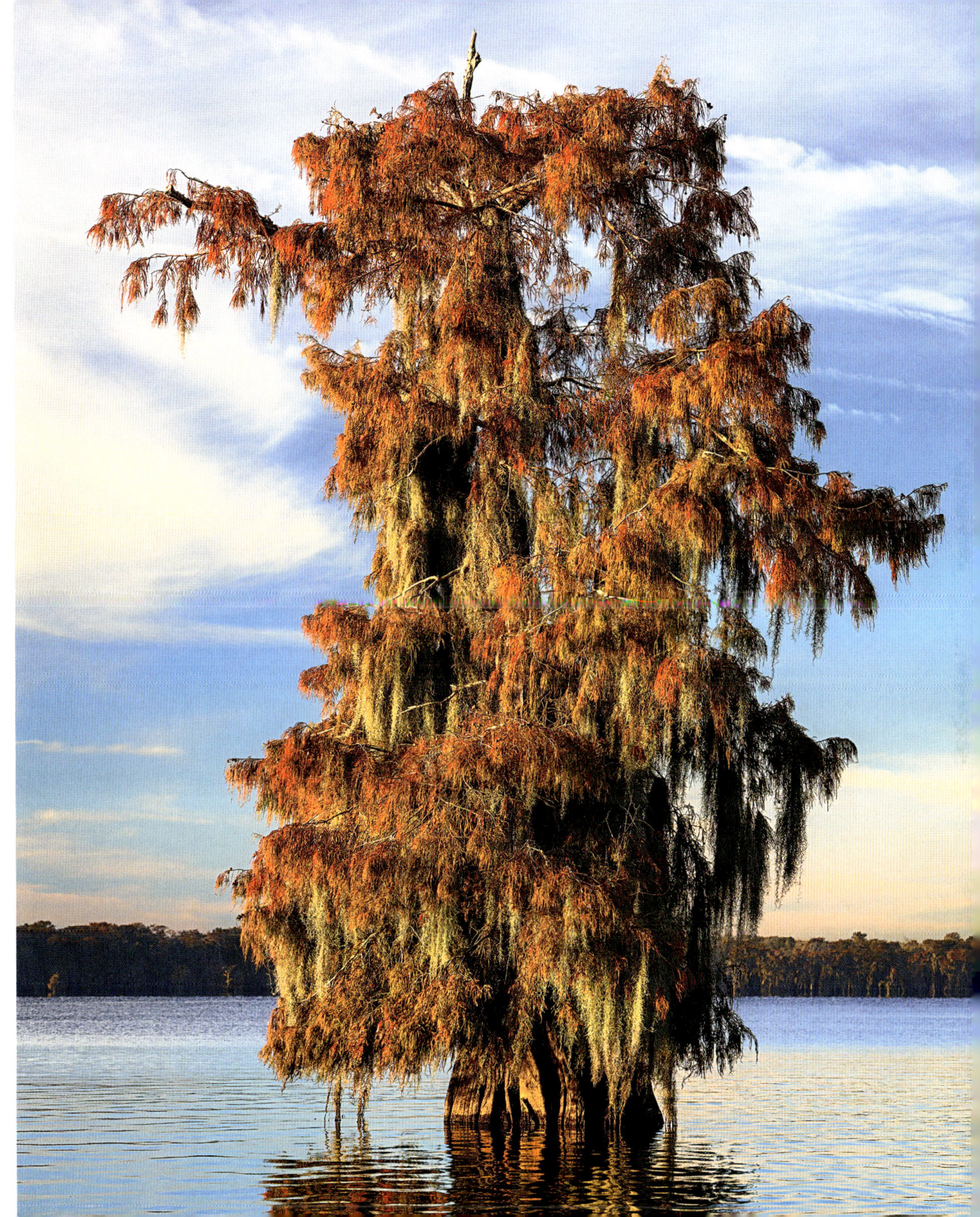

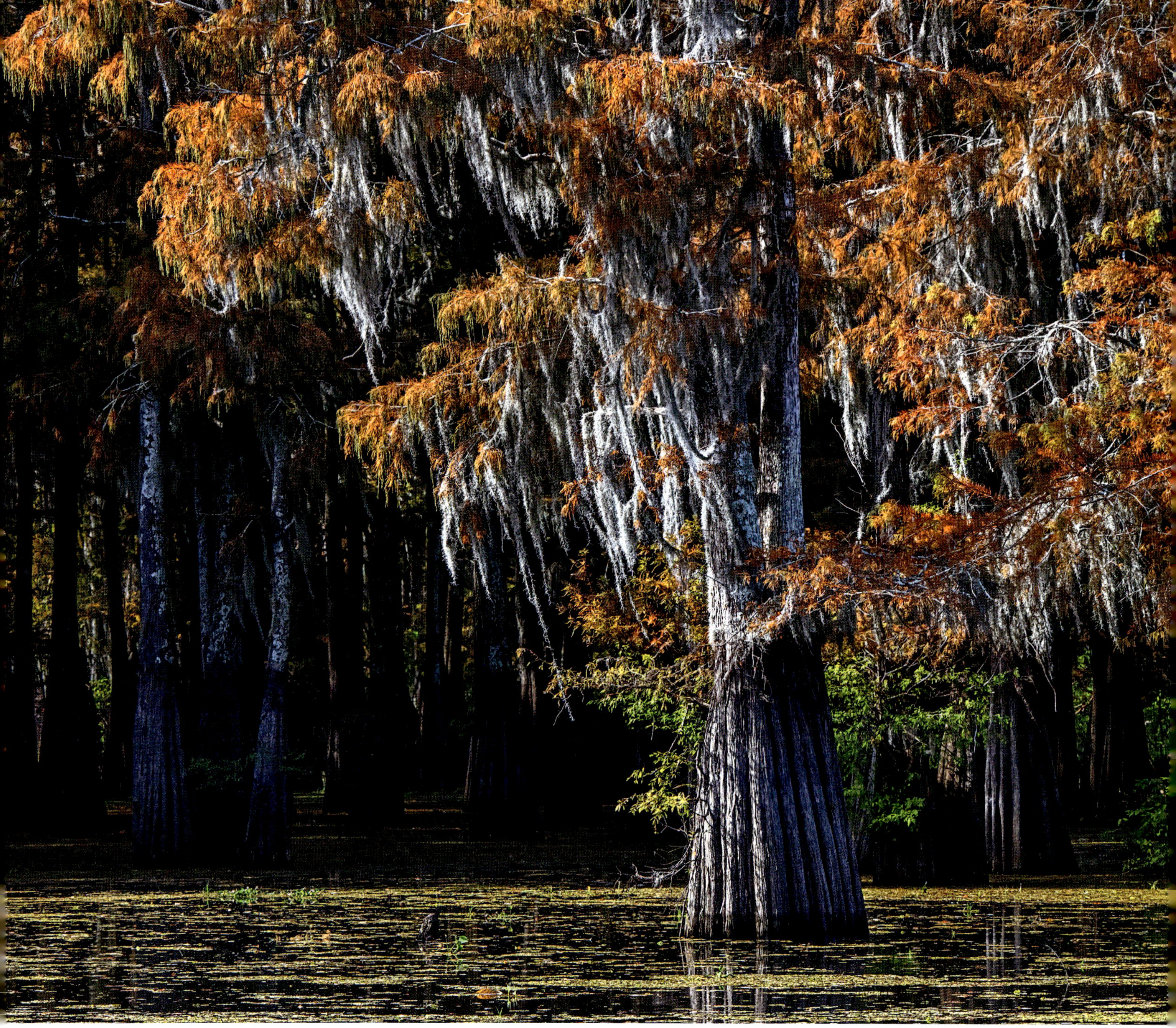

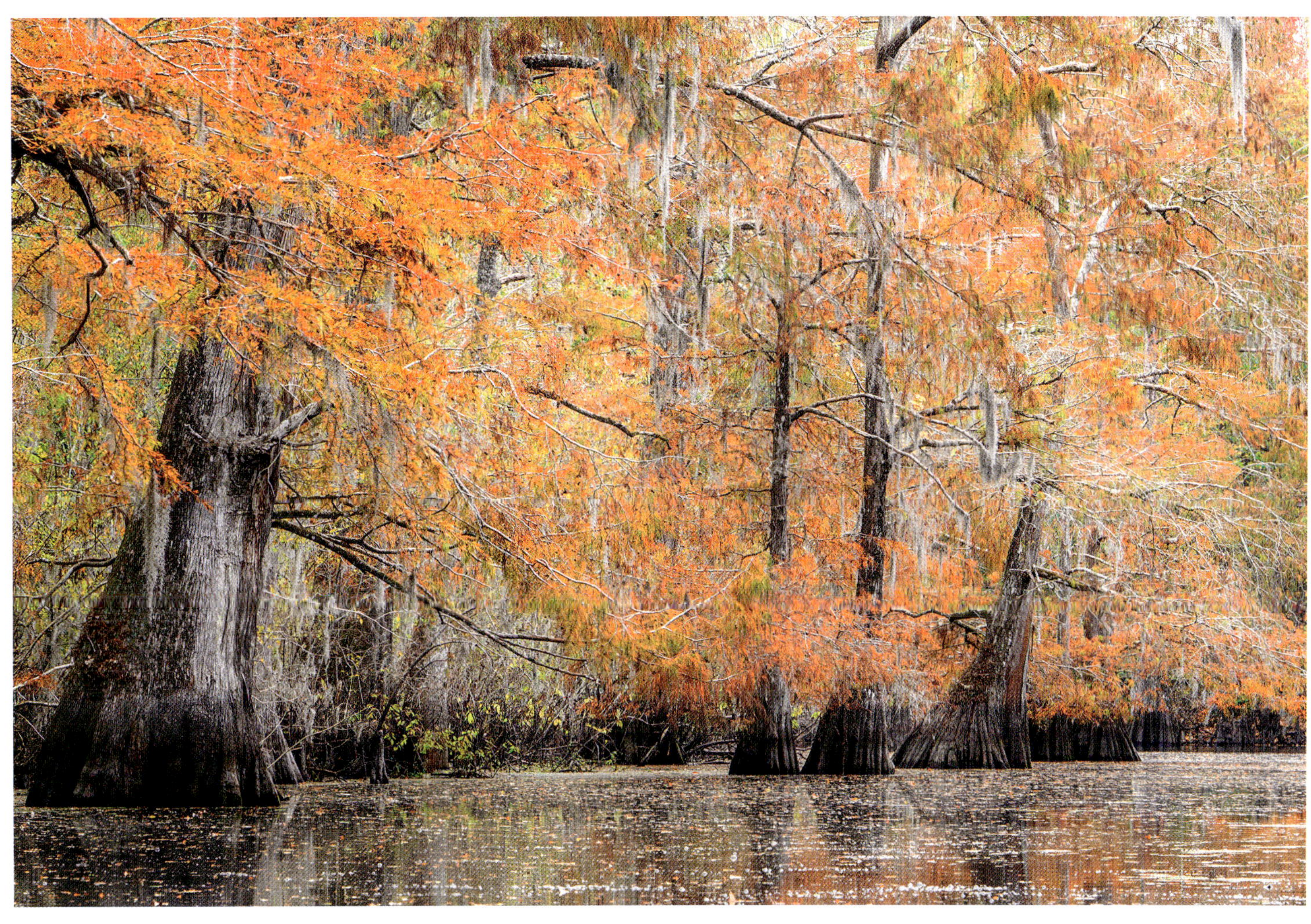

Opposite page: I was floating through a thick forest of flooded cypress trees in Henderson Swamp when I saw this amazing tree glowing in one of the few openings. The darkness of the forest in the background offered the perfect contrast to show off the colors of the grand old tree.

There are times when fall creates a kaleidoscope of color, as along this bayou located on the northern end of the Atchafalaya Basin.

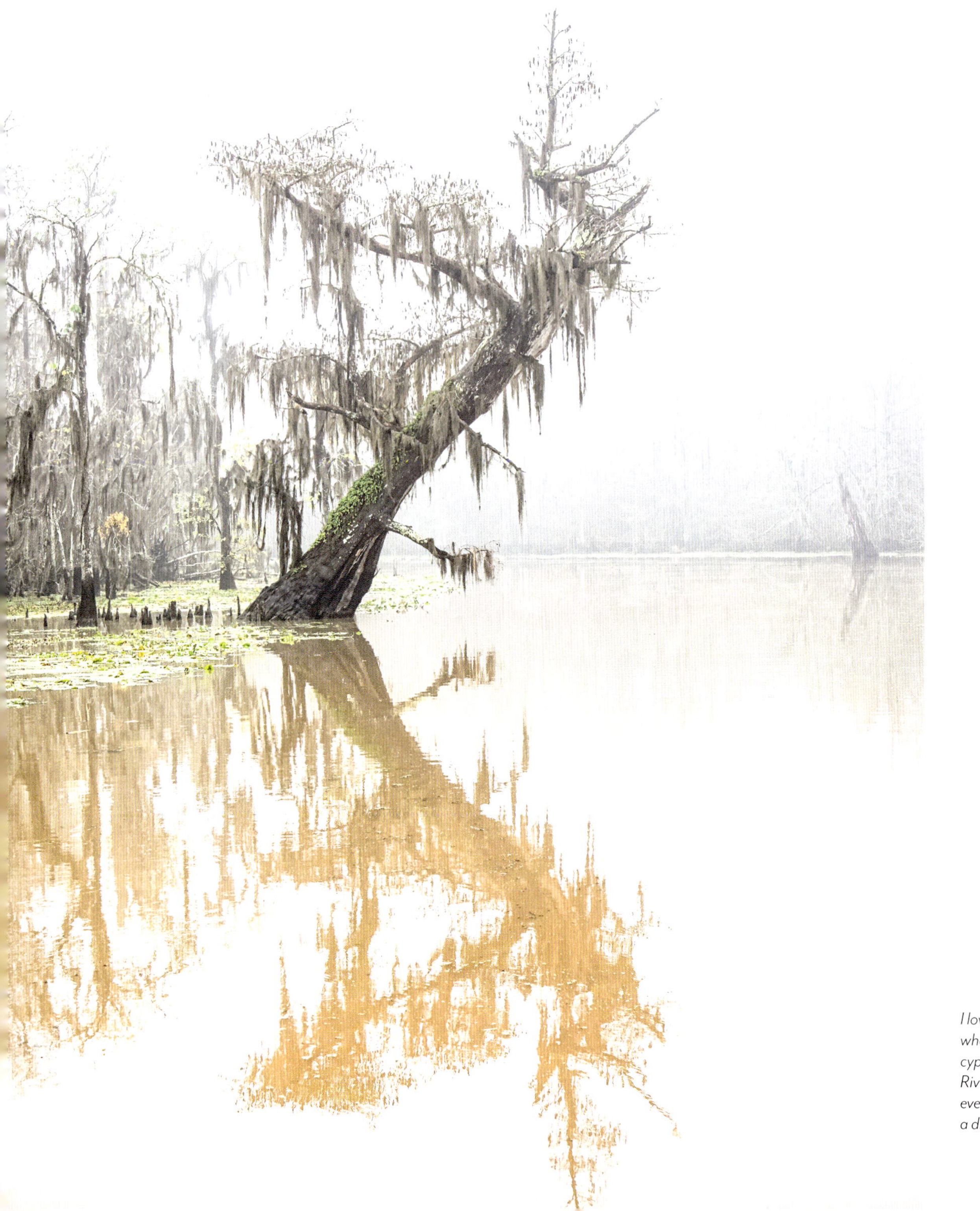

I love the reflectiveness of foggy mornings, when waters go slick smooth. This old cypress tree stands on the edge of Blind River on a day so foggy that you couldn't even see the fall color in its branches from a distance.

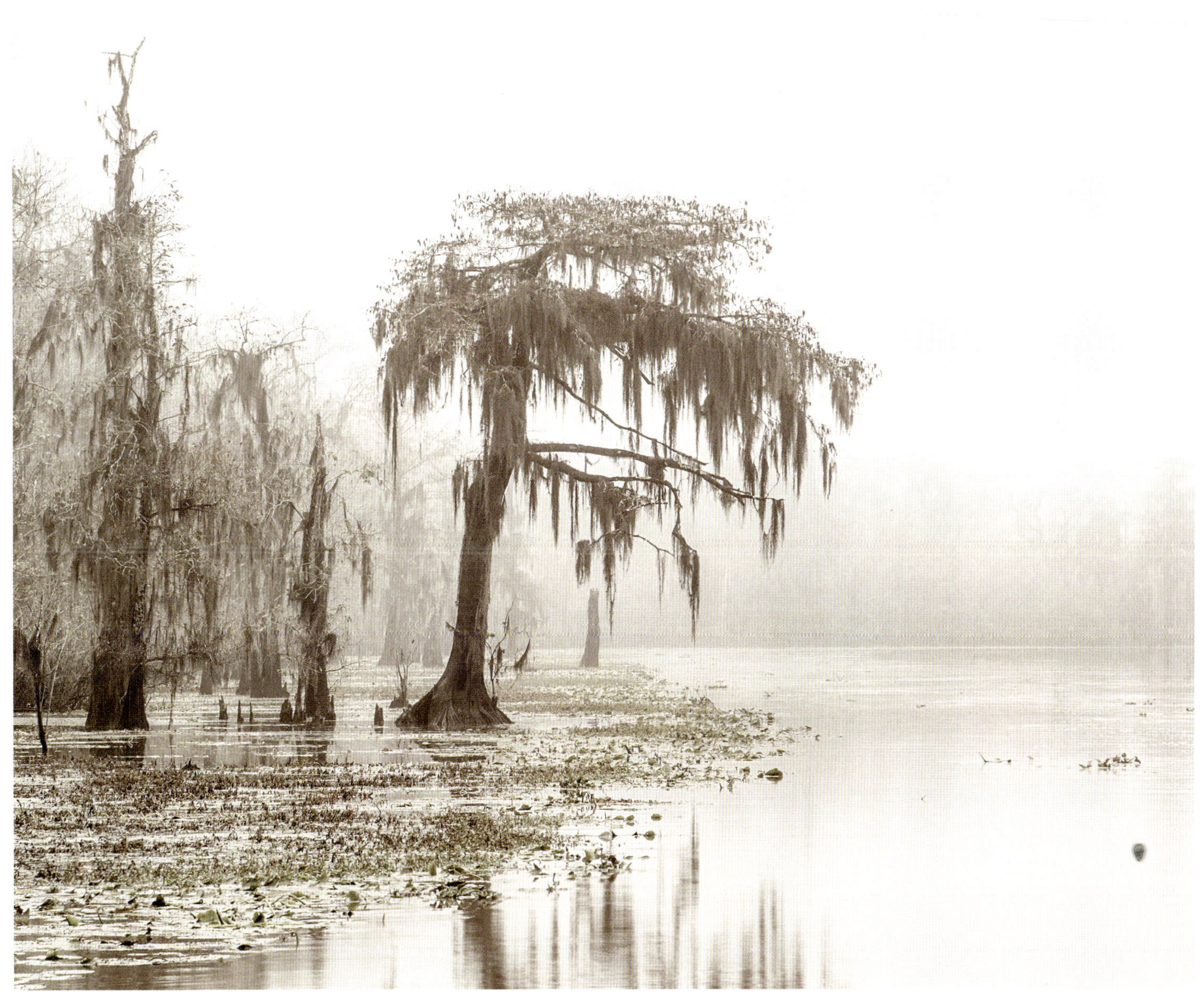

Fog seems to suck all the color out of some scenes, creating natural monochromes. That's what happened on this day when very thick fog seemed to hang in the trees along Blind River.

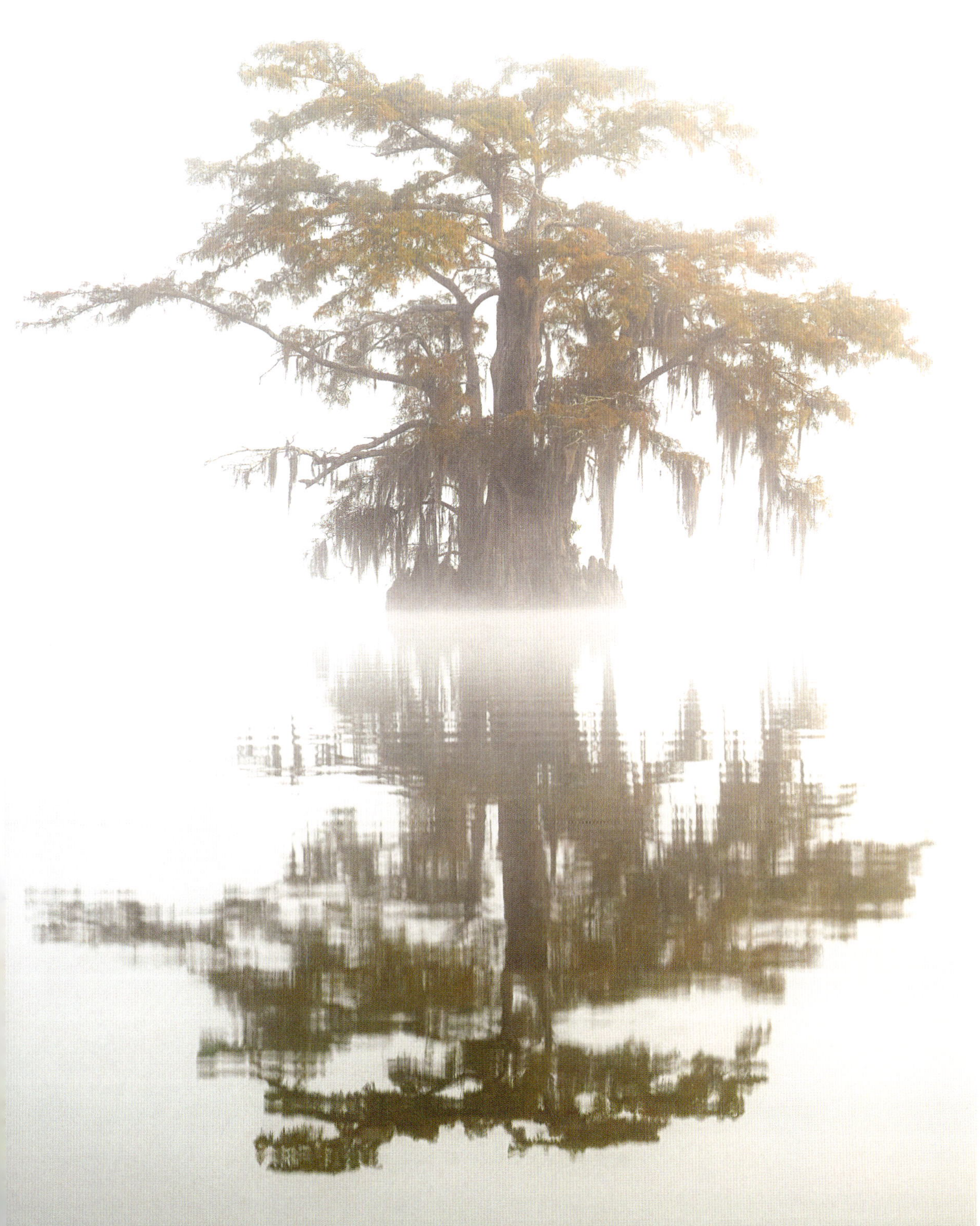

I had barely begun my Lake Dauterive paddle when I saw this character-filled tree barely peeking through thick fog. I loved how the fog muted the colors and added mystery to the scene.

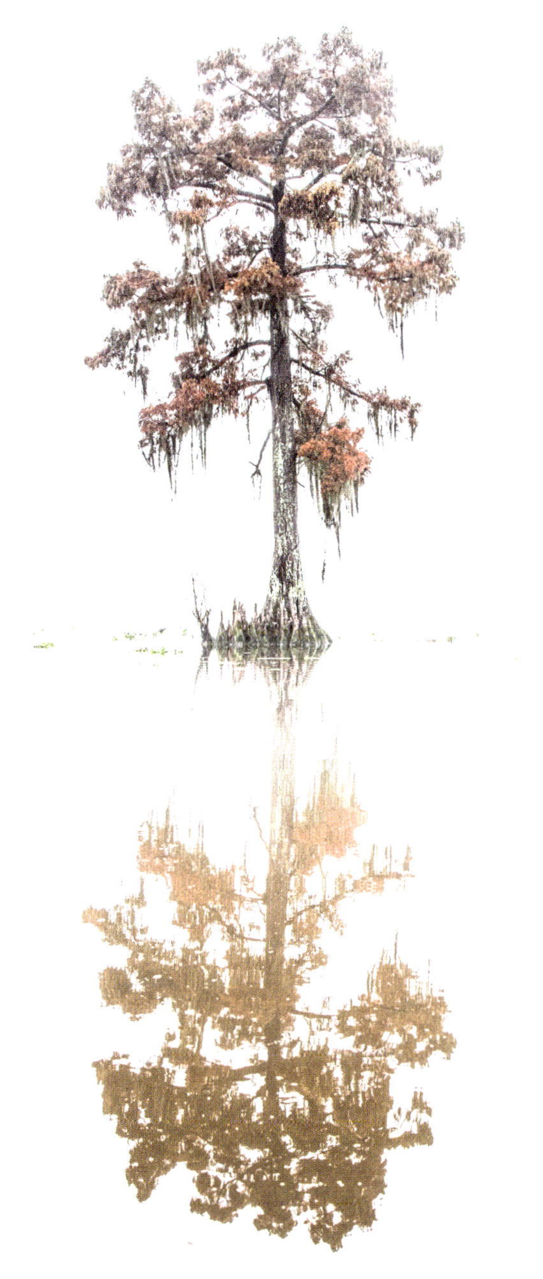

This tree stood in a fog bank so thick that everything around it was hidden, while the still waters created a perfect reflection of the colorful tree. It was surreal.

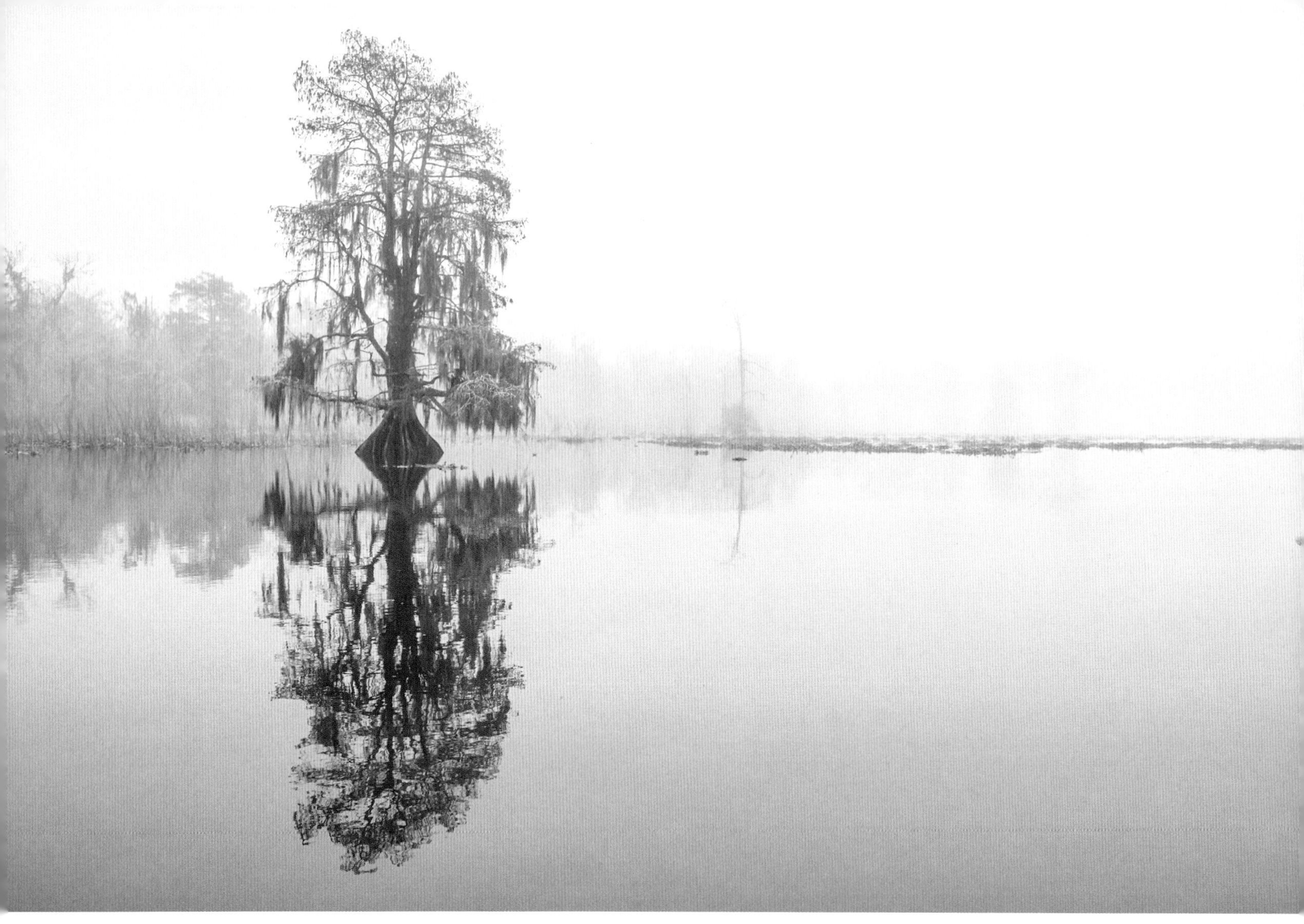

The fog was so thick in the Maurepas Swamp on this day that it was disorienting. I was easing over a shallow flat when this tree materialized out of the mists at the mouth of Blind River, which snakes through this vast swamp from near the Mississippi River (to which it was once connected) before emptying into Lake Maurepas about 35 miles northwest of the famed New Orleans French Quarter.

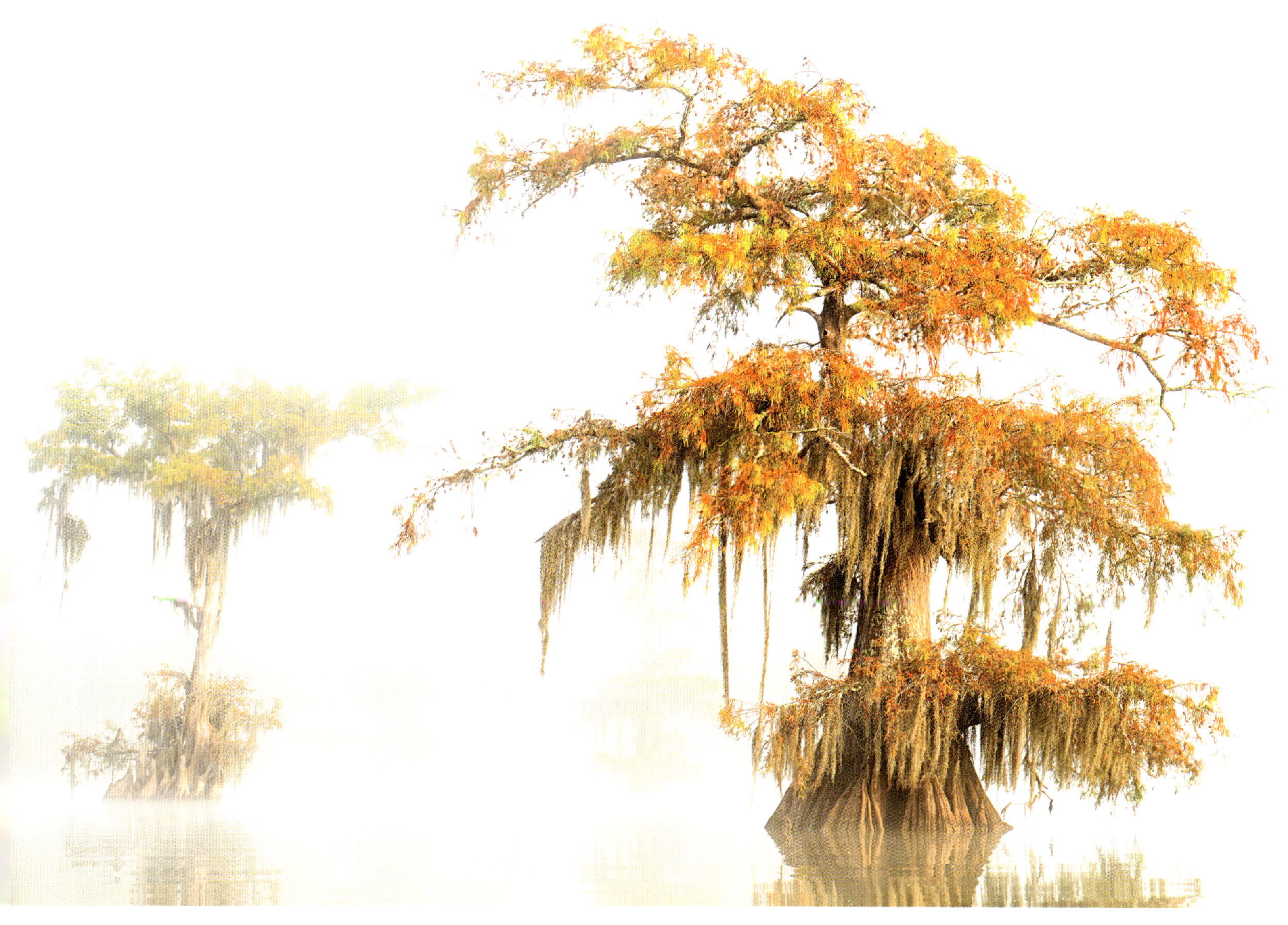

I absolutely love the mood of foggy fall mornings, especially when a colorful tree has this much character and the trees in the background can be seen only through the opaqueness of the mists in the air.

CHAPTER SIX

SUNSETS

And then the day comes to a close. The sun races toward the western horizon, and the wildlife of the swamps begins transitioning to nighttime routines. Alligators slip into the dark waters for their nightly hunting patrols. Wading birds gather in roosting trees. Mosquitoes and other bugs emerge from the moss hanging on the trees, creating an incessant buzzing.

Light softens as the sun touches the horizon and slips out of sight. Clouds light up. Haze glows. Languid waters reflect the colors above. Trees and cypress knees are painted with warm light that brings out every detail.

Darkness begins directly overhead, while the horizons burn with color. Sometimes it's all about the western horizon and that beautiful, final burst of sunset. Other times, the real magic happens on the eastern horizon as softer pastels skitter across the undersides of the clouds.

Finally, darkness snuffs out the last vestiges of sunset, and the swamp is left in darkness.

All that remains is the quiet paddle back to the truck.

Opposite page: Lakes give scale to the swamps, which can sometimes feel tight and constricting. This cypress tree stands well out in Grand Lake, in the heart of the sprawling Atchafalaya Basin, and you can see the main forest of flooded cypress trees on the far horizon.

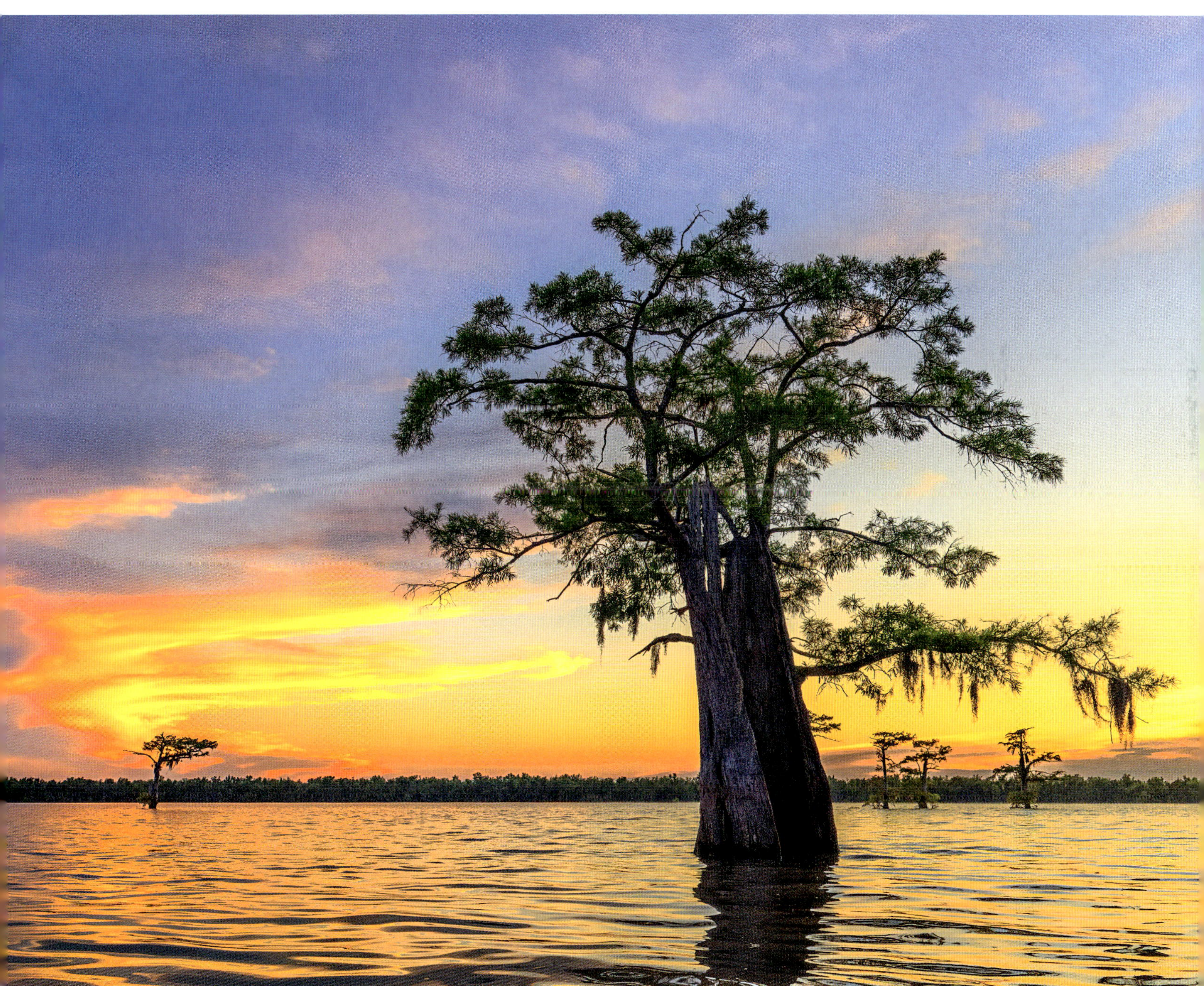

The tone of light during sunset can be incredible, casting amazing colors over the swamp. On this evening, sunset came and went with very little color. Ten minutes later, the clouds blossomed with amazing rose-colored light that reflected in the still waters of Lake Verret and added a glow to the trees and cypress knees.

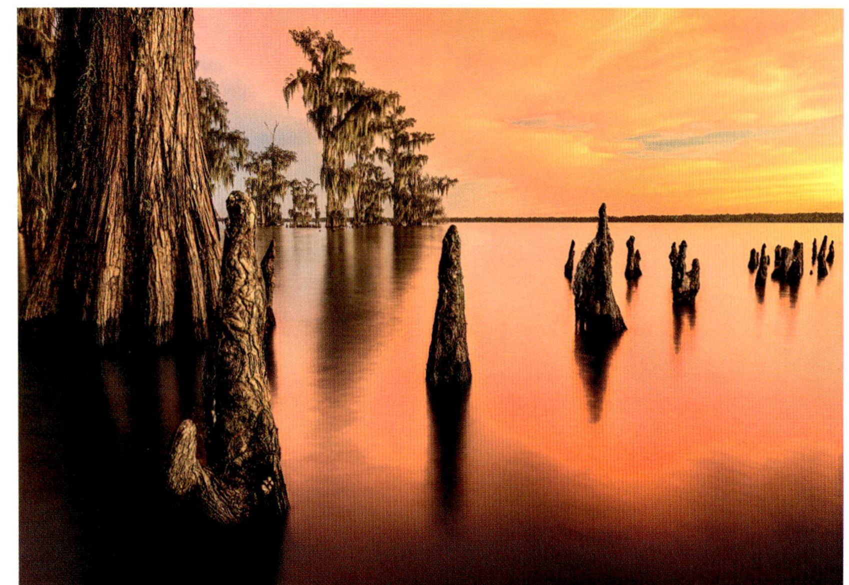

I had paddled far into the Lake Verret swamp for this sunset, and as the sun raced to the horizon, I saw the opportunity to use one of the iconic cypress trees to frame the ball of fire. Atmospheric haze burned red, and the sun cast gorgeous light through the veil of Spanish moss hanging from the tree. The row of cypress knees to the right of the tree balanced the final photo.

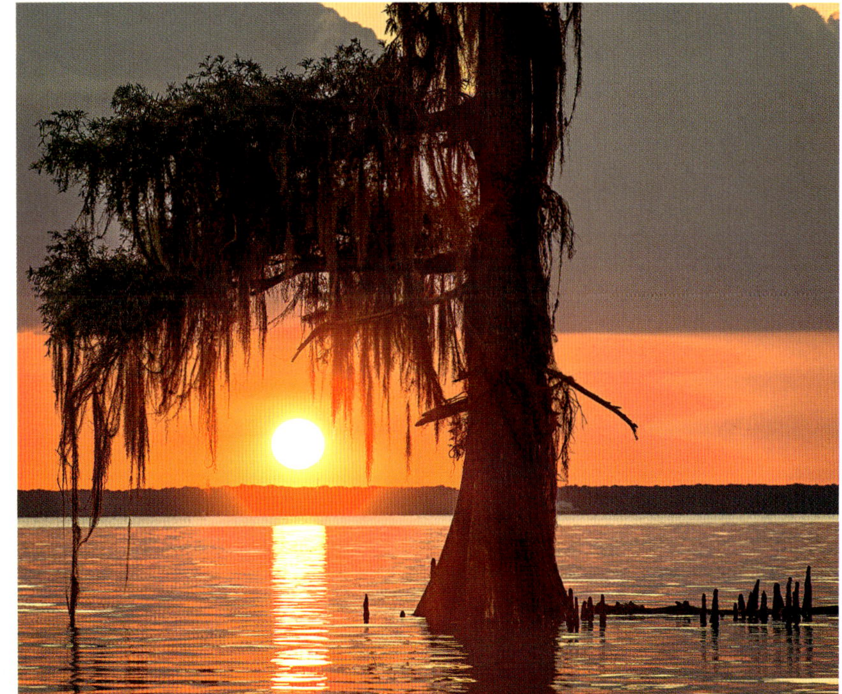

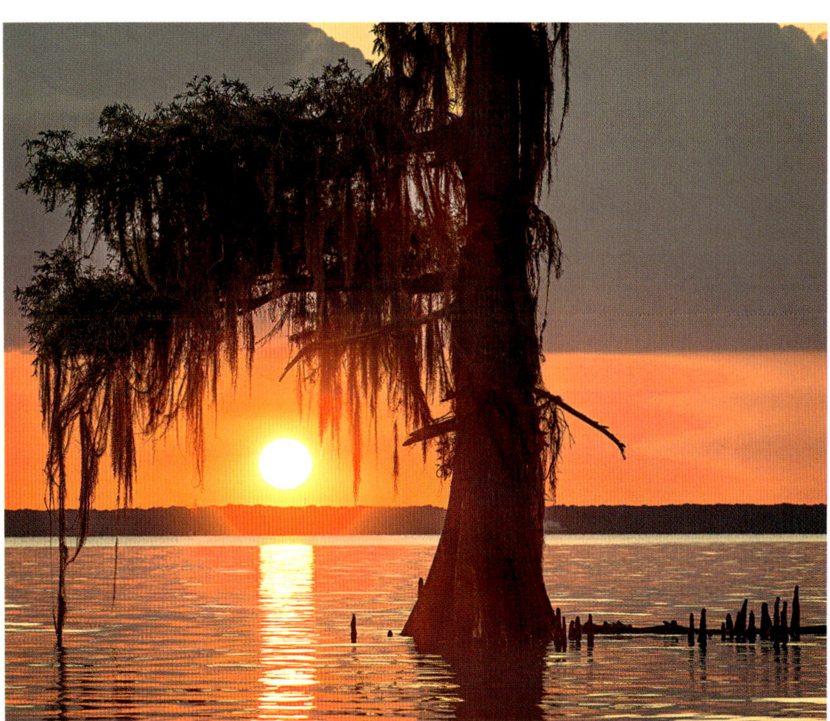

Opposite page: The Louisiana coast is defined by swamps and marshes, and the meeting of the two can be magical. This scene near the edge of Lake Pontchartrain, just west of the Big Easy, perfectly illustrates the conjunction of the two coastal habitats. I was blown away by how the golden light bursting through the distant cypress trees tipped the tops of the marsh grass.

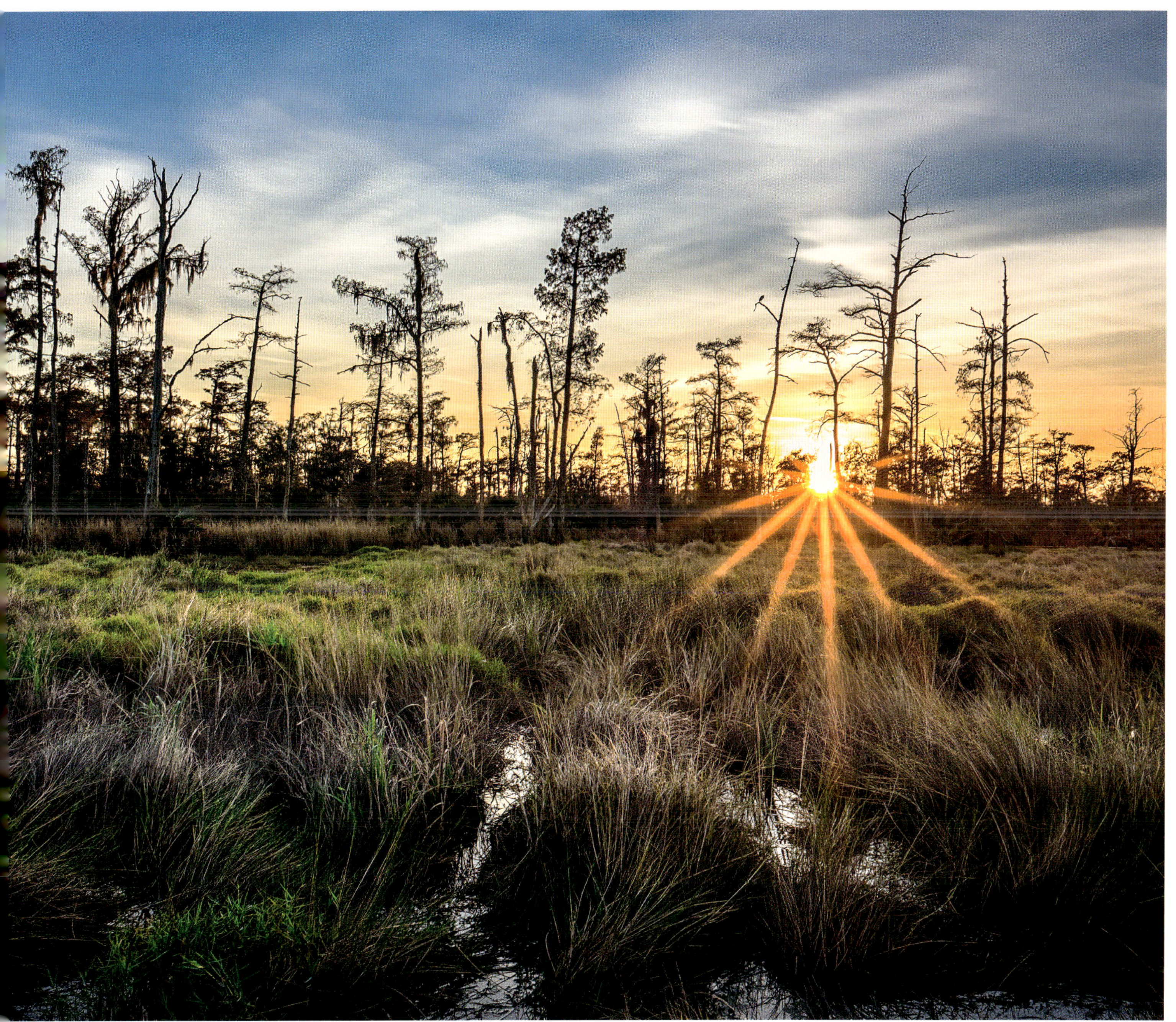

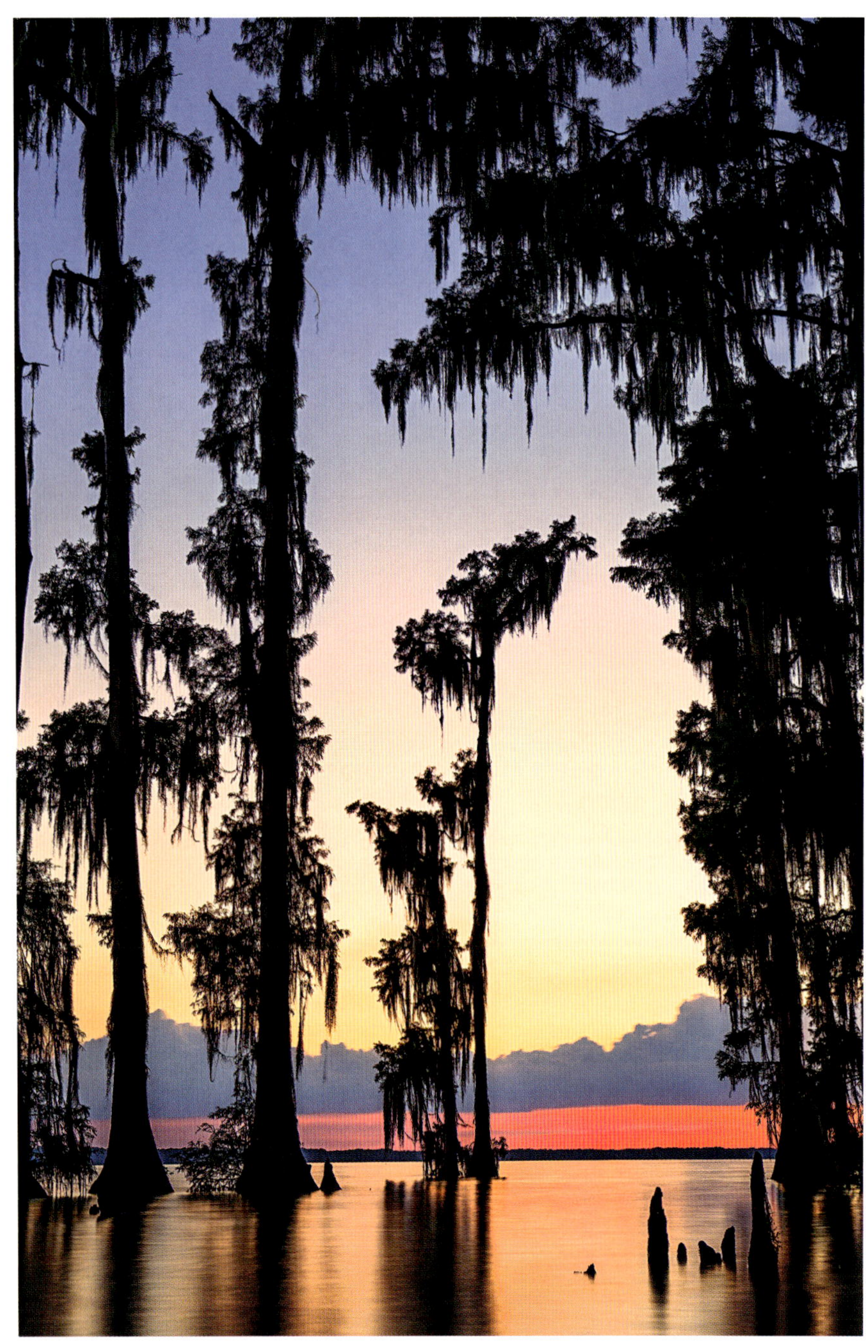

Towering cypress trees form a window for the colorful summer sunset. I paddled far back into the swamp to find this composition, braving hordes of mosquitoes that had awakened for the night. Even numerous bites from these bloodthirsty insects couldn't ruin the beauty of the moment.

Opposite page: Three cypress trees perfectly frame the setting sun as wind ripples the surface of Flat Lake on the south end of the massive Atchafalaya Basin.

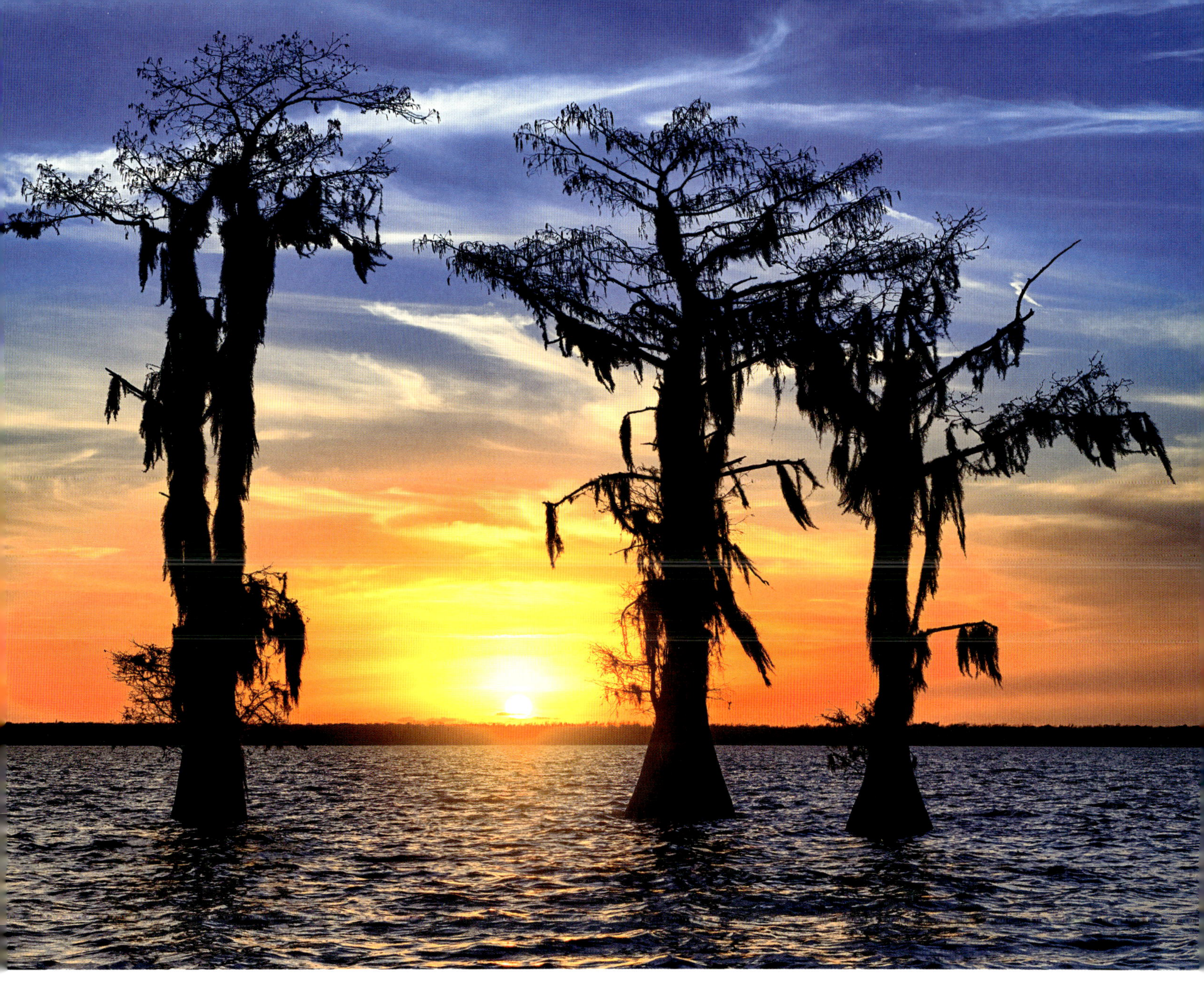

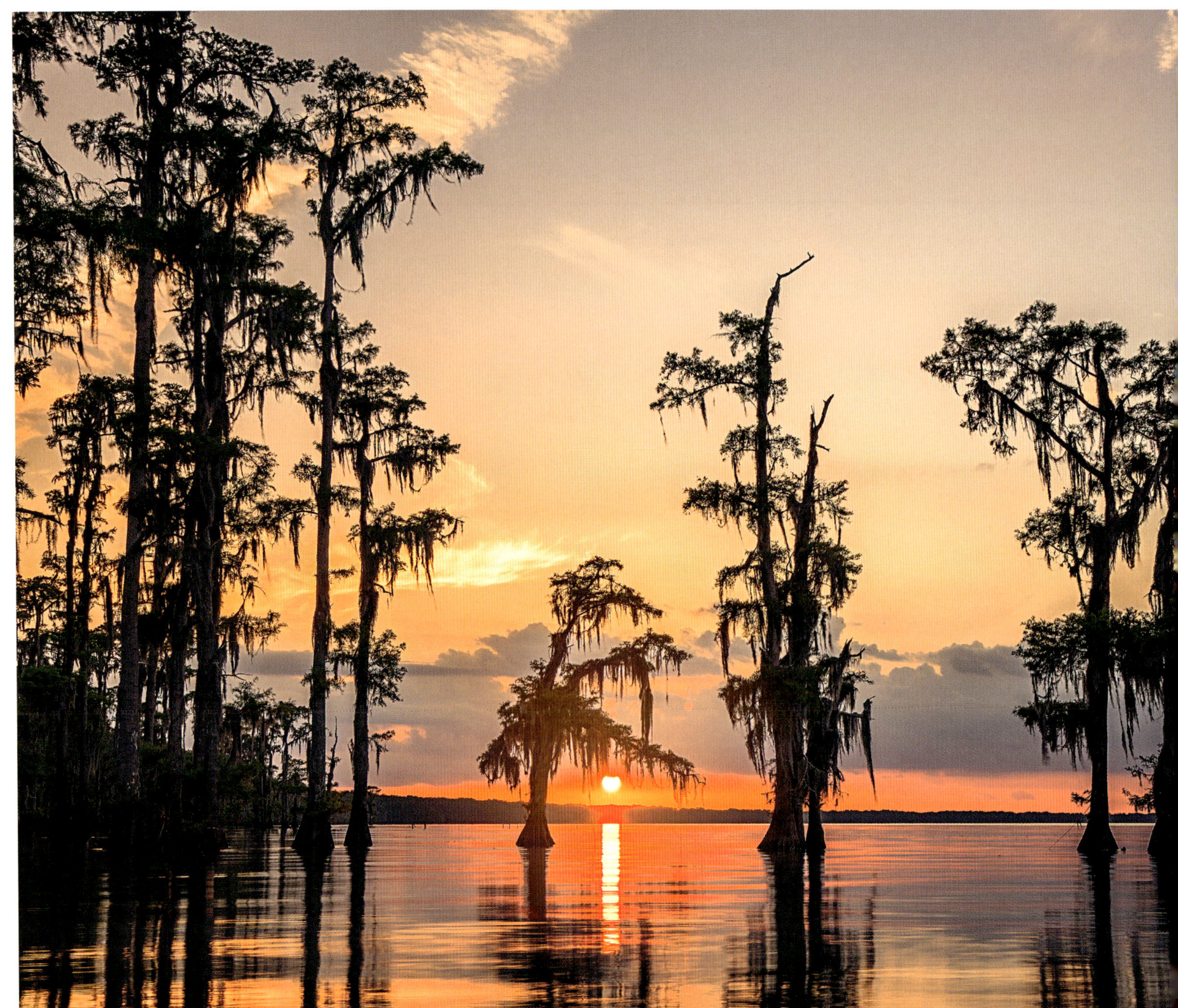

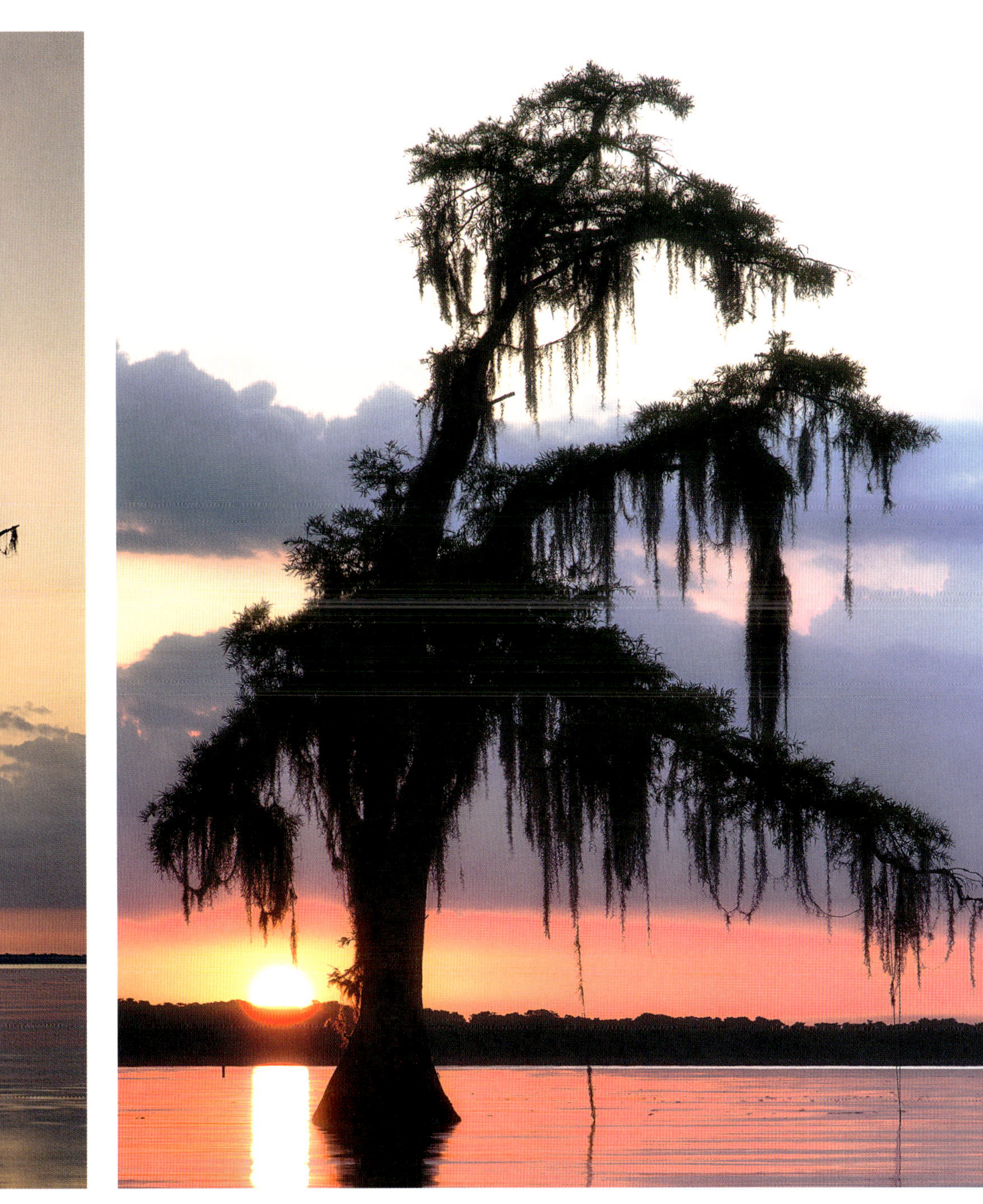

Opposite page: Standing waist deep in the waters of Lake Maurepas while watching the sky take on the first of the sunset glow is always amazing.

As sunset progressed, I switched lenses to capture a tight shot of the same tree framing the burning ball of the sun. The horizon hummed with color beneath the thick clouds. Standing in those dark, still waters made for a wonderful few minutes.

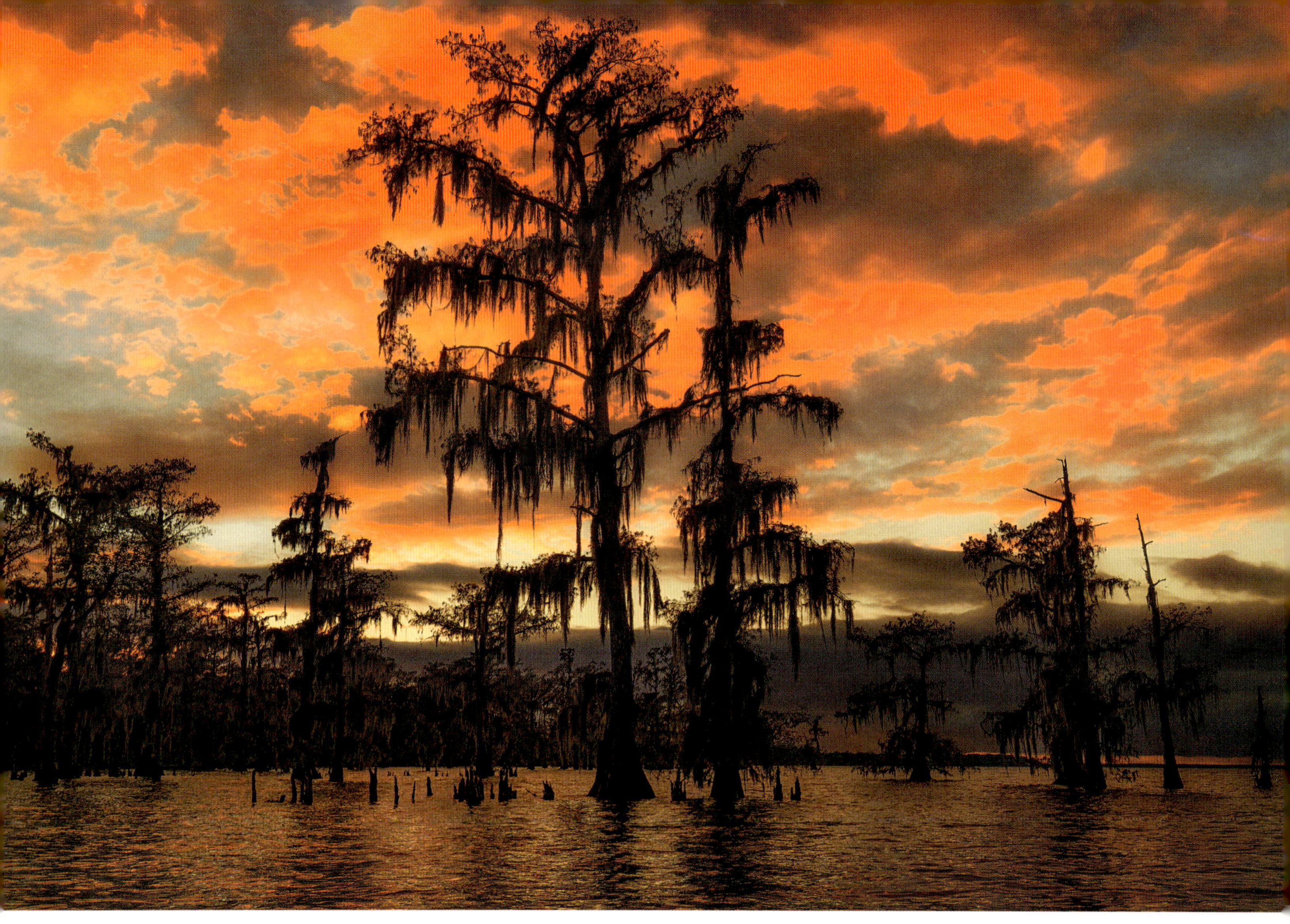

Sunsets can often turn garish, especially when cracks form in thick storm clouds. On this evening, pessimism turned to excitement when the setting sun found one small opening that momentarily allowed vibrant orange light to explode across the bottom of the low clouds.

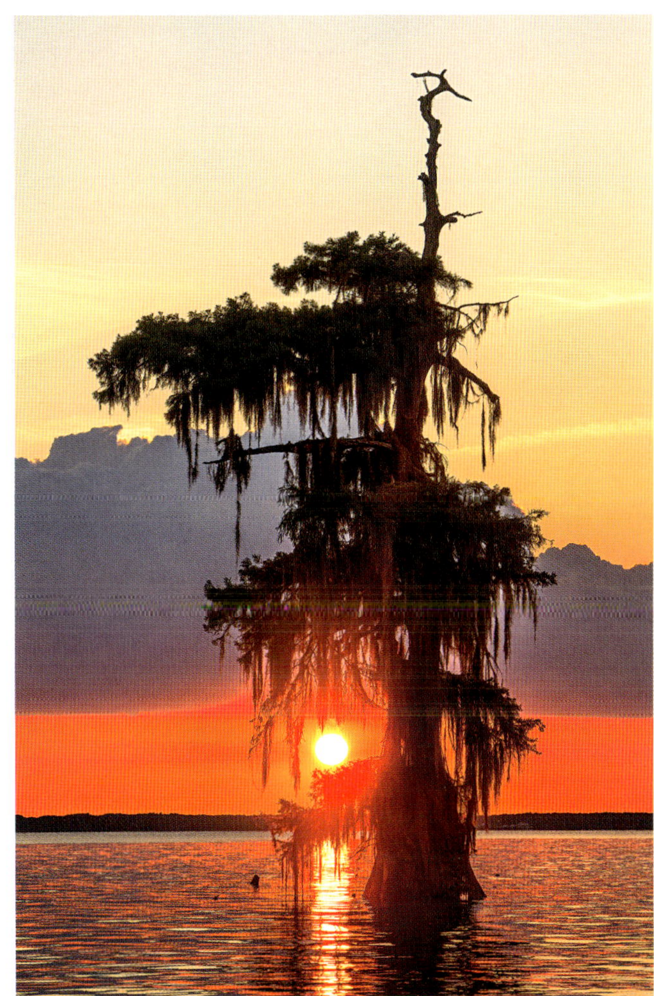

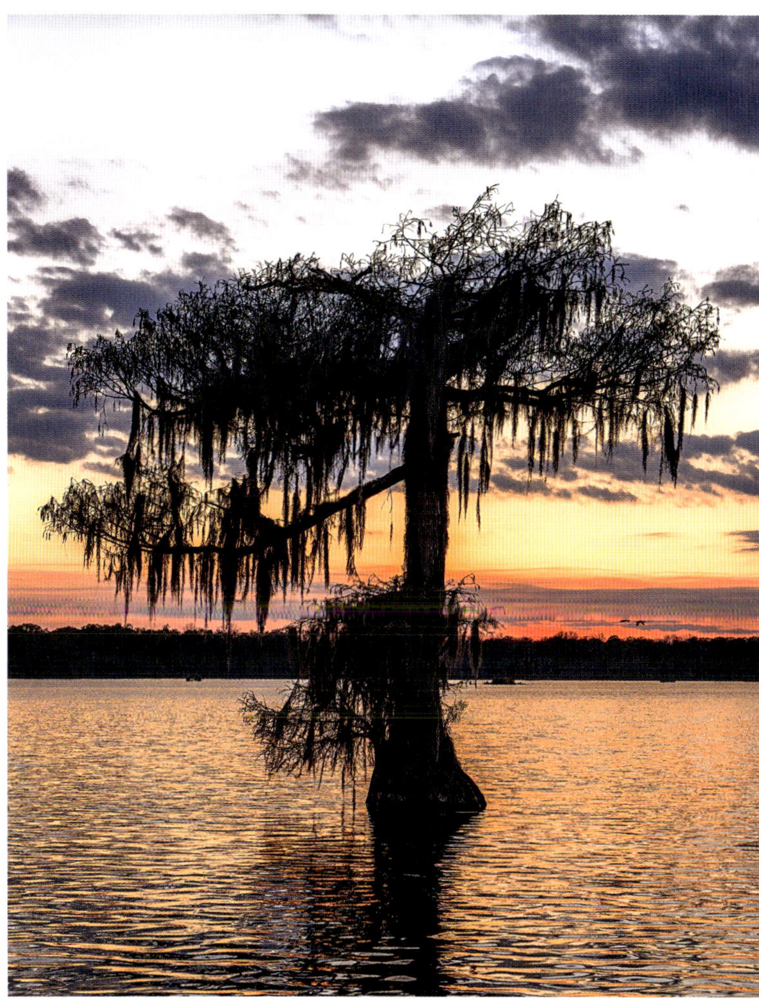

Patience is a virtue when photographing sunsets. On this evening, I saw that the sun would eventually position itself between the branches of this tall cypress tree, so I set up and waited. The gorgeous light through the surrounding Spanish moss was amazing!

Lake Martin near Lafayette, Louisiana, is part of the Cypress Island Preserve, which serves as a major bird rookery. It's also one of the few swamps in Louisiana offering drive-up access. Sunsets are very popular, with small crowds often forming to watch the light show.

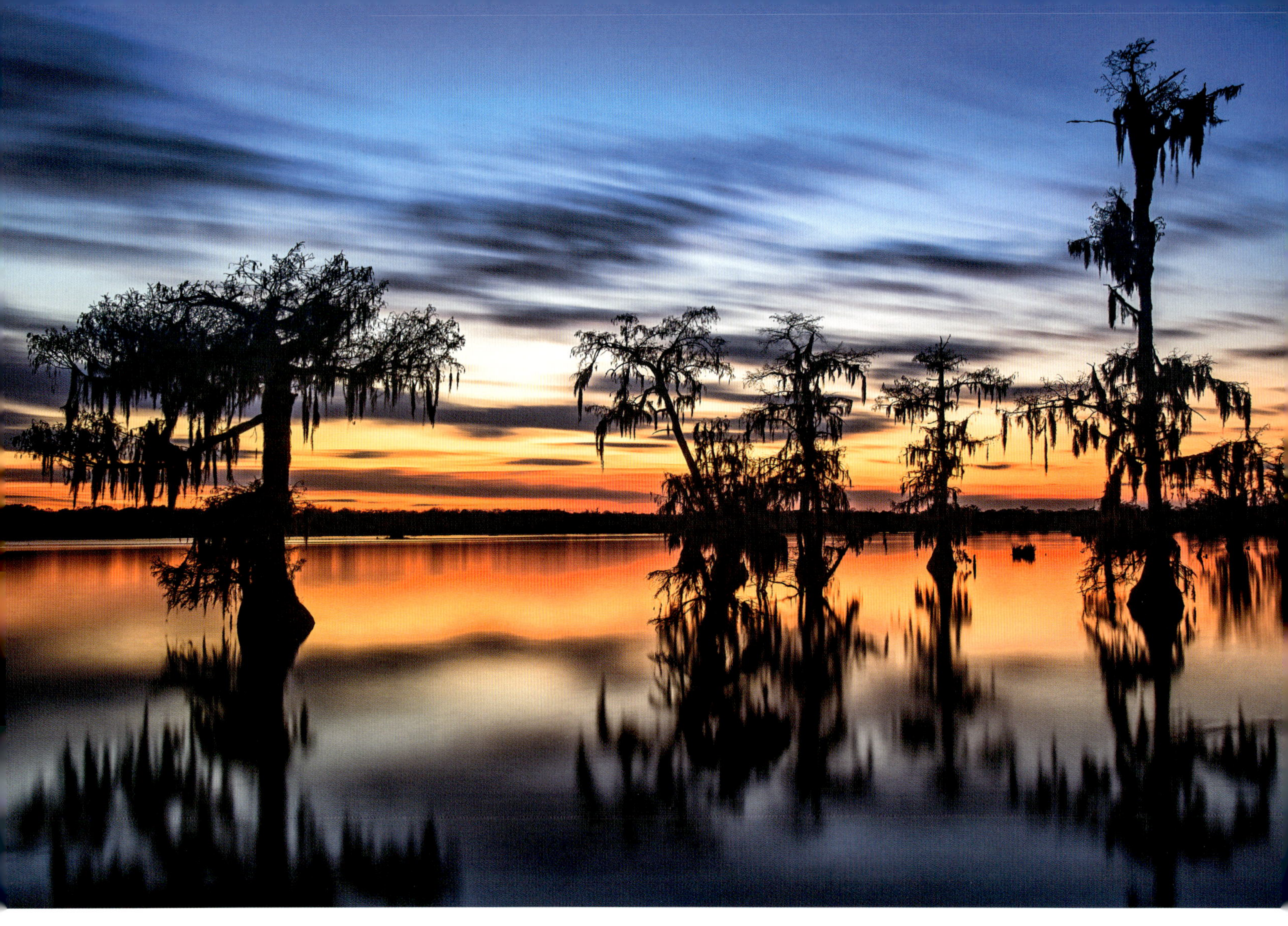

This is the view for those who drive to Lake Martin for sunset. It's amazing to watch the last light of day in the very heart of the Acadiana Region.

Opposite page: The many isolated cypress trees on lakes, rivers, and bayous provide unending options for sunset photographs. I look for trees that have different shapes or beautiful character.

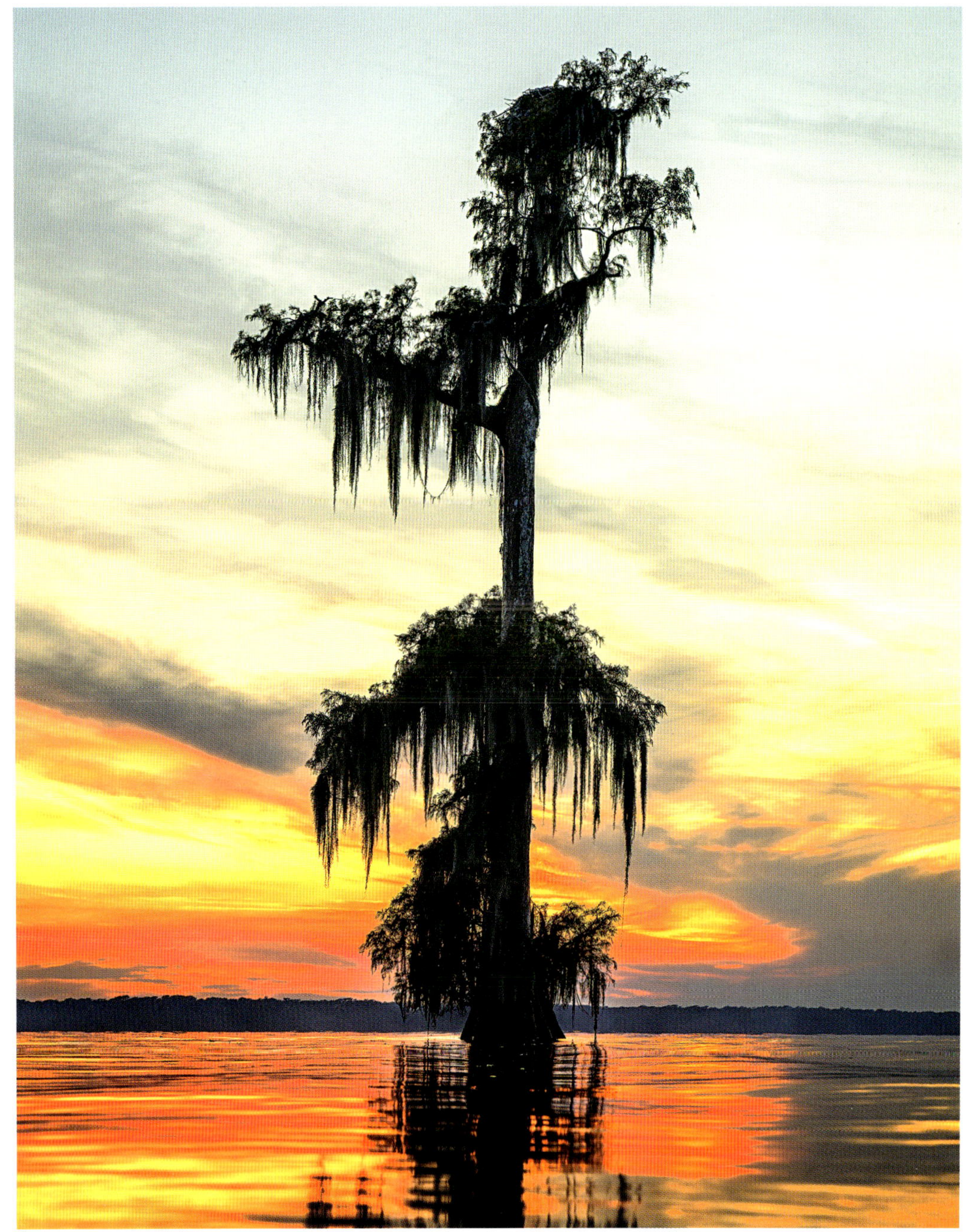

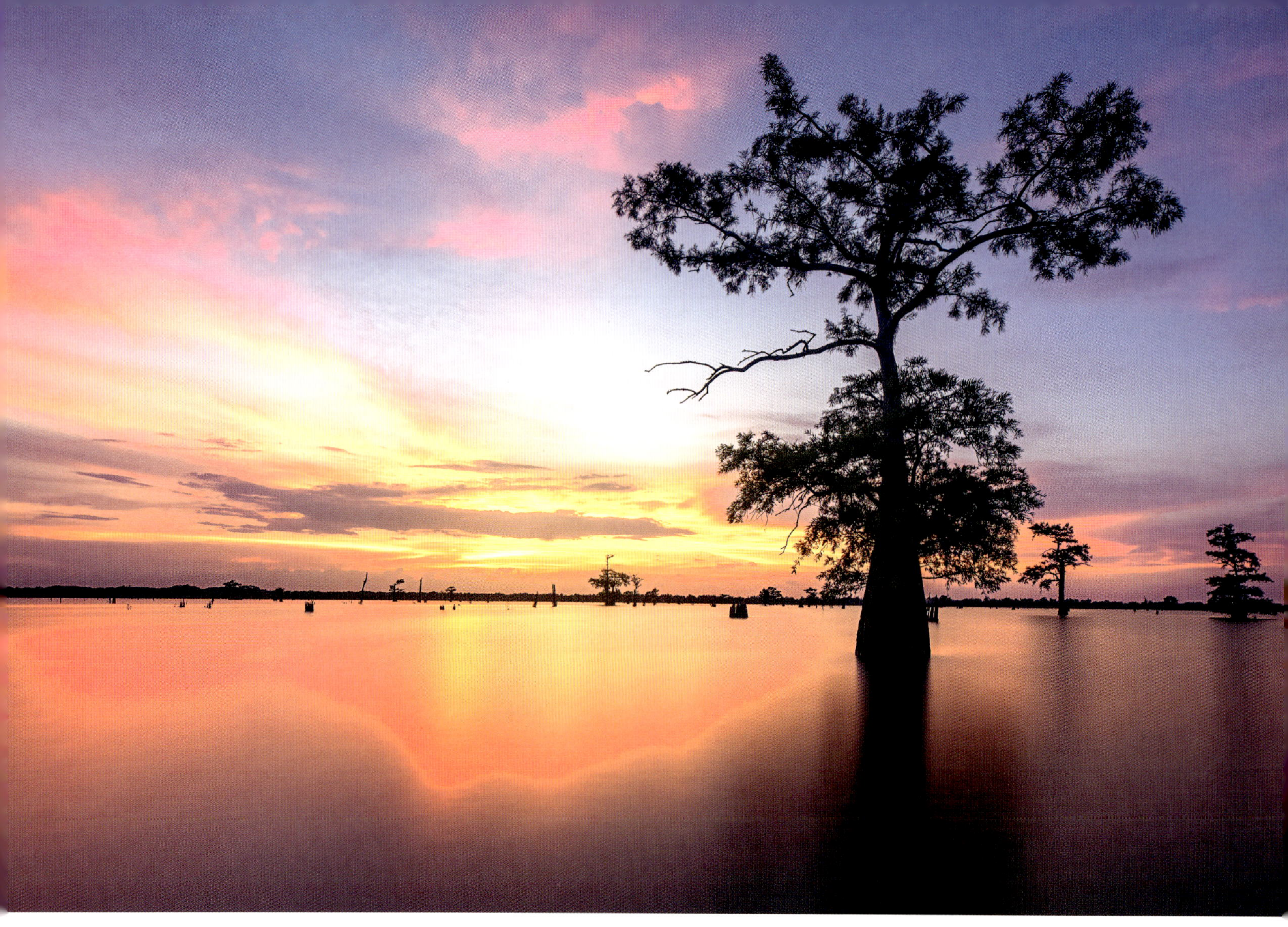

A single cypress tree in the gorgeous Henderson Swamp bears witness to sunset on the summer solstice. I created the beautiful mirror-smooth water, which reflects the colors in the sky, by using a filter that slowed my shutter speed.

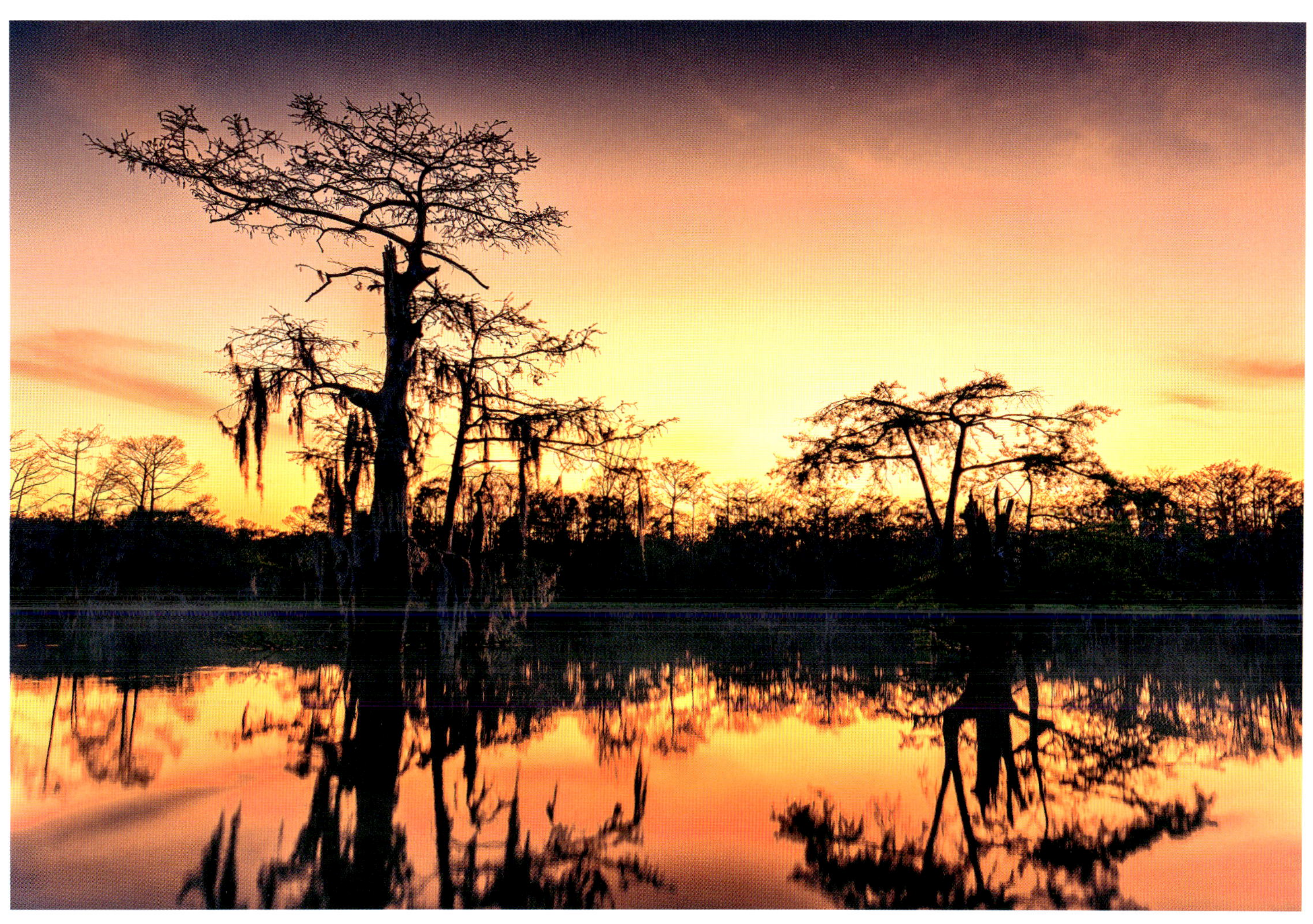

A light fog rises from the waters surrounding a pair of cypress trees as the sky burns above the Atchafalaya Basin, the nation's largest river swamp.

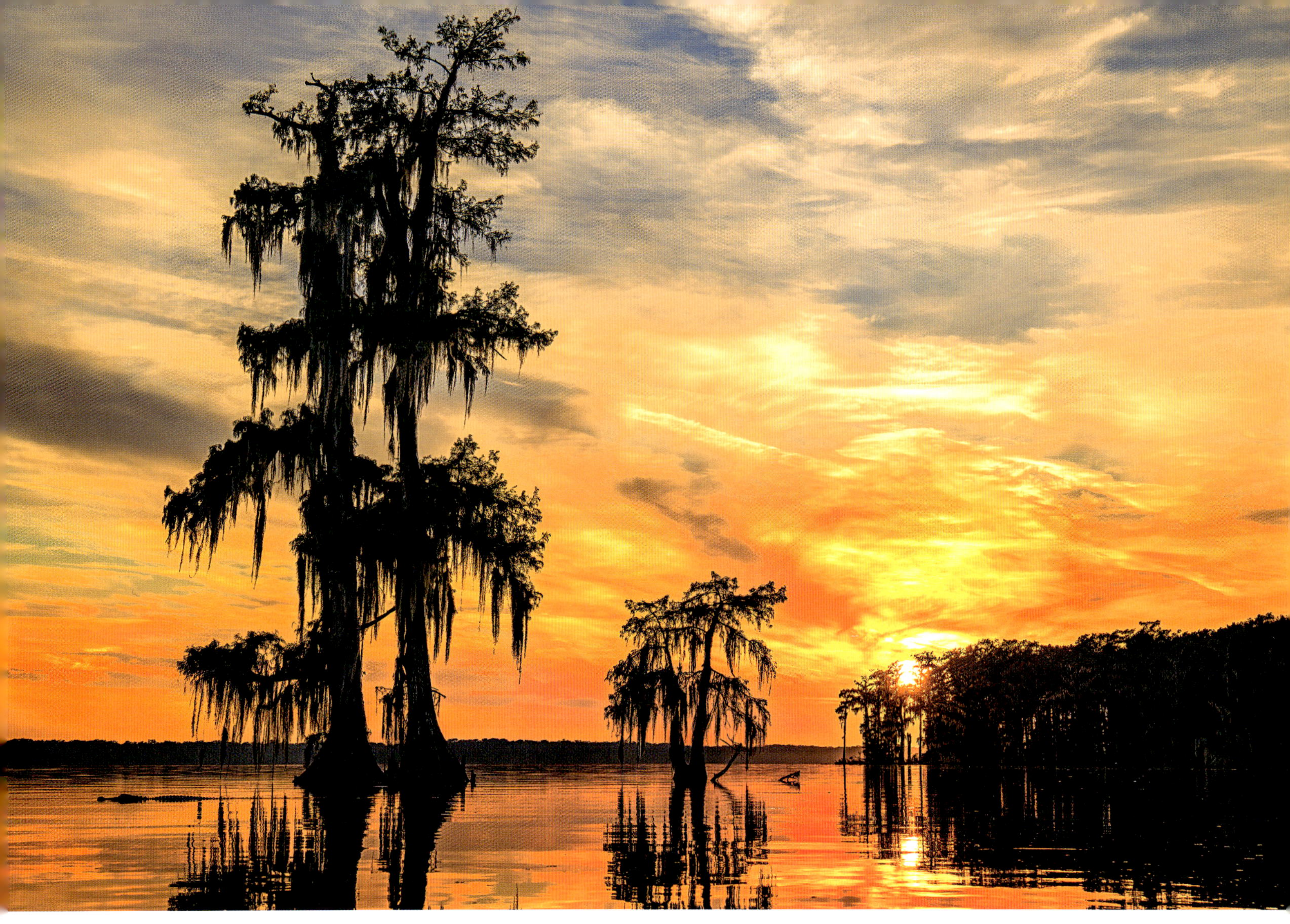

I often use cypress trees to create visual lines from the foreground to the setting sun. On this evening, a large alligator even joined the scene to make this photo iconic.

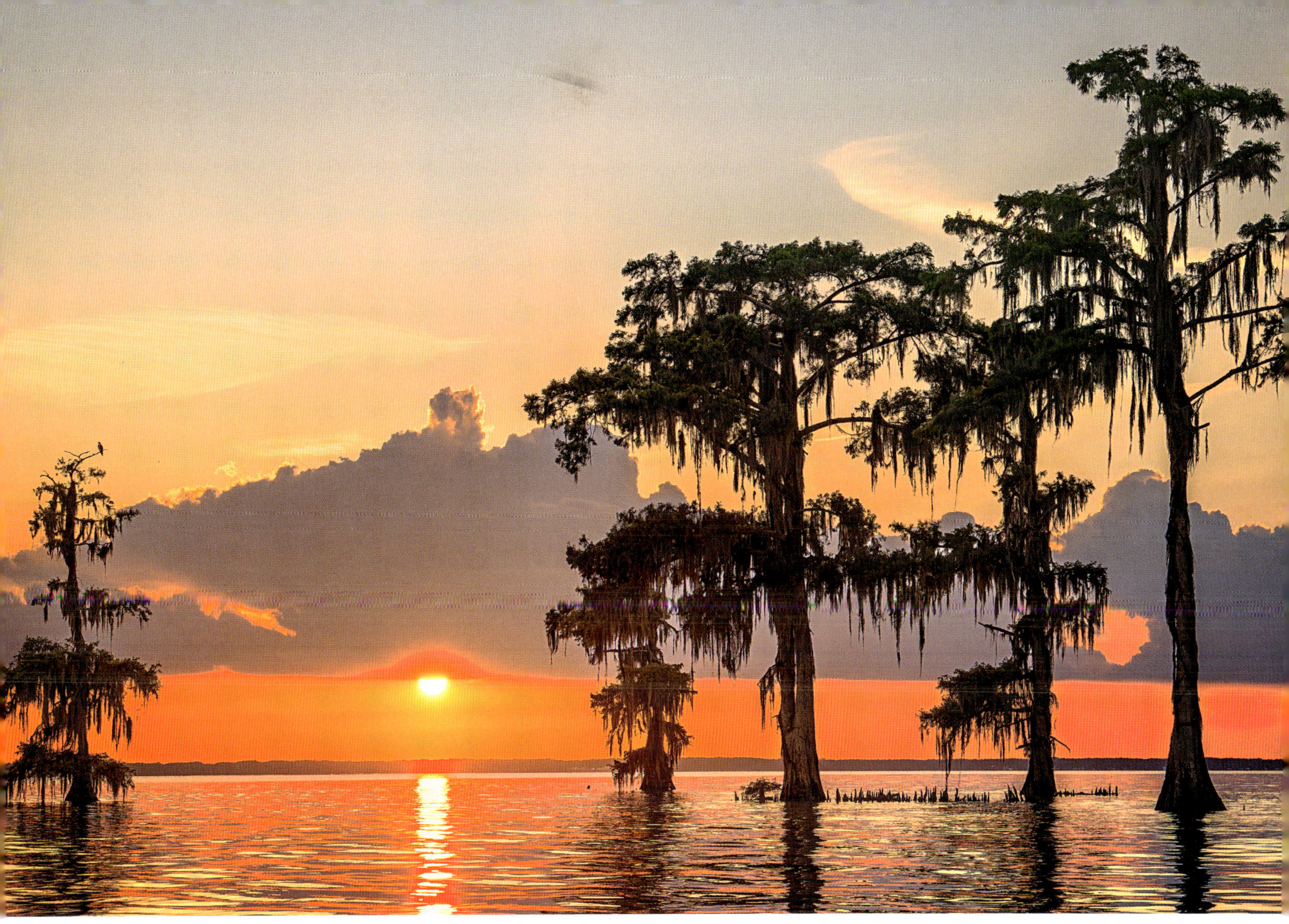

Some sunsets just have more meaning than others. I captured this beautiful sunset, which includes an osprey seemingly enjoying the view, the evening before the passing of my father-in-law, Jean Fairchild. He was an avid outdoorsman, and he would have loved this view.

ABOUT THE AUTHOR

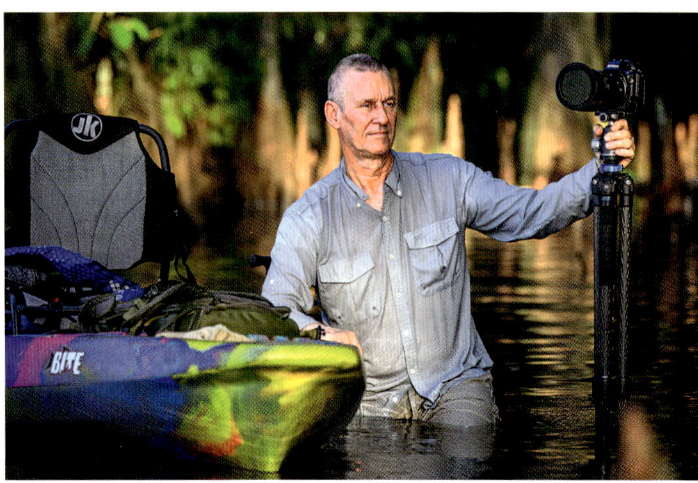

Photo courtesy of Kevin M. White

Andy Crawford was born and raised in South Louisiana and has spent untold hours in the swamps near his home. After spending more than twenty years in the outdoor industry as a writer, he turned to photography full-time. As part of a team of photographers covering Bassmaster fishing tournaments, Andy travels extensively and photographs some of the most beautiful locations across the United States along the way. He also has fallen in love with the American West. A major goal is to visit and photograph every national park in the contiguous United States.

As much as he enjoys every trip outside of his home state, he always looks forward to reuniting with his first love: the amazing Louisiana swamps.

In recent years, he has largely traded his motorboat for a kayak, preferring the quiet, intimate experience of paddling through those amazing flooded cypress trees and watching the sun cast its golden light through the Spanish moss.

To share the majesty of these swamps, Andy hosts annual Into the Swamp Photo Workshops during which he guides small groups of photographers into some of the most beautiful, untouched, and unknown wilderness areas in the country.

Andy has been married for more than thirty-five years to the perfect woman and has two children and a growing cadre of grandchildren.

Andycrawfordphotos.com